DATE DUE

FACES OF THE STATE

FACES OF THE STATE

SECULARISM AND PUBLIC
LIFE IN TURKEY

Yael Navaro-Yashin

PRINCETON UNIVERSITY PRESS   PRINCETON AND OXFORD

Library of Congress Cataloging-in-Publication Data

Navaro-Yashin, Yael, 1969–
Faces of the state : secularism and public life in Turkey / Yael Navaro-Yashin.
p. cm.
Includes bibliographical references and index.
ISBN 0-691-08844-6 (alk. paper)—ISBN 0-691-08845-4 (pbk. : alk. paper)
1. Anthropology—Turkey.   2. Political culture—Turkey.   3. Islam and
secularism—Turkey.   I. Title.

GN585.T9 N38 2002
306′.09561—dc21   2001050026

British Library Cataloging-in-Publication Data is available
This book has been composed in Caledonia Typeface
Printed on acid-free paper. ∞

www.pupress.princeton.edu
Printed in the United States of America

10   9   8   7   6   5   4   3   2   1

To Mehmet

Contents

Illustrations

Acknowledgments

I WOULD LIKE to first thank all the people in Istanbul who generously opened their lives to me and did not mind the sharing of a critical and engaging space, even when we came from very different points of view. The Islamist and secularist individuals, whose privacy I have attempted to protect in the following pages, will probably disagree with the analysis provided here for their worlds. But, in spite of what appeared like political or other differences, it is due to the open-mindedness of each one of my informants that I was allowed in as a researcher as well as a fellow, yet different, citizen.

I was very lucky to be trained by some of the most amazing teachers. I owe the most sincere gratitude to Abdellah Hammoudi, who closely supervised this piece work throughout the process of its fruition and who has been the greatest source of learning, inspiration, direction, and spirit. I owe special thanks, as well, to Kay Warren for her faith in this project and her long-term support. Rena Lederman, Vincanne Adams, John Kelly, James Boon, Gananath Obeyesekere, Brinkley Messick, and Zachary Lockman taught and supported me at various stages. Their input and influence will be visible in this book, as well.

This work developed through close friendships: I owe the most special gratitude to my dearest friend Begona Aretxaga for her reading of chapters of this manuscript when it was still a dissertation and her encouragement to send it for publication at the most crucial stages. I would also like to thank Darini Rajasingham-Senanayake, Kaushik Ghosh, Davida Wood, Ayfer Bartu, and Derin Terzioğlu.

Most of the writing and revision of this work was done when I was already in Britain. I would like especially to thank colleagues in the departments of social anthropology at the University of Edinburgh and the University of Cambridge, who provided much needed support and space for the completion of this work.

Deniz Kandiyoti, Charles Stewart, Çağlar Keyder provided helpful commentary on different chapters of this work. I would like to thank them and the anonymous reviewers for Princeton University Press for their suggestions.

In the editing process, I was assisted by Con Coroneos in Cambridge and Mary Murrell at Princeton University Press. Thanks to them, as well.

The research and writing of this work was supported by several funding bodies. I would like to acknowledge the support provided by the Princeton University Fellowship, the Mellon Foundation Training Grant, the Social

Science Research Council (SSRC) and the American Council of Learned Societies International Doctoral Research Fellowship, the American Research Institute in Turkey (ARIT)–National Endowment for the Humanities Fellowship for Doctoral Research, the Center for International Studies (Princeton) doctoral research grant, the Society of Fellows of the Woodrow Wilson Foundation Dissertation Fellowship, and the American Association of University Women (AAUW) International Dissertation Fellowship.

A section of chapter 1 was published in an earlier version as "The Historical Construction of Local Culture: Gender and Identity in the Politics of Secularism Versus Islam," in *Istanbul Between the Global and the Local*, ed. Çağlar Keyder (Lanham, Md.: Rowman & Littlefield, 1999); a version of chapter 3 was published in *Fragments of Culture: The Everyday of Modern Turkey*, ed. Deniz Kandiyoti and Ayşe Saktanber (London: I. B. Tauris, 2002); and a section of chapter 4 was published in an earlier version as "Uses and Abuses of 'State and Society' in Contemporary Turkey," *New Perspectives on Turkey* 18 (Spring 1998). I would like to thank the editors and publishers of these works for their permission to reprint them.

I owe the most special gratitude to my treasured parents, Leyla and Daniel Navaro, whose support has always been boundless, and to my beloved husband, Mehmet Yashin, whose mark on me will be evident in this work.

FACES OF THE STATE

Introduction

Semiconscious States: The Political and the Psychic in Urban Public Life

Entering the City

Imagine a public square in the center of a metropolis crowded with hundreds of policemen, in identical uniforms, chanting slogans to demand more "rights" from "the state" to use their authority over "the people." Imagine this taking place in Taksim Square, Istanbul, a site often selected for public demonstrations in critique of the state. Taksim Square—emblematic site in urban public consciousness for the enactment, production, and regeneration of the political—was built around the memorial monument for Mustafa Kemal Ataturk, the secular/modernist founder of modern Turkey. Imagine a group of mothers and a father throwing themselves in front of the rushing cars in Taksim Square traffic, or another group sitting on the main street and waving their banners at hurried drivers blowing their horns. Picture the banners reading "Our children are dying on hunger strikes in prison." Envision, then, pedestrians passing by, cursing and spitting at the demonstrating parents. Imagine hundreds of people gathering to watch what is happening, and doing nothing: a public voyeurism. Visualize a young man emerging from the crowd, his face red and his fists clenched, in an attempt to attack the parents demonstrating for their children. Imagine, then, the police approaching to force the parents out of the traffic and to threaten them with arrest. Picture, too, journalists running about, cameras clicking, their flashes encircling the incidents. Figure the stories produced by street dwellers and their rumor, as well as the TV news coverage of the latest events in the city center. Think about millions of people watching TV, reproducing and magnifying the political as framed by the journalists.

The public square, so imagined by social theorists as symbol par excellence for the public sphere or for civil society, is a site, here, for the production of the political. If it pretends to be a domain for rationalized communication and disagreement (Habermas 1989) or if it is idealized and represented as such in public discourses, the public square is interrupted with multiple interventions by representatives of the state. But who, what, and where is "the state" in the incidents just described? Here the police claim to be more "stately" than the state and demonstrate against it. There is a pedestrian, an ordinary young man from "the public," emerging to attack the parents of the hunger strikers thereby assuming a representation of the state through his action and persona. The state appears in many guises and constantly transfigures itself. If now it stands as a monument and symbol of the Republic in the garb of the statue of Ataturk erected in the middle of the public square; next it appears as a flash in the journalist's camera. The state is represented in the police officers' words of threat; it is there, as well, in the gazes of idling pedestrians. The state circulates in the political imaginations of consumers of news, sitting in their homes and watching TV. Events in public life are reflected and magnified within a culture of news, alarm, and sensation. Indeed, in this exemplary and emblematic public square, there is no space that is not arrested with one or another face of the state.

Faces of the State is a study of the production of the political in the public life of Turkey in the 1990s. Public life in Istanbul, with its complexity and absence of boundaries, is the main site for this ethnography. I construe "public life" as a site for the generation of the political, against the grain of such analytical categories like "the public sphere," "public culture," "civil society," and "the state," all frameworks that, in different ways, assume a distinction between domains of "power" and "resistance."[1] I would like to employ the notion of public life to lead the reader into a precarious political arena where it is the public (ambiguously referring to both the people and the state) that produces and recasts the political. When configured as such, the notion of the public in public life enables us to analyze people and the state, not as an opposition, but as the same domain.

Most recent anthropological studies of the political have followed the strategy of picking a social institution and studying its production of public discourse. We therefore have ethnographies of education, law, bureaucracy, and medicine, imagined out of fieldwork in characteristic institutional sites: schools, courts, public offices, clinics. As important as such anthropological work has been, I argue that its analytical frames of the political are precisely that—"frames." There is an assumption, in such strategies for research, that the political can be "sited" in its characteristic contexts, that the political appears in the garb of institutions and their discourses. I do not disagree with this proposition, but I would like to suggest that it is limited.

The work of Michel Foucault, as is well known, has been productively influential in anthropology and its many fields. When anthropologists used to construe "politics" as a distinct domain, beside that of "kinship," "economy," or "religion," the work of Foucault challenged them to envision the political in each and every domain. However, anthropologists have predominantly reflected Foucault's work in only so many ways, employing his studies of schools, courtrooms, prisons, and clinics to expand their imaginations about "sites" for the production of the political. But if Foucault wrote ethnographies of "institutions," he was actually a critic of the very notion of "the institution." In the same way that he would not construe "the state" as a "site" or an "institution," he also did not imagine medicine, the law, and education as distinct and limited domains. And yet, his work on the army, the hospital, and the psychoanalyst's clinic has led itself to be read in a certain way, producing a forceful anthropological imaginary of the political as rationalized institutional practice. The figure of "discipline," in Foucault's sense, has triggered the fantasies of anthropologists about the political, seducing many to write ethnographies of the production of selfhoods through disciplinary institutional mechanisms. Institutional "discourses" have been the focus of ethnographies studying such diverse yet related topics like gender, immigration, illness, and so forth.

As much as this study builds on such contributions to the study of the political, it also attempts to break the boundaries and limitations in analyses that would bind the political in its seemingly rationalized institutional and discursive forms. In the context at hand, public life in 1990s Turkey, the political was not just a product of public discourses as fabricated in the obvious social institutions. As in the multiple garbs and guises implied by the metaphor "faces of the state" the political was precisely unsitable. There were no institutional or other boundaries that could be analyzed around it; no "site," as such, for it. Public life, as I construe the term in this study, is not an institution or a site, imagined as domains with limitations. Instead, it is intended as a category that would allow the study of the political in its fleeting and intangible, transmogrified forms. In the chapters that follow, readers will be led through the production of the political not in the rationalized garb of institutional discourses and mechanisms, but in what I call its multiple metamorphoses. There is no face in which the political does not appear. And therefore the ethnographer must follow it in all its boundless guises. In fact, I take very seriously Foucault's proposition that power is everywhere (1980). In the context at hand, the concept of power figures in multiple forms that muddy the circumscribed institutional arena. Moreover, it is possible to comment that the institutional site, so privileged in many recent anthropological studies of power, is a reflection of a particular and historically specific imaginary about power in which these anthropologists are complicit. In the intention of critiquing modernity, anthropologists have reproduced modernity's own discourse about itself under the metaphor of the institution with its modes of rationalized practice and accountability.

Versions of such institutions exist and proliferate in contemporary Turkey. If I have not picked yet another institution to decipher its production of discourse, it is because the study of the political led me to a more messy

arena. Against the grain of the privileging of Foucault's notion of discourse
in anthropological studies of the political, I would like to introduce here,
via the work of Slavoj Žižek (1995), a study of "fantasy." Studies of political
discourses have generally focused on the construction of the political, the
analysis of which follows a deconstructive strategy. I would like to argue
that there is an element of the Marxist notion of ideology in poststructural-
ist uses of the notion of discourse. Similar to Marxist hopes for a lifting of
false consciousness with an exhibition of ideology, there is an implicit assumption, in deconstruction, of a revelation after the exposure of discursive construction. My argument, following Žižek, is that the political endures and survives deconstruction. The critical capacities employed in
"ideology" or "discourse" critique are not only the prerogative of trained
intellectuals. In the context for this ethnography, Turkey during the 1990s,
critique was a central, common, and ordinary mode of relating to the state.
People from all sections of society were constantly involved in criticizing
various manifestations of the state in the most sophisticated manner. In
other words, I argue that the so-called public in Turkey has already critiqued and deconstructed the state. And yet, simultaneous practices of reproduction, regeneration, and re-reification keep re-dressing "the state" in
a variety of garbs. If the political survives critique and deconstruction, if
the state endures, as it has, then the anthropologist must venture other
arenas and analytical frameworks for the study of the political. For the very
people who critique the state also reproduce it through their "fantasies" for
the state.

Fantasy, according to Žižek's reading of Lacan (1995), is a psychic symptom that survives analysis, critique, or deconstruction. The work of "fantasy" generates unconscious psychic attachments to the very object (e.g.,
the state, the nation, public discourse) that has been deconstructed in the
domains of consciousness. In other words, fantasy escapes deconstruction.
It invisibly and intangibly regenerates and supports the reconstruction of
the political, just as it had been critiqued. The concept of fantasy, more
than the Foucauldian notion of discourse, enables us to study the enduring
force of the political. Indeed, the symptom of the state survives sabotages
of its power. How? Force and physical might is not the only answer. The
state lives on in the fantasies of its subjects who would regenerate and
reerect it after its multiple crises. As Begona Aretxaga (2000) has argued,
the state is an object of psychic desire. It can be maintained even after it
has been deconstructed with rational capacities and thought processes.
Fantasy, and not a lack of consciousness about ideology or discourse, is
what reconstitutes and regenerates state power. Fantasy does everyday
maintenance work for the state.

The state does not figure in this book as a concrete entity, as if it were
"citable in all its moments," to use Walter Benjamin's idea of totalizing

endeavors (1968). In using the work of Žižek, I engage with scholars who have deconstructed the state—studying it as an idea (Abrams 1988), a discourse (Mitchell 1991), or a fetish (Taussig 1992)—through the notion of fantasies for the state.[2] Fantasies for the state is a concept that may help us challenge the limitations of a deconstructionist approach.

Though Foucault construed discourse as a mechanism that transcends consciousness (that could not be available to consciousness), many anthropologists who have employed Foucault's work have researched discourse in the domains of consciousness. For example, anthropologists have studied institutional publications as well as the formalized narratives of their informants as sites for discourse. Such studies of the political that would confine the political within the domain of consciousness are not only misreadings of Foucault; they also leave the psychic and unconscious domain of the political unstudied. For, even when the political is deconstructed in the realms of consciousness, it survives and returns to life in psychic forms.

Imagine once again the central public square in Taksim, Istanbul, leading into Beyoğlu, one of the main centers for bookshops, cinemas, and cafés. Picture hundreds of people strolling down the main İstiklâl street in a leisurely manner as policemen stand in groups on the sides of the street. Visualize young people walking by the policemen, going in and out of the bookshops, sifting through magazines, checking out new books, listening to heavy metal, rock, or protest music. Imagine people sitting for hours on end in cafés, critically discussing politics in response to the public agenda or the news. Envision them unable to imagine that anything will change. Visualize them getting used to the crises in the state that they criticize. And picture them passing by the policemen, once again, months later, and not noticing them. Imagine them going in the coffeeshops once again. Are these traces of the public sphere in Habermas's sense, with its coffeeshops for the production of rationalized communication? Is this the archetypal domain for civil society?

In this book, I study "cynicism" as a central structure of feeling for the production and regeneration of the political in Turkey's public life. Cynicism, as a mechanism employed by members of the public in Turkey, is an approach that reproduces the political by default. But in contrast to Peter Sloterdijk (1988) and Žižek (1995) who would study cynicism as a mode that exists among formerly leftist intellectuals, I study it as a feeling of political existence in Turkey, a more common and ordinary way of managing existence in a realm of state power.[3] Public life is precisely the arena for the production and maintenance of this approach to the political.

News has been central to the making of public life in contemporary Turkey. In fact, when I didn't follow the news during my fieldwork, I felt out of the loop when my informants were discussing politics and their lives as a reflection of it. References to the latest public events were picked from and circulated through television reporting. Everyday discussions were dominantly focused on the agenda as set and presented in the news.

The culture of news, as I would like to call it, is a crucial component of this study of urban public life. But against the grain of discourse analysis in media studies, or in works that would institutionalize the media and study its formative power in creating public discourse, I study the force of a culture of news in inciting a political structure of feeling. Stuart Hall et al.'s (1978) study of "moral panic" about mugging in Britain, as such panic was created by the news, is much more insightful on this account than a study of the construction and dissemination of mediatic discourses.[4] Against the rationalizing implication of the notion of public discourse, the framework of moral panic allows one to explore the nonrational dimensions of the political in public life. In this book, the media is not an object of study, but one important agent in the making of public life. The hype, scandal, and alarm produced by journalists around political issues in the 1990s created successive cultures of panic and fear in public life. In the culture of news, "the political" was turned into a consumer item. In the quick consumption of "political issues," under the influence of the media, public cultures of alarm were quickly followed by public amnesia. Issues that were central in public discussions for two months, were almost forgotten and pushed to the public unconscious very soon after. In his work on bureaucracy, Michael Herzfeld wrote, "I shall open the analysis with a brief account of my sources (especially newspapers) as representing the national level of discourse most clearly analogous with the play of gossip and reputation in the local community" (1992, 132). It is in this vein that I argue that television news becomes crucial for the analysis of this particular public formation.

Secularism in Public Life

The conflict over secularism was probably one of the most central issues that shaped public life in Turkey in the middle of the 1990s. In Turkey, a study of secularism cannot be dissociated from a study of the state, for secularism is the state's preferred self-representation or selected idea about itself. Secularism is not a neutral paradigm, but a state ideology as well as a hegemonic public discourse in contemporary Turkey. For example, the army has presented itself as the ultimate bastion and guard of founding leader Ataturk's secularism. Therefore, a study of the culture of secularism in Turkey is also, necessarily, a study of militarism, authoritarianism, and the culture of the state. Statism (or reverence for the state) in Turkey's public life is often represented in the garb and language of secularism.

But then, if secularism is the state's preferred narrative about itself, why study it? Why privilege the secularist / Islamist conflict in this ethnography of public life? Indeed, the conflict over secularism is the state's and the army's favorite story about the political in contemporary Turkey, against other issues (Kurds, Cyprus, and so forth). "The rise of Islamism" has been construed and presented as the most major threat to the integrity of the state in Turkey. A study of secularists and secularism in public life is a central topic of this book. But my intention is to problematize "secularism," rather than reproducing discourses and ideologies that employ its terms. A culture of the state was the context for the secularist/Islamist conflict in late-twentieth-century Turkey. Secularism and Islamism competed in a public arena, both wearing different faces of the state.

This book takes the apparent schism between secularists and Islamists as one of its topics, but it does not take this seeming "schism" for granted. Indeed, rather than framing the problem as a communal conflict between secularist and Islamist communities or social groups, I choose to problematize "secularism" itself. Most studies of conflicts over religion in public life have objectified "religion" as the problem, focusing on the religious community as an anomalous or emergent social group. Many studies of Islamists have been produced under such a framework, sometimes employing the dubious notion of "fundamentalism." Instead, in this work I take secularism to task because it is, by and large, the most dominant discourse that forms the basis of public life in Turkey. Beyond isolating Islamists as a community or Islamism as a phenomenon, I study Islamists working within conditions of possibility of a public life dominated by secularist discourses. Islamism in Turkey is imbued with the language of secularism. In fact, I argue that secularist fantasies about Islamists in public life have been complicit in producing versions of Islamism in Turkey. So every comment on Islamism in what follows should be read, as well, as a comment on "secularism," challenging the very analytical distinction of secularity versus religion. I argue that "secularity" and "religion" are in a dialectic. The relationality between secularism and Islamism is therefore at the conceptual center of this book. Here, in relation to Islamists, secularists, too, emerge as main informants. If secularists in Turkey would like to present their life practices as transcultural or neutral against Islamists, I problematize their references to "culture" as much as I do those of Islamists.

In the 1990s, public life was a central arena for the reconfiguration of the meaning of "Turkish culture" and "nativity." In debate with one another, secularists and Islamists pit different interpretations of Turkish culture against each other. They argued over Turkey's proper "region"; they disagreed on Turkey's positionality vis-à-vis Europe. The chapters in this book study this conflict over Turkish culture. And at no point do the references to culture appear stable.

The Turkish Astronomer and the Little Prince

In a reflective moment, the narrator of Antoine de Saint-Exupéry's *The Little Prince* (1943) remarks,

> I have serious reason to believe that the planet from which the little prince came is the asteroid known as B-612.
>
> This asteroid has only once been seen through the telescope. That was by a Turkish astronomer, in 1909.
>
> On making his discovery, the astronomer had presented it to the International Astronomical Congress, in a great demonstration. But he was in Turkish costume, and so nobody would believe what he said.
>
> Grown-ups are like that . . .
>
> Fortunately, however, for the reputation of Asteroid B-612, a Turkish dictator made a law that his subjects, under pain of death, should change to European costume. So in 1920 the astronomer gave his demonstration all over again, dressed with impressive style and elegance. And this time everybody accepted his report (12).

Since 1943, it is possible to amend Saint-Exupéry's story. I have observed that even when the Turkish astronomer is dressed in European costume, "grown-ups" do not believe in his report. These grown-ups—let us call them anthropologists—still imagine that the layers of European costume are transparent to an underlying Turkish culture. And so, in spite of all his trials and tribulations, style and elegance, the astronomer is ignored.

The problem of positivism in the politics and the study of culture is one of the framing questions of this book. Indeed, there is a residual positivism with regard to "culture" even in those ethnographies that have employed the theoretical tools of deconstruction. Examples include studies that, after Edward Said's *Orientalism* (1978), have targeted Western discourses and anthropological categories as their subject for critique in the anthropology of the Middle East (e.g., Mitchell 1988, 2000; Rabinow 1989; Messick 1993; Abu-Lughod 1998). Indeed, the critique of modernity, whether it be of colonialism or of Westernization, has been the project of a certain anthropology and post-Orientalist scholarship. Yet such projects have risked reproducing essentialism in leaving a precipitation of cultural authenticity or tradition underneath the layers of European costume, thereby overlapping, by default, with cultural revivalisms or nationalisms in the contexts studied. Many a critique of representation, employing post-structuralism, has ended up implying that a reified discourse of modernity is a misrepresentation, stopping the process of deconstruction in its tracks. From such a reading, some of the people whose lives inform this ethnography, "secular Turks," could be understood to be misrepresentations of themselves, in contrast to "Islamist Turks," who, claiming to revive the culture of the Ottoman-Islamic past, could be studied as representations and representatives of Turkish culture or nativity. For this paradoxical political return to culturalism in the postcolonial critique of modernity, Deniz Kandiyoti has coined the term "neo-Orientalism" (1997, 114).

And yet, a critique of the critique of modernity does not in turn, in canceling the negatives, have to be an affirmation or reification of modernity or of politics constructed in the name of modernity. Instead, following Abdellah Hammoudi's strategy of "double-edged critique" (1997), I study power in both its Western and Turkish references. There is something missing from the paradigm that would study "the West," "modernity," or "the anthropologist" as representations of "power" and examine "the rest" as "culture." Here, I attempt to engage the context of research with a study of power through and through. The study of the political must be dissociated from the culturalist reservoir that is implicit in the framework of postcoloniality and the critique of modernity. Even if represented as Western or Turkish in specific historical contingencies, power belongs to neither culture. The attempt, here is to work against the grain of both Western and local discourses of power.

Though as of 1999 the European Commission has granted a candidacy to Turkey, the idea of Turkey's otherness to Europe persists. With a long-standing European historiography that assigned the Ottoman Empire to "the East," "Turkey and Europe" are still conceived both within and outside Turkey as a contradiction in terms. In contrast, I argue that there is no inherent conflict or necessary difference between Turkey and Europe, Islam and the West. Ethnography that draws a radical distinction between "native" and "Western" categories, as in the project of cultural relativism, will find itself at sea in the study of Turkey, given the Ottoman Empire and Turkey's historical placement within and vis-à-vis Europe. The cultural relativist project of analytically distinguishing Western or anthropological categories from local or native ones would be limiting in the study of Turkey, as it is arguably problematic in the study of other comparable historical contexts. It is not possible, in the context at hand, to distinguish native from Western points of view because there is no space where they have not been integrally and historically engaged with one another. Turks, like Arabs and Jews, have been Europe's internal and not external others. The Ottoman Empire was central to European history, intrinsically related to and informed by Byzantine forms of governance, and rivaling the Hapsburgs. And yet, Turks and Muslims are still interpreted as counter- or extra-European. To challenge the notion of Turkey as "non-European" is not to reproduce the terms of Turkish nationalist discourse with its Westernist aspirations, as in the project of Mustafa Kemal Ataturk, but to write the meaning of "Europe" anew through the prism of a crucial internal other.[5] For the very meaning and connotations of Europe would have to change if Muslim and Jewish histories were placed at its historical center.

The history of Turkey has generally been conceived, in scholarship as well as in political discourse, as a history of "Westernization," whether it be in secularist praise or Islamicist criticism (e.g., Lewis 1969; Berkes 1964). We do, indeed, have at hand a history of radical state-imposed Westernizing reforms. Yet I argue that the category "Westernization," as a category of historical analysis, is a positivist notion that assumes an original distinction and incommensurability between a constructed "East" and "West." It is interesting that there should be such an implicit overlap between modernizationist / Orientalist constructs of "Westernization" and postmodernist / post-Orientalist references to "modernity."[6] The concept of Westernization, like notions of a major historical rupture with modernity, is based on the assumption, by default, that an essentially separate "culture" existed prior to the development or the shift. In turn, to write against the grain of the notion of Westernization in the historical analysis and trajectory of Turkey is not to legitimize the politics of state-regulated Westernization, nor to suggest that "anything goes." It is only to set in train a long-term ethnographic and political process of unmasking categories that reproduce claims to originality.

The Construction of "Turkish Culture"

The argument of this book is that "Turkish culture," as such, does not exist. From the vantage point of the politics of culture between Islamists and secularists, when the meaning and components of "Turkish cultural practice" have been debated, produced, transformed, and repeatedly displaced, it would be misplaced to employ the notion of Turkish culture as an anthropological or analytical category.

The notions of Turkey, Turks, and Turkish culture, arguably like other terms of state or identity, have been entangled in a history of multiple constructions. According to historian Cemal Kafadar (1995), "Turchia" was not a term through which Ottoman subjects identified themselves or their polity in the early Ottoman centuries. Ottomans called themselves "Rumi," a term adopted from the Byzantines. The self-appellation "Turk" was derived, through the formative period of Turkish nationalism, in relationship with Europe. "Turkey" and "Turks" were the terms used by Europeans to classify the Ottomans, and when these terms did not have a place in the self-identification of subjects of the Ottoman Empire, they came to signify cultural identity under a nationalist construction.

Thus, an anthropological search for Turkish culture in its own "native" terms, or the project of understanding "the native's point of view" (e.g.,

Geertz 1983) is set to be reconsidered. "Turkishness," arguably like other cultural categories, was already and always a misnomer. It was never a category that existed independently of Ottoman relations with Europe. Not even in the formative stages of the Ottoman state, in the fourteenth century, was there such pristine "Turkish" cultural space.

Far from being natural or straightforward concepts, then, the notions of Turkey, Turks, and Turkish culture are products of historical agency and contingency. To situate these notions more accurately, one would have to turn to the early stages of Turkey's national formation. Late-twentieth-century discussions on nativity make references to constructions of "Turkish culture" in early-twentieth-century nationalism. With the foundation of an independent republic to replace Ottoman sovereignty, there was an effort to define what was culturally native to the new polity, "Turkey." The founders of the republic, led by Mustafa Kemal Ataturk, aspired to Westernization, following the example of the Young Turks before them. But as they were informed by the European Enlightenment, the forerunners of the idea of "the Republic of Turkey" were also implicated in the contingency and discourse of rising nationalisms. The Ottoman Empire had disintegrated by the early twentieth century, and, giving up the project of sustaining the Empire, Ottoman-Turkish leaders geared efforts to constitute a nation-state in the model of Balkan and Arab nationalisms that had developed in their midst. Nationalisms, as they were formulated at the time, were based on primordialist claims to represent the unitary and original "culture" of circumscribed pieces of territory.[7] To be legitimate in a world of nationalist discourse, a nation-state had to have claims to cultural continuity between the past and the present. The builders of "Turkey" had mobilized themselves against European powers who were partitioning the remaining portions of the Ottoman Empire among themselves. But they had also organized, with Republicanist aspirations, against the Ottoman dynasty and the sultan who had surrendered to the Europeans. The Republicanists did not have much interest in identifying the new nation-state with the culture of the Ottoman Empire. And yet, for their nationalism to be commensurable with the primordialist discourses that abounded under the conditions of possibility at the time, connection to a certain past had to be claimed. The paradox was resolved when the early nationalists began to suggest links between the Westernized (or "modern") national culture that they wanted to institute and the culture of Turkic groups in ancient Central Asia.[8] As Deniz Kandiyoti has insightfully noted, "the 'modern' was thus often justified as the more 'authentic' and discontinuity presented as continuity" in efforts to reconcile Europeanization with nationalism (1993, 379).[9]

Memory of a Turkic past in Central Asia was nonexistent among inhabitants of Anatolia in the early twentieth century.[10] Moreover, with the migrations, multiple conversions, and intercultural marriages that characterized Ottoman society, the Muslim individuals who came predominantly to compose the citizens of "Turkey" were of mixed ancestry, not necessarily speaking or identifying as "Turkish."[11] But in the interest of claiming a shared "national culture," the founders of the republic constructed links with "the culture of Central Asia."

Under the new construct of "Turkey," the capital city Ankara was founded, railroads were designed, schools were built, the postal system was changed, measurements were reformulated, the legal system was reframed, borders were patrolled, soldiers were conscripted, women were employed in the labor force, and so forth. All of this material construction took place as nationalists claimed organic links between modernizing implementations and national culture. And to a significant extent, the new notions of Turkey and its "culture" were internalized by citizens of the republic. Through enrollment in state schools, attendance in Community Houses,[12] subjection to army discipline, and exposure to radio, newspapers, novels, and the like, people came to organize their lives, to a certain extent, around the new notion of what being Turkish (and hence, modern) was now about.

"The Anthropology of Turkey"

"The anthropology of Turkey," conceptualized as such, has been composed primarily by British-trained structuralists. The project, for the likes of Paul Stirling, was to describe structural survivals of the Westernizing history of Turkey. The "Turkish village," in his terms, conceived as a unit of analysis, was a perfect setting for such an enterprise.[13] Here, one would collect statistical information on society, kinship, agricultural systems, and economy to be generalized into indices. The material product of positive scientific research would be taken to reflect Turkish society or Turkish social structure. Younger anthropologists introduced history into their depictions of Turkish society, producing ethnographies of "structure and change." The state figures in these more recent accounts as an entity that is essentially external to village life.[14] Change is a new but alien phenomenon. Structure and change are conceptualized as entities distinct and dissonant from one another. The entry of American-trained anthropologists in the field did not radically shift the project of the anthropology of Turkey. Cultural anthropologists have only located their anthropological "truths" in different sites. Rather than presenting an economic average, a household count, or mean kinship figures as an account of society, Carol Delaney, for example, has studied the gendered cosmological meanings that villagers associate with the symbols of seed and soil to come up with an account of Turkish culture.[15]

Approaches that would imagine an underlying Turkish culture are prevalent among scholars in cultural studies, too. Kevin Robins, for example, positions himself as a critic of Westernism, Westernization, and Western discourses in Turkey. He writes, "As much as it has been shaped by the assimilation of Western culture, modern Turkish identity 'is also a product of various negations': Turkish society became 'practiced in the art of repression'" (1996, 68). By employing the terms of "negation" and "repression," does Robins have an argument about what is (or was) "positive" to Turkish culture and identity? Members of the Islamist movement, in Robins's reading, exemplify such positive identity: "Once the psychic repression had been lifted, lost identities and experiences began to be recovered" (1996, 74). In critique of "Westernized Turks" and in reference to Islamists, Robins writes, "Of course, the real people could never be banished" (1996, 71). Robins's work accentuates a latent nativism in the critique of modernity.[16]

Faces of the state avoids the conventionalized anthropological project of describing Turkish culture and society. There is no such essential "Turkishness" to be found, no Westernizing curtain to pull back and reveal a hidden cultural reservoir. From this point of view, attempts using interpretivist methodologies to understand "culture" share a project with structuralist measures to chart "society."[17] The material presented in this book works against the grain of the essentializing notion of the "anthropology of Turkey." Instead, in following Stuart Hall's (1993) radical social constructionism, this ethnography describes enactments, productions, and contestations over culture.[18] In contrast to Robins, Hall would not allow a notion of an original culture to appear through the back door after attempts at deconstruction.

The object of anthropological inquiry, the study of "local" or "native culture" is critically juxtaposed in this book with a study of the intrinsic entanglement of culture with the political. But the deconstruction of the notion of Turkish culture is not activated, here, from the position of the anthropologist alone. It is the experiences of the people whose lives inform this ethnography that predicate an unsettling of the idea of Turkish culture (and therefore, of the anthropological category of culture) with their politics of culture. As the content and meaning of Turkishness is created, contested, and consumed, so-called Turkish culture undergoes constant and several displacements.[19] The Islamist and secularist characters represented in this book are involved in questioning one another's life practices in a politics of culture. The narrative here attempts to match their experiential unknowing (or lack of ground) with an epistemological unknowing.

The Not-Too-Native Anthropologist

Recently, it has become an anthropological convention to involve the ethnographer's subject-position in the writing of the ethnographic text (e.g., Clifford and Marcus 1986). While I agree with the critique of "objectivity" that motivates "anthropology at home," I am uncertain about the category of "the native anthropologist," which it, by implication, celebrates. The notion of "the native anthropologist" has been problematized and complicated by anthropologists who have positioned themselves as "halfies" (e.g., Narayan 1993, Abu-Lughod 1988). But I think that the concept requires further criticism. I would not like to position myself as the "native" critic of Western discourses on Turkey, a role I would have found easy to assume, having "returned home" to Istanbul to do my research. Rather, I attempt to deconstruct the notion of the native. The celebration of the native anthropologist and anthropology at home falls far short of problematizing the notion of "nativity" and "the native's point of view," which has informed nationalisms as well as anthropology. For there is no space, at least in the context here studied, where nativity is not always and already entangled in political discourses of exclusion. The anthropology that would privilege the native anthropologist, in a "progressive" attempt to unsettle anthropology's external / western gaze, cannot be disentangled from local nationalist discourses that would employ the terms of nativity for constructed and implemented cultural division.

The notion of the native is not an innocent concept and neither is a native positionality. As a person of "minority" status in Turkey, I was not perceived as a "proper native" by many of my informants, whether Islamist or secularist. In encounters in my own city Istanbul, the first thing that incited curiosity on an everyday basis was my name. Immediately, people expressed surprise to hear Turkish spoken as a native language by someone with a non-Turkish name. Many of my informants were meeting someone from what they knew as "the non-Muslim minorities" (*gayrimüslimler, ekaliyet*) for the first time in their lives. Some, especially Islamists, were puzzled by the presence of "a Jew" (*Yahudi, Musevi*) in their midst. In all cases, upon meeting me, people would ask, "Where are you from?" "From here, from Turkey," I would respond. "How long have your ancestors lived in these lands?" would be another question. I would be forced to respond in primordialist logic that "some of them were Greek-speaking Byzantine Jews, others arrived in the Ottoman Empire after the Inquisitions in Spain." "Does your family still live here?" I would be asked by informants who would simply assume the transitory nature of non-Muslim minorities in Turkey. "How come you speak Turkish so well?" "Turkish is one of my native languages," I would say. My positionality as "native" was ambiguous, from my informants' nativist points of view. They would simply consider themselves as more native than I. In the available conditions of possibility, I, like others of comparable status, was an object of othering nativist discourses in Turkey.[20] This book goes beyond those that would reify "the native" or "the native anthropologist," in its attempts to problematize the notion of nativity in anthropology and in nationalist discourses.

Researching the Political

The questions posed in this book demand that I employ a different and nonconventional research strategy. Nationalism and cultural politics in Turkey could be studied with a "methodology" that would have recorded articulated, conscious, and formalized narratives of secularist, Islamist, nationalist, and / or statist informants. Moreover, such a study, which would have expansively used the "sources," could have documented the place, placement, and context of secularists and Islamists as "communities," a notion that still dominates the anthropological imagination.

A study of public life in urban Turkey, such as this one, would have been very limited, however, if constrained by such methodologies and frameworks. "The political" is forceful in a manner that is available, and yet, also not available to the consciousness of its subjects. Studies researching "the political" in informants' consciously articulated narratives or ideologies (to analyze it as elements of "a discourse") are only partially revealing. Both my secularist and Islamist informants were ready to give me framed ideological accounts of their political views, their identities, and their cultures. But if I had focused my research on these proliferating narratives and counter-narratives between secularist and Islamist communities, the political would have slipped away.

As an imaginary register for research, the aphorisms of Walter Benjamin are deeply insightful. In his "Theses on the Philosophy of History" (1968), Benjamin has argued that "only a redeemed mankind" would be able to study a situation, a context, or a concept in its totality. Instead, Benjamin grasps knowledge as it appears, in his terms, in the form of "flashes," as they dart by. Moving beyond research that presents totalizing conscious accounts as exemplary of cultural or political narratives, Benjamin incites us to maintain ourselves within streams of consciousness: that which is not stable, not re-articulable, but which blinks, momentarily shows itself, and escapes (see Pandolfo 1997). Benjamin's aphorisms are much more insightful as a strategy of tracing the political than the research strategy or anthropological methodology that would constrain and locate the political in place. They push one to study the political against processes and frameworks that rationalize or normalize it (see Aretxaga 2000). Research on public life in Turkey—the panic, the uproar, the alarm, the excess—requires just such a tracing of the political against accounts that would normalize it. As transient and ephemeral as they are, states of semiconsciousness or "fantasy," which are of interest to me in this book, require such an imaginary of research. More than an anthropology that locates sites for research, single or multiple (Marcus 1995), Benjamin's writings urge one to imagine the intangible: that which escapes formalized articulation, normalization, citation, siting. In what follows, informants' entanglements with the political are followed through different and simultaneous forms of consciousness: crisply articulated, hazy, or submerged.

How does one research the movement of public life? What method is suitable for a study of the force of fantasy in generating the political? In chapter 1, I study humor, rumor, imaginary stories, projections, and irrational fears as intangible sites for the making of the political in Istanbul's public life. The attention to out-of-focus or fuzzy consciousness is followed through in subsequent chapters. Chapters on the state move with the flow of public life in Istanbul—from a farewell party for a soldier-to-be to the celebration of Republic Day—to study the phantasmatic forces that effect and the psychic work that regenerates the state. The strategy of research is to sense and follow the movement of public life in Istanbul in order to grasp the flowing, fleeting, or submerged forces that produce and regenerate the political.

Part I

CULTURAL POLITICS

1

Prophecies of Culture:
Rumor, Humor, and Secularist Projections
about "Islamic Public Life"

"The Native"

On an afternoon in March 1994, two Turkish women, one veiled, the other not, encountered one another in front of the Ayasofya museum in the old quarter of Istanbul.[1] The short-haired woman, dressed in a skirt to her knees, a trimly fit blouse, and a short coat, asked the other woman who was wearing a black veil, whether this was the line for tickets to the museum. The veiled woman was surprised. "You speak Turkish?" she asked in amazement. "Yes, I am Turkish!" asserted the short-haired woman, put off by the question. "Oh! You don't look Turkish. You look like a Westerner," said the veiled woman. "You don't look Turkish either," said the other. "I thought you were an Arab." "Oh!" said the veiled woman, "thanks to God, we are Turkish and Muslim." "Well, we are too," said the short-haired woman. Both these women were claiming exclusive "nativeness" through their own respective manners of dress and public comportment, mutually ascribing "foreignness" to one another, each wanting to dissociate the other's appearance from her respective notions of "Turkey."

In the course of the mid-1990s, this sort of verbalized disagreement about the content of "Turkishness" had become extremely commonplace in Istanbul's public life.[2] The debates centered especially around the question of women's dress. What was the form of public appearance that best fitted "the Turkish woman"? Should she veil herself, as demanded of Muslim women by Islamic law? If so, was it sufficient to cover one's head with a scarf, no matter what the color or style, or did she have to practice abstention to the point of wearing only a black veil? Focusing on such discussions, this chapter explores the implication of politics of gender in competing discourses about nativeness to Turkey.

In the formative stages of the republic, Kemal Ataturk had advocated for women to present themselves in western clothes. His Hat Law (*Şapka Devrimi*) of 1925 prohibited the wearing of the fez, a symbol of "Orient" in the eyes of Westerners, and decried its associated Ottoman social rankings. The bowler hat to be donned by men was to symbolize the association of

the new republic with Western as opposed to Islamic civilization. With the
Hat Law, Ataturk also encouraged men to be tolerant of their wives' and
daughters' dressing habits. Women in Turkey had started to take up Westernized forms of dress, making themselves up according to an image of the
proper Turkish woman, as institutionalized through disciplinary state practices in the early Republican period (the 1920s and 1930s). In the 1990s,
Turkish women dressed in a whole range of outfits and styles, much determined by class, position, and rural or urban context. And women who used
forms of Western gear began to argue, against Islamists, that this was the
proper way for Turkish women to dress.

There was also heightened interest, in the 1990s, in the Turkish term for
"nativeness" (yerellik). The meaning and components of nativeness were at
the heart of public discussions and debates. What constituted Turkish nativeness? There was no consensus about this question. The content of
"Turkishess" was picked apart, contested, and unfolded as the Islamist
movement rose to popularity and power. What was Turkey going to look
like? What was the country's image going to be in the eyes of Westerners?
These were the issues framed and expressed by secularists. All took to
mapping, constructing, and debating the appearance of the proper Turkish
native.

The Turkish word for nativeness (yerellik) contains an implicit reference
to place, signifying "locality" or ingrainment to the land. Also, in contemporary Turkish it signifies "local culture." In the contemporary context of a
reframed and rekindled nationalism, the term yerellik has had extra symbolic resonance, implying primordial connections with the national motherland (vatan). In the 1990s, yerellik was used as antonym for yabancılık,
standing for foreignness or external origin.[3] Yet there was no consensus
about the content (the reference) of these notions. Instead there was a
proliferation of arguments over the meaning of nativeness in Turkey. There
was intense public discord over what being native to Turkey or acting like
a native meant. The debate was especially acute on the axis of secularist / Islamist politics of culture.

In sorting out their differences, secularist and Islamist women found
that they had to justify their lifestyles by claiming organic unity with Turkey. In doing so, women often wrote their opponents' ways of life out of
their own respective narratives of nativeness to Turkey. In the 1980s, Islamist women legitimized their resumption of the veil through a version of
a nationalist discourse, the Turkish-Islamic synthesis.[4] They argued that
they were reviving what was "Turkey's local culture," which they said "had
been repressed through years of Westernization." Those who did not veil,
Islamists argued, were, in their words "not being true to themselves," were
"copying the West," were no longer "behaving like natives."

In political and moral struggles with Islamists, secularist women did not at first realize that they had to justify their lifestyles through a competing discourse of "being native to Turkey." For many secularist women, Westernization, as instituted by Ataturk, signified women's liberation, freedom from the constraints of religion. Yet, as they interacted with and lost ground to Islamists in the political arena, secularist women realized that they had to claim an "organic unity with Turkey," as well, in order to be convincing. They had to create their own discourse of Turkey's local culture. To do this, many of them returned to early Republican sources dealing with Turkey's national culture. Through a reified version of the early Republican period (or Ataturk's lifetime), they found what they wanted to see: a validation for their struggle to survive with their lifestyles in the context of present-day Turkey. According to early nationalist discourses on Turkey's culture, it was secularist and not Islamist women's practices and clothes that were properly Turkish and local. In the course of public contestation, it became unclear through whose discourse (women's or men's, civil society or the state) women were writing their stories of belonging in Turkey. Women found that their concerns about their rights and freedoms had to be articulated through narratives of nativeness to Turkey. Their life practices had to be legitimized in the terms of alternative nationalist discourses, Islamist or secularist. Secularist and Islamist women spoke through seemingly conflictual narratives of an underlying nationalist structure.

If we were to attempt a social history of the concept of culture in the Turkish domain, in the manner that Raymond Williams did for England (1958; 1985, 11–20), we would be able to isolate certain historical periods when contestation of the concept of culture became public. At certain points in the history of Turkey, culture was transformed from tacit knowledge into an abstracted concept to be discussed, dissected, analyzed, and theorized.[5] The mid-1990s was one such important period, when the rise to local administrative power of a significant branch of the Islamist movement reproblematized the issue of Turkey's local culture in public debates. The foundational years of the republic, the 1920s and 1930s, were an important period for debating the question "What is Turkey's culture?" So too were the 1990s, with the success of the Islamist Welfare Party in securing an electoral majority in Turkey's version of democracy. Once again, people across class, gender, and ideologically based differences, became anthropologists of themselves, arguing over what nativeness signifies, what sort of everyday comportment—manner of walking in the streets, dressing, or talking to strangers—Turkish authenticity requires, or what sort of worldview, belief, or loyalty to the state Turkish local culture calls for. The conflict between secularists and Islamists was a central arena for the production of such fantasies for Turkey's local culture. On the axis of this politics of identity, women's practices of everyday life were the central focus of arguments over the meaning of Turkish culture.[6]

Because change occurs swiftly in the volatile climate of contemporary Turkey's public life, the ethnographic material I present in this chapter should be understood to concern a particular historical contingency: on March 27, 1994 the Islamist Welfare Party won the municipal elections in Istanbul and a majority of other cities throughout Turkey. This chapter is an account of a dominant public discourse on local culture in the month before and the month after these elections in Istanbul.[7]

The appropriate ethnographic question here is not what is (or was) culturally local to Turkey given its history of state enforced Westernization and secularization. This, by implication, is the question posed by scholarly critiques of modernity in anthropology and other disciplines. I rather prefer to ask what is being reformulated as "local" in a history that has been construed as a process of modernization or Westernization? I do not, in other words, take for granted the framework of Westernization, so dominant in the social science of Turkey as well as in the scholarly study of modernity generally. In this account, both Islamists and secularists imagine the history of the Ottoman Empire and Turkey as a story of Westernization. Secularists and Islamists position themselves differently, as characters in this story. Here, I position my analysis not in critique of modernity but against the grain of the framework of Westernization itself, which has so dominated both public-political and scholarly discourses. The point is to displace the narrative of westernization, not to re-reify modernity through a critique.

Tales of Nightmare

The municipal elections of March 1994 did not merely consist of a competition between political parties each of which promised better management of the city's infrastructure. The campaign was a contest in cultural politics. As the winning potential of the Islamist Welfare Party became obvious in early 1994, all the other political parties claimed to be the sole guarantee for the future of secularism in Turkey. It was one of the first times that an Islamist group was going to assume significant official power in the history of republican Turkey. And a certain kind of secularism was so much taken for granted up to that point in the public unconscious, that upon awareness of a real Islamist threat, the other political parties put all other issues aside to promise the maintenance of a cultural status quo. According to its political rivals, the Welfare Party threatened the meaning and unity of "Ataturk's state" as founded in 1923 and instituted through decades of secularist and modernist practices.

Most public polls conducted by big mainstream newspapers and private research firms had not predicted that the Welfare Party would win the municipal elections.[8] Even as the actual poll results were being announced, district by district on TV, many viewers had a hard time taking in what had happened. In metropolitan Istanbul, the Welfare Party came to power with 25 percent of the total votes (Çakır 1994, 222–24). In a system where winner-takes-all, most of the city's district municipalities as well as the municipality of greater Istanbul were obtained by the Welfare Party. According to the reports, the party had gained most of its support from the shantytowns of Istanbul. The Welfare Party's own constituency (its actual activists, rather than those who merely voted for it in the booths) were Islamists of various political and sufi affiliations.

Toward the end of March 1994, many of the city's secularist inhabitants who had not seriously anticipated such an event imagined that they were in for a nightmare. There was an atmosphere of uncertainty, sometimes ridden by panic, depression, and serious anxiety. What would happen to life in Turkey now that an Islamist political party had gained municipal power? An older woman who grew up under the strictly secularist regime of the early republic complained of high blood pressure. A young university student said that she was walking around with "zero morale." For a few days, many people were fearful of passing through places that were to be administered by the Islamist Welfare Party. No one was sure what awaited them on the streets of Istanbul.

Times of social hysteria create many imaginings. In the state of fearful suspense, many jokes and stories were invented and exchanged. Indeed, Welfare's victory was largely and significantly received through the medium of black humor on the part of its opponents—the sort of humor that exaggerates an anticipated calamity to render it ridiculously funny, thereby relaxing the seriously anxious. It was in the domain of this informal production and sharing of humor and rumor that secularist discourse on Islam had its force.[9] This orally produced popular fiction tells much about a certain secularist-Turkish discourse on Islam.[10] The site of humorous and rumor-filled imagination about "the Islamic future of Istanbul" was one of the most effective arenas for the consumption and production of discourse on local culture.[11]

The domain of humor and rumor reflects discursive knowledge in the form of "flashes," in Walter Benjamin's sense of the term. The jokes and the gossip are like glimpses of "memory as it flashes up at a moment of danger" (1968, 255). Benjamin's work is useful in identifying *streams of consciousness*, a concept that, I argue, ought to be important in anthropological analysis. More than in consciously formulated ideology or formalized conversation, humor and rumor reveal an unconscious precipitation of remembered discursive forms in the present. My ethnographic examples reveal that Islam was conceived, on the part of secularist joke-tellers and gossips, as a plea for the rejuvenation of local and native (*yerel*) against contemporary and civilized values (in Turkish the word *çağdaş* encompasses both the latter notions). The fleeting stream of references here were to the early republican period, which has been cultivated in discourses that circulate in contemporary Turkish social institutions. What I will now recount are examples of humorous secularist projections about Islamist mayors' notions of locality and nativeness.

A day or so after the election results, a secularist businessman ironically said, "My attire is settled. I already have a beard. All I need are prayer beads and I am fine!" A small shop owner asked his employees, "Tell me what color veils you want, so I can order them wholesale for you to wear from now on!" Some joked with female acquaintances on the street suggesting that they would no longer be able to stroll around without proper Islamic cover. A writer said that he would volunteer to wear a turban: "At least no one will see the bald spot on my head!" Like this, many of the humorous comments produced by secularists had to do with dress and appearance. Indeed, one of the main things that secularists imagined Islamists would do would be to impose Islamic public attire in place of versions of European-style clothes now customarily worn by many of Turkey's urbanites. In their discursive association, Islamic attire was mapped onto tradition, nativeness, or the past, in contrast to "Westernized attire," which was linked with the modern and contemporary.

In the week that followed the elections, a young bus driver of Istanbul was making funny sarcastic remarks in reference to what he called "the Islamist takeover." "From now on everyone goes to bed at twelve," he said. And, "how nice, Turkey sleeps after midnight! No more fun in bars or drinking places!" "What are we going to do?" middle-class youth asked one another while laughing nervously. "Well, we're sure to find some new ways to entertain ourselves. Perhaps we can learn to chant and whirl like dervishes!" Those who could partake in the social and cultural life of the metropolis were unsure of the future of their habits. They feared that they would be forced to resort to Islamic or local ways of socializing and entertaining themselves instead of enjoying the lifestyle available in the bars, restaurants, cafés, movie houses, theaters, and discotheques of Istanbul, which were said to match those of the world's biggest metropolises.

Mostly, secularists speculated about possible restrictions on women's lives through the enforcement of "Islamic ways." An apartment tenant, associating "Islam" with polygamy, told his neighbors, "I will visit you with my four wives next time!" "Awful! Awful! Especially for us women," a young bank employee complained with a grave-looking grin. "They won't allow women to work, women will sit at home, will not vote, will have to wear the veil, et cetera." She was sitting alone by the bar tender in an inexpensive bar. "This must be one of my last nights out like this!" she ironically gasped. Shocked by the election result, secular Istanbulis were attempting to relax by humorously getting themselves ready for what they perceived was the worst that could happen.

Those unfamiliar with Istanbul might not comprehend why the thought of such things as enforced veiling and polygamy or as controlled public space could be so outrageous for citizens of a Muslim country, especially if those readers maintain such a preconception about what is native or authentic to "Muslim cultures." Curiously, many citizens of Turkey who identify themselves as secularists share versions of such Western constructions about what is normal to Muslim countries. Yet one thing that native secularists knew was that as far as they could remember, the religious order that they demonized did not exist in their country. In their mental associations and categorizations, Turkey was different from other Muslim countries, and especially distinct from Iran and Saudi Arabia. In the mid-1990s, a common slogan chanted by secularists in counter-Islamist demonstrations was "Turkey will not become Iran."

Under cultural reforms introduced by Ataturk, as secularists had been schooled to remember, there had been a clothing reform in 1925, when the wearing of the fez, the turban, and the robe was abolished and that of the veil officially discouraged. Since then, Turkish urbanites mostly followed domesticated versions of West European fashion variable by class. In fact, it would be wrong to classify such clothing as "Westernized" or "European," for they are so much part of Turkey. Women's pants, trimly fit skirts, and sweaters are as authentic to Turkey as the veils and overcoats worn by contemporary Islamist women. But, in the constructions of those citizens brought up under republican institutions, not only secularists but also Islamists, such clothes as the turban, the robe, and the veil symbolized Islam or what was local to Turkey as opposed to European modernity, into which Turkey had been slowly assimilating through years of Westernization. The voters in the March 1994 elections were not used to encountering large numbers of veiled or turbaned people on the streets of Istanbul. Even though many women wore scarves in public at that time, there was no official requirement and many of the scarves worn by immigrants from small Anatolian towns or villages did not necessarily indicate religiosity. Secular Istanbulis knew the city as a metropolis with numerous locales for public entertainment, including bars and restaurants, cafés, casinos, and nightclubs. Drinking alcohol was part of social life. Most of the public spaces they frequented were open to women especially in daytime, if not also at night, and most women worked outside the home. It was from the vantage point of such marks of urban middle-class sociality that secular Istanbulis preemptively imagined what could happen with enforced authentication or a return to Islam.

Humorous speculations about a dystopian future under an Islamist city administration reflected genuine unease. Concerns revolved around a cluster of issues. Islam or local culture signified only specific things to those who were anxious at the time.[12] As the jokes reveal, covered public appearance, especially for women, was central to the resonance of "Islamic order" in the stream of secularists' consciousness. Restrictions on drinking and public entertainment presented another conviction about "Islam." And most important, there was speculation about control over women's public lives. All these markers of everyday public comportment had been surpassed, secularists thought, with national leader Ataturk's Westernizing cultural reforms, which they believed to have moved Turkey to a more "modern echelon of culture." A revivalist movement, they imagined, would want to unearth local or Islamic cultural ways that had historically been overcome. And, somehow, again and again "nativeness" was related by these secularists to the public practices of women (Göle 1991). Islam, in their construction, was primarily about a restriction on women's liberties and lifestyles.

Cultural differences between secularists and Islamists at that time of crisis were mapped onto the question of gender. This should not be much of a surprise to anyone attuned to the gendered component of social formations. But what is more interesting to point out was the *excess* of emphasis placed on gender at this time. According to secular Istanbulis, Islamists were different particularly in terms of the moralist restrictions that they would impose on women. Curiously, in international othering discourses on Islam—with their constructions that implicate Istanbul's secularists and Islamists—Islam surpasses other socio-cultural domains in its attention to women. Islam is portrayed as obsessed with gender, as if other domains were less so.

There is, of course, also a historical explanation for secular Istanbulis' mapping of their difference with Islamists especially onto the question of the public practices of women. In the formative years of the Turkish nation-state, Ataturk had tried to differentiate the "new" Turkey from its past, and from its Muslim neighbors, especially by instituting two important reforms for women. In 1925, he and his associates discouraged the wearing of the veil, and, with girls' institutes all over the country, institutionalized a new mode of dressing for Turkey's women.[13] In 1934, women were granted voting rights, long before Swiss women received it. Turkey had a stake in illustrating to Europeans that it was even more modern than they were.[14] In the historical consciousness of today's secularists, the culture of Turkey had been differentiated from its Ottoman-Islamic past, especially on the axis of gender. Turkey, in this secularist narrative of progress with deculturation, had detached itself from its local culture to ascend to civilized ways, especially in "liberating" women. So much symbolic weight had been attached to the question of women in the period of the new nation-state's character formation, that it is no surprise for contemporary secularists to differentiate themselves once again from local culture or Islam especially on the basis of gender. As a secularist woman from Istanbul remarked on the eve of the last national elections, when the Islamist Party was due to win, "It's all about gender!" ("*hepsi cinsiyet ile ilgili!*").

The public imaginary about Islam that I untangle here, in studying the secular middle class of Istanbul, might seem to resonate with versions of Orientalist constructions of Islam, especially as articulated in contemporary Western media. Compare, for example, Turkish-secularists' notions of Islam with the subject matter of Edward Said's criticism in his *Orientalism* (1978) and *Covering Islam* (1981). One can indeed argue that images of Islam that were institutionalized and popularized under secularist regimes in republican Turkey, as well as contemporary secularist ideas about Islam, have been influenced by past and present Orientalisms. What is even more interesting to note is the comparable implication of Islamists in Turkey in Orientalist discoursing on Islam. In other words, Turkish-Islamists have been Orientalizing themselves. The gender emphasis in secularist-Islamist politics of culture in Turkey is as pronounced as it is because internalized Orientalist discourses on Islam are significantly gendered.

One of the most humorous speculations about the Islamic future of Istanbul appeared in a fax that was circulated during the elections of 1994. There was a traffic in signed and anonymous faxes throughout private and public offices of Istanbul at this time, calling upon people to unite in the name of the legacy of secularist and modernist leader Ataturk. Indeed, communication technology has been a central medium in the formation of politics of culture in the contemporary Turkish public life. And among a heavy load of panic-stricken invitations "to do something," was a letter from one Cüneyt Kurt, "owner of Şans Restaurant," that was most likely intended as a joke:

> As you all know, our party [Welfare] is the strongest candidate of the March 27, 1994 municipality elections in Istanbul. With the permission of God and the power of the faith granted to us by our Prophet, we will win these elections. In fact, we will not be satisfied with this, we will win national elections and build the just order [*adil düzen*—the motto of Welfare's utopia].[15]
>
> Below we indicate the new order that will be enforced in restaurants, night clubs, and casinos run by infidels like you.
>
> **1.** The sale or maintenance of all alcoholic beverages will be forbidden. Moreover, beverages such as Coca-Cola and Pepsi, which are inventions of the infidels [*gâvur icadı*], will be disallowed. Only the sale of boza, ayran, şıra, demirhindi, and lemonade ["local beverages"] will be permitted in these establishments.
>
> **2.** The sale and maintenance of dirty and sinful pork products will also be forbidden. In these places, only meat butchered according to religious prescriptions (*helal*) will be allowed.

3. These establishments will be organized anew and separated on the basis of gender [*harem-selamlık*]. Only a special section will be reserved for families. Women will enter these places with faces and bodies covered in the black veil and will never reveal their heads in any way that may provoke adultery.

4. In these establishments only Arabic music and yalelli will be allowed, all sorts of infidel music and songs will be disallowed. Moreover, electrical instruments of music, which are once again inventions of the infidels, will not be used, instead the ud, the tef, the string saz and blow instruments ["local instruments"] will be used.

5. One room in these establishments will be kept as small mosque [*mescit*] for prayer.

6. All these establishments will be required to close before the nighttime *namaz*.

We consider it an obligation to send this written warning to all imitators of the infidels and all those who are skewed religiously like yourself. In case you accept to abide by the just order until we come to power, we may forgive you and accept you as one of ourselves. Otherwise, the destitute homes of sin run by people who do not follow these rules will be burnt and destroyed and the owners will be stoned in public.

Those who remain alive after this stoning will be punished by the annihilation of their private parts. For your information.

This was a self-conscious exaggeration and ironic caricaturization of what was a latent idea about Islamic order (read: "local culture") shared by many secularists in Turkey, at least before the Welfare Party assumed power. Surely the witty author did not know whether such an order, including stoning and castration, would really be enforced. He meant to be bitterly funny. Yet, beneath the mockery is secularist Turkish discourse about Islam. The inventers of this anti-utopia thought that their everyday habits of "living like modern Westerners" would no longer be available, to be replaced by something of the local past. They imagined that they would be forced to drink what they constructed as native drinks, *ayran* and *boza*, and no more Coca-Cola. They would have to attune themselves to what they construed as Arabic-sounding music and no longer listen to Turkish disco or English jazz. Instead of strolling with their significant others dressed in pants and dresses, they would have to assume Islamic dress and sit separately in public. In other words, they thought that they would have to localize or "Islamicize" what they defined to be their civilized and up-to-date (*çağdaş*) or "secular" (*laik*) ways of comporting themselves.

Secular Istanbulis, much like white Europeans, tended to think at the time that their ways were not cultural. Culture, in their construction, was what Islamists had, praying five times a day, celebrating religious festivals, reading the Kuran in Arabic script, dressing in Islamic gear, and so forth.[16]

In contrast, secular Istanbulites imagined that they themselves had transcended culture.[17] They were modern; they were civilized; they had attained global norms, leaving behind a local abberation. It is hence that secularists thought that the Welfare Party's campaign for the municipalities, unlike that of other political parties, was about culture. They thought that Welfare would force them to localize their up-to-date and civilized ways. In fact, however, as time went by after the initial two months of Islamist municipal rule, secularists shifted their discourse on local culture and found that to be publicly convincing, they had to argue that their ways were local, too.

Rumor or Reality?

The period after the elections produced not only humor and story, but also much rumor. Within the two weeks that followed the announcement of election results, rumors spread in the city that Welfarists were harassing people in public. Many people returned home with stories, either experienced in person or heard from someone else, of street confrontations.[18] On March 29, 1994, two days after the day of election, I heard, via word-of-mouth, that "some men approached women without headscarves as they were walking in a central district of the city and told the women that they would no longer be able to promenade in that fashion." One middle-aged man said that "a woman who went to a children's park was told by some covered women that she couldn't enter that place without covering her head." On those tense days that followed Welfare's electoral victory, many people were sitting around, exchanging overheard stories of street events. I heard, for example, that "a woman who was getting on a public bus in the neighborhood of Sarıyer in Istanbul was not allowed in because she wasn't properly covered." Then there was a story about men dressed in turbans and robes attempting to separate train passengers (traveling from a suburb of Istanbul) by gender into different compartments.

Mass media, print or broadcast, also had a role in spreading or catalyzing the dispersion of hearsay. The secularist newspaper *Cumhuriyet* reported the following on April 1, 1994: "Fanatics kidnapped a bus in Istanbul. . . . Four turbaned and robed aggressors who halted a public bus in [the neighborhood of] Ortaköy ordered the women passengers out and threatened the men to abide by the order of the segregation of genders [*harem-selamlık*]." He added, "After the Welfare Party won the municipality of greater Istanbul, . . . gangs in favor of Islamic order have been continuing their attacks against young girls and women."[19] Similar coverage appeared in mainstream newspapers and TV broadcasts as well.[20] The news items were based on calls made to press offices by people who had experienced the events. But, even more than word-of-mouth, press coverage had the further effect of confirming, validating, and enhancing the power of rumor.

In the everyday life of Istanbul in March 1994, women were used to being subjected to sexual harassment on the street, but not especially on the basis of whether they followed Islamic prescriptions to cover. Men and women ordinarily used the same vehicles for public transportation, standing or sitting beside one another. There were few public places, among them traditional coffee shops, certain restaurants and bars, certain schools, and mosques, that had gender-based rules of entry. It was to city people used to this kind of public life that rumor of harassment on the basis of attire or the use of public space appeared unnerving and absurd.

Hearsay is not produced or consumed in a cultural or historical vacuum. I argue that if opponents of Welfare were complaining, then, of attacks on their freedom of movement in the city, or if they were spreading such warning far and wide, it was because they were already afraid of the possibility of such attacks. Long before Welfarist officials made any first moves to institute change in the urban domain, secular urbanites speculated humorously about what would happen with an Islamist administration. Slavoj Žižek has interpreted the reception of the sinking of the *Titanic* by Europeans at the turn of the last century in a similar way:

> The sinking of the *Titanic* had a traumatic effect, it was a shock, "the impossible had happened," the unsinkable ship had sunk; but the point is that precisely as a shock, this sinking arrived at its proper time—"the time was waiting for it": even before it actually happened, there was already a place opened, reserved for it in fantasy-space. It had such a terrific impact on "social imaginary" by virtue of the fact that it was expected (1995, 69).

Žižek is studying the historical context for the excessive interest in interpreting the meaning of the *Titanic* wreck. He notes,

> [A]t the turn of the century, it was already part of Zeitgeist that a certain age was coming to an end—the age of peaceful progress, of well-defined and stable class distinctions, and so on: that is, the long period from 1850 until the First World War. . . .
>
> In other words, the wreck of the *Titanic* made such a tremendous impact not because of the immediate material dimensions of the catastrophe but because of its symbolic overdetermination, because of the ideological meaning invested in it: it was read as a "symbol," as a condensed, metaphorical representation of the approaching catastrophe of European civilization itself. The wreck of the *Titanic* was a form in which society lived the experience of its own death (1995, 70).

It is likewise that I study the reception of the Welfare Party's victory in Istanbul's municipality elections. Following Žižek, I will argue that the time was ripe at this historical contingency for secular urbanites to interpret the success of the Welfare Party in the way that they did. Was there fear about the flimsiness of the modernization project in the seventy-year-old Turkish republic? That was to be sure. But what is significant to point out is that the Welfare Party, before it even realized itself in practice, was received through the sieve of an already existing secularist discourse about Islamism. Secularists projected their fears about restrictions on public life across gender. With an imaginary of beheading as a form of punishment in Islamic law, secularists thought that Welfarists would institute this upon assuming power. They feared that all Turkish women would be forced to veil and to confine themselves to the private sphere of the home. In other words, when the Welfare Party won, the context was already there for this sort of interpretation.

A point needs to be made about self-fulfilling prophecy. Othering discourses about Islam and Islamism preceded the Welfare Party's bureaucratic practices in the municipalities, and they proved to have some actual consequences. Michel Foucault has written about what he calls the "truth effects of discourse":

> The individual is no doubt the fictitious atom of an "ideological" representation of society; but he is also a reality fabricated by this specific technology of power that I have called "discipline." We must cease once and for all to describe the effects of power in negative terms: it "excludes," it "represses," it "censors," it "abstracts," it "masks," it "conceals." In fact, power produces; it produces reality; it produces domains of objects and rituals of truth. The individual and the knowledge that may be gained of him belong to this production (1979, 194).

Here Foucault makes a provocative statement about the generation or the emergence of subjectivities through specific mechanisms of power. Power, in this understanding, does not shape by curbing, abolishing, or repressing individuals. Rather, individuals, as the desired objects of power, are constructed as such through productive and generating mechanisms.

The content of the imagistic humor and rumor that prevailed in Istanbul's social networks during the 1990s was constructed in the domain of an influential media as a technology of power—media in the broad sense of the term, implying a journalistic gaze on the world enhanced by photographic and video cameras. Islamist individuals were gazed at, interviewed, photographed, filmed, broadcast, framed, followed, and inspected by journalists of the mainstream Turkish press. The images of women in veils and men in turbans were fixed through sensational exposition on TV. Humor and rumor, as it wandered through private and public domains, was fed and regenerated through the technologies of mediatic power. Islamist individuals were produced, in a certain sense, on these sites of power.

Black humor had the power to effect seemingly essentializing truths about Islamists. It did not, however, incite the sorts of truth that secularists and Westernists desired. It rather worked mostly to engender what secularists dreaded.[21] This was production in the negative sense of the term. Hence the use of Žižek's notion of "prophecy." The context is set for the receipt of a catastrophe from the point of view of secularists. There was anxiety about the coming-of-age of the republic.

Indeed, secularist discourse on Islam to a certain extent contained "effects of truth," in Foucault's sense of the term, proving to have power in inciting historical change. Prejudices aired about the Welfare Party had the uncanny ability actually to engender events, at times like a self-fulfilling prophecy. Humorous exchanges about calamities brought on by an Islamist city administration preceded the actuality of such events. The rumor struck a familiar chord in the cultural imagination of a specific secularist public about Islam. Whether the rumored events were real or not, whether they had actually materialized or not, the way in which the events were interpreted and felt through rumor was specific to the discourse of secularists. For many people, the stories matched a preexisting structure of feeling about Islamists and their quests for the enforcement of a certain Islamic local culture. Otherwise, why would there be humor only about particular sorts of incidents? Or, when the rumored events really materialized, why did only particular sorts of things take place?

The incidents I narrate in this section are about the truth effects of discourse. A dominant secularist discourse about Islam managed not only to imagine but, at least to a certain extent, also to produce truth about Islam. This is an argument, pace Foucault, about the inherency or inseparability of discourse and event or construction and experience. However, the dynamism of the political in the city demands that we study further than the determinism that Foucault's notion of "truth effects" implies.

Slavoj Žižek writes about the tendency for a psychoanalytic / political context to bring about by default the feared event. Žižek studies this in reference to Lacan's notion of "the lack," where the subject so much identifies with his psychoanalytic weakness that he produces situations that will trigger his pain. He writes,

> The Oxford philosopher Michael Dummett has written two very interesting articles included in his collection of essays *Truth and Other Enigmas*: "Can an Effect Precede its Cause?" and "Bringing about the Past." [T]he Lacanian answer to these two enigmas would be: yes, because the symptom as a "return of the repressed" is precisely such an effect which precedes its cause (its hidden kernel, its meaning), and in working through the symptom we are precisely "bringing about the past"—we are producing the symbolic reality of the past, long-forgotten traumatic events (1995, 56–57).

One of Žižek's characteristic joke-stories, this time an interpretation of Greek mythology, perfectly illustrates the point:

> We find the same structure in the myth of Oedipus: it is predicted to Oedipus's father that his son will kill him and marry his mother, and the prophecy realizes itself, "becomes true," through the father's attempt to evade it (he exposes his little son in the forest, and so Oedipus, not recognizing him when he encounters him twenty years later, kills him . . .). In other words, the prophecy becomes true by means of its being communicated to the persons it affects and by means of his or her attempt to elude it: one knows in advance one's destiny, one tries to evade it, and it is by means of this very attempt that the predicted destiny realizes itself. Without the prophecy, the little Oedipus would live happily with his parents and there would be no "Oedipus complex" (1995, 58).

Žižek's study of the prophecy is insightful, to a certain extent, in studying the self-destructive effect of discourse. And, in one reading of the Turkish elections, one could study the historical turning point in the two critical months that preceded and followed the success of the Welfare Party in municipality elections as an apparent actualization of "prophecy." We could say that the secularists, knowing that Islamists were rising to power to challenge a secularist system, enabled or catalyzed its course in their attempts to evade it with black humor. The Welfare Party represented the negation of the being, life, presence, and identity of Istanbul's secularists. That is why discussion about Islamism proliferated in that period when the Welfare Party had widened its constituency. A Welfarist success was the worst thing that could happen from the secularist point of view. It was imagined as a catastrophe. And, at least in the beginning, what was feared was realized. Moreover, the symbolic content of the anxieties to a certain extent materialized, too. Secularist speculations about Islamists centered on a few central symbolic issues: the use of public space across gender and the wearing of the Islamist-style headscarf. In the months that followed the election victory, these issues became central to certain Welfarist officials' knowledge of themselves and to strategizing about urban administration, as well. History took shape in a relational manner.[22]

The rumors I have mentioned revolve around the public separation of men and women, either through women's attire or through the physical segregation of space. Is this Islam? Is this Turkish local culture? Does this reflect what is native to Turkey or what was there before Turkey moved to Westernize? I would argue that contemporary Islamist life practices do not represent the repressed native striking back, as certain cultural critics and social scientists of Turkey have argued (e.g., Robins 1996, Göle 1991), but it is what has been reconstituted, reformulated, or constructed as native on the part both of secularists and Islamists after years of so-called Westernization in Turkey. For in actuality the new practices of Islamists are very contemporary and have little to do with those in the Ottoman Empire or in the times of the Prophet Muhammad, as Islamists would claim or secularists would imagine.

When rumors of harassment spread, the preempted anxiety of secularists was confirmed. The Islamic order that they had been creatively imagining and fearing had begun, in certain incidents, to take the shape of an Islam that they were actually experiencing on the streets of Istanbul. When Welfarist street dwellers indeed disturbed people in one way or another on the basis of their public manners, they realized the secularists' nightmares. In the instance of reporting on harassment, image and event were indistinguishable. So much symbolic bearing had been given to women's public appearance that, in time of crisis, the notions of Islam and locality came to be identified with the veil, even for some of their Islamist proponents. In certain coincidences of feeling between secularists and Islamists—one fearing, the other realizing the fear—events were indeed produced and engendered.

And yet, there were others who reacted to secularist prejudice in a different way. A study of the shaping of the political in urban public culture demands a more dynamic theoretical framework than allowed by either Foucault or Žižek. Events in the city were indeed related to public discourse and prophecy. Yet, if public worries, as circulated in the city and magnified in the media, were initially actualized by Islamists, the political relation (or dialogue) in itself produced other, more indeterminate, eventualities.

"It is not us [Welfare's cadre] who are doing this," a municipal police officer of the neighborhood of Beyoğlu complained to me one day. We were sitting in a corridor of Beyoğlu's municipality building a couple of days after the election finale. The building was crowded with Welfare Party officials joyously settling in. The officer had just returned from a call to work on the main street of Beyoğlu. "We were called because there were four men walking around with turbans, robes, and sticks, hitting women with miniskirts on the street," he said. "They are accusing us [Welfare's workers] of this sort of event. In fact, these turbaned men are provocateurs. They are doing this in order to divert public opinion against us." With a few other officers of the new municipality, this man had turned in the harassers to the central police station. Welfare officials were worried about these events because they did not want to be associated with them. Having just assumed power, they wanted to show that they would be effective in managing urban affairs, doing what city municipalities were supposed to do.

For certain Islamists, like the gang of Welfare supporters on the streets of Beyoğlu, negative propaganda about Islam had the effect of a pre-scripted mise-en-scène. The group of young men dressed in turbans and robes were out actualizing secularist discourse on the supposed essence of what would happen under an Islamic order. Why was this gang especially picking on women walking around in miniskirts? Did Islam not signify any other practice, or anything else, for these believers? On the other hand, among some officials of the victorious party itself, more pragmatic about sustaining rule, reaction to secularist discoursing was different. As my discussion with the municipal police officer reveals, certain workers of Welfare wanted to disprove and not to realize the fears of their opponents. In fact, many of the Welfarist administrators and workers to whom I spoke at the time were attempting to escape secularist pigeonholes, by trying to divert attention away from controversy over veils or miniskirts, Coca-Cola or lemonade.

In light of this historical turn of events, contemporaneous with the events on the street, one could reread the Oedipus myth in a manner that differs from Žižek's reading. Žižek's approach to "prophecy" is much too deterministic. In the Oedipus myth, Žižek envisions no other historical consequence, but that which was predicated in the prophecy. There is too much closure and predetermination in his approach to history. But history can take many courses and there is much more human agency involved. We could also read the Oedipus myth in a different way. We could suggest that it was only out of some unhappy coincidence that Oedipus ended up killing his father. The king believed in the prophecy and there *is* a truth effect there, in that instance and incidence, as far as the king decides to send his son away in order to prevent patricide. But Oedipus had never met his father when he committed the murder. In fact, he did not know that he was killing his father. He might have not encountered this man in the forest and history would have taken a different course. Ultimately, it was a coincidence that made it seem like the prophecy was realized.

Here, there is coincidence and uncertainty. Discourse has truth effects only if the receiver of the oracle transfers his or her structure of feeling onto it. And there too, there is an uncertainty. One may relate to the oracle and one may not. In Turkey most secularists transferred their fears onto Islamists. And yet the final result was not predictable. While certain Islamists related to the othering images that secularists had projected onto them, other Islamists did not. In certain coincidences of structure of feeling and contingency, secularist and Islamist discourse merged to engender "the prophecy." In others, Islamists went off on their own course, refusing to be objectified by secularists, and attempting to define themselves and shape their practices of everyday life in their own terms. There is much to be learned in exploring the difference between the turbaned Islamist men on the streets of Beyoğlu who had taken to harassing unveiled women on the streets, as prophecied in secularist humor, and the lower-level Welfare

Party officials who tried to dissociate themselves from such acts of enforcement. And indeed, Islamists in Turkey cannot be studied in holistic terms. They related to secularists in different contingent terms at different times, through one coincidence of feeling in relation, or through another in reaction, but always in charge of a certain level of agency.

A comparison of the reaction of Welfarist street dwellers with that of Welfarist officers vis-à-vis an objectifying secularist discourse is important. Secularist and Islamist individuals, in many other incidents, revealed more agency in managing their ways within discursive conditions of possibility than Foucault and Žižek allow their historical subjects of study. In this case, negative discoursing about Islam is shown to have always relational, yet indeterminably diverse effects on Turkish-Islamists. One negative has multiple positives. Welfarist gangs assertively realized prejudice about themselves, upholding the negative image of themselves as a positive, desirable, and moral way of living from an Islamist point of view. On the other hand, Welfare's officials were attempting to dissociate themselves from these images. Discourse, then, had no predeterminable effect, only situational effects that became knowable in the aftermath of events, events that were the making of engaged human agents.

The Issues at Stake

During the first couple of months after the election results, journalists of secular mass media were preoccupied with the affairs of the new municipalities. The new leaders, victoriously sitting in their democratically earned seats, indeed provoked much attention. In awe of the first Islamist takeover of significant official power in the history of republican Turkey, the new leaders seemed to be amused in declaring their dreams for "a more Islamic Istanbul." In those first interactions between journalists of secular mass media and the new Islamist mayors, all broadcast nationwide on TV and published in detail in newspapers, the secularist discourse on Islam and nativeness was at play once again. When Welfare administration became reality, journalists posed only certain sorts of questions to the new mayors: what might seem like trivia, but what I would name pseudo-trivia.

"What will you do with the brothels in Beyoğlu?" asked a young TV reporter in one of the very first public addresses of Istanbul's new mayor Tayyip Erdoğan. "I will shut them down and send their workers to resthomes," responded the victorious mayor, seeming to enjoy the pleasure, at that time, of announcing his most provocative visions. A day after the election results were formally announced, an article appeared in a secular mainstream newspaper, in which Istanbul's police chief assured readers that "municipalities can only inspect brothels' hygiene, they have no authority to shut these down by themselves. . . . As long as the governor of Istanbul [who is appointed by the state] does not approve, nobody can close any brothel."[23] The question of brothels was also high on the agenda of foreign journalists who had flocked to Turkey at that time to report on what they thought were the outrageous election results in the only secular state in the Middle East. I was present when a reporter from the French news magazine *L'Express* was interviewing Nusret Bayraktar, the new mayor to the district of Beyoğlu on April 2, 1994, in the municipality building. When the question was put differently, a different answer was produced. "Is the problem of brothels one of the main issues on your agenda, or is the press exaggerating this?" proposed the French journalist. The mayor attempted to make it clear:

> Brothels are not our first, not even our second, but one of our very last preoc-
> cupations. Our first tasks will be routine ones. We will visit different neighbor-
> hoods and ask, "What are your needs?" and we will meet those specific needs.

In this instance, the mayor attempted to sidetrack the effect of the Western journalist's discourse. Yet, despite the mayor's intentions, such a big deal had already been made out of the shaky future of brothels on the part of secular mass media, that, indeed, one of the very first tasks of the mayor turned out to be a general inspection of the brothels of Beyoğlu.

"Are you going to remove the portraits of Ataturk from office buildings?" journalists queried the new mayor of Beyoğlu, imagining he would do so as the Welfare Party defined itself against the national leader's secularism. "Or will you hang a portrait of Fatih Sultan Mehmet by it?" suggested the French reporter, referring to the Ottoman conqueror of Istanbul much revered by Welfarists. "We are not bothered by such obsessions with form," Nusret Bayraktar snapped, irritated by the questions. "If there are people who have served our society in the past, we remember them, but we are not into such formalisms."[24] Here Bayraktar reflected the othering discourse back, refusing to produce it in his subjectivity and intention. But the attitude of Ankara's new Welfarist mayor was different vis-à-vis this question. When reporters wondered, "Will you visit Ataturk's mausoleum before assuming office?" Melih Gökçek responded, "Don't ask me such silly questions!" He was not intending to abide by the state decree that required all officers to visit Ataturk's tomb before taking office. Gökçek was realizing secularists' prophecy. In a press conference, Hayri Kozak-çıoğlu, the state-appointed governor of Istanbul reassured the public that "in case the photographs of Ataturk are removed from municipality buildings, [he] will take legal action. In public offices, people are obliged to have a picture of Ataturk on the wall."[25]

As the new mayors assumed public office, there was much uproar about the inaugural ceremonies. "Welfarist mayors took power by praying and

offering sacrificial animals," was the news, "when mayors of the Social
Democratic People's Party (SHP) and the Republican People's Party (CHP)
placed flowers by Ataturk memorials."[26] A couple of weeks later, the new
mayor's manner of inaugurating the municipal parliament of Istanbul came
under alarmed criticism. While the normal procedure asked that members
silently stand in respect to Ataturk and sing the national anthem, the
mayor opened the ceremony by reading a prayer (the *fatiha*). Outraged by
the incident, the social democratic mayor of the district of Beşiktaş ran
forward and asked the Welfarist mayor to stand in respect to Ataturk. In
response, the Welfarist mayor said, "As Muslims, we read the *fatiha*, which
is the best gift to our elders. There is no logic in idly standing up." But in
spite of slurs on the part of Welfarist parliamentarians, the secularist mayor
of Beşiktaş tried to move people to stand in respect to Ataturk. As members of the parliament began to chant the national anthem, the Welfarist
mayor felt obliged to stand, but could not keep himself from criticizing the
ordeal by saying that standing in respect to the deceased was a Western
tradition. "What good does it do to the dead if we stand for them?"[27] In
this incident, the Islamist mayor produced an effect of a secularist discourse by voicing his opinion on the procedure and reading the prayer. But
he also deflected this discourse by ultimately standing in respect to
Ataturk.

Notice that a discursive distinction between foreignness and nativeness
as mapped respectively onto secularism and Islam runs in this controversy,
as well. A revivalist movement would, in the imagination of secularist journalists, replace secularist symbols such as the portrait of Ataturk and the
national anthem with Islamic ones like the picture of Fatih or the prayer,
fatiha. It turned out, in this case, that the Welfarist mayor himself reproduced this dichotomous discourse through his actions. In definining the
habit of standing in respect to the deceased as "a Western tradition,"
against the Islamic prayer as "authentic" to Muslims, the mayor was putting the secularist distinction between the foreign and the local to effect.
But let us not forget that the mayor also ultimately stood in respect to
Ataturk. Through such everyday incidents and their interpretation, a particular kind of Islamism was taking shape in Turkey, one that no holistic
social science would be able to place.

In another exchange, a TV reporter, addressing the representative of the
ladies' commission of the Welfare Party, asked, "Will you bring restrictions
to women's clothing? Will women still be able to wear miniskirts if they
want to?" "We will ask social scientists to do research on the moral values
of the average Turkish citizen, and we will study the results and bring
regulations accordingly," Welfare's representative Sibel Eraslan replied.
She was suggesting a normalization of public appearance on the basis of a

supposedly objective evaluation of general local values. Implicitly, miniskirts would have to fall outside this category of native Turkish culture.

Indeed, the future of brothels, Ataturk portraits, and miniskirts were on top of the agenda of secular mainstream journalism on those first days after Welfare won. And through the media, the concern trickled down to anxious viewers to an important extent. These issues were discussed as the markers of cultural difference between secularists and Islamists. Discussion was directed constantly to the future of such symbols of modernity and civilization or of "the state of being up-to-date with the world" (in Turkish, *çağdaşlık*).

Part of the anxiety of secularists indeed turned out to be well founded, but in this case the attack was easily repelled. One of the very first measures taken by Beyoğlu's new mayor was to order the removal of tavern tables that were set out on the street or sidewalk. Restaurant owners were asked to put opaque curtains on their windows to conceal indoors. This interdiction was justified with a rhetoric of populism, with Welfarist officers arguing that the street would become more accessible to pedestrians who could not afford to eat out. A few days after the event, a group of secularists organized a sit-in on Nevizade street, moving the tables outdoors and drinking beer, *rakı*, and wine in public. They demanded their right to socialize and drink in public space. One of secularists' worst fears had been realized on the very first week of Welfarist takeover. Islamists had begun to regulate the use of public space, pushing social life forcefully indoors. There was no conceivable way the outdoor facilities of Beyoğlu locales could be forced shut, for there was vast demand for these to remain open. Within a few weeks, the mayor had to allow tables out onto the streets once again.

This incident shows that in crafting an ethnography of the ways in which discourses on local culture affect the actualization of municipal policy, one has to be very specific historically, for the first months that followed the election results were different from later ones. In the first month of intensity, discourse had much the effect of truth; prophecy was almost realized. In the latter months of sharing space and institutions, discourse began to dissipate, leaving way to newer formulations of public notions of culture. In other words, if some of the first Islamist actions in urban public space were loaded with older structural projections about Islam and local culture, later, as cross-political relations inevitably developed on the site of urban affairs, new matter was culturalized and unpremeditated issues were raised.

Indeed, in the period that followed the initial workings of the Welfare Party's city municipality, secularists shifted their discourse to identify *their* ways of comporting themselves as more local and native (*yerel*) than the ways of Islamists. In this new contingency and turn of events, secularists, *too*, began to sidetrack the discourse of nativeness that they were self-destructively producing through black humor. Prominent secularist artists, actors, professionals, and intellectuals came forward in declaring themselves Muslim (*Müslüman*), something that they had never cared to do before. They wanted to argue that they were Muslim and they did not veil, they did not perform the *namaz*, they drank alcohol, they watched movies, and socialized in public places across gender. In this strategic turn of discourse and prophecy, secularists came to assert their own nativeness, their belonging in Turkey.

Before the elections and soon after, only particular sorts of things were issues in identity politics. At that time, everyday events were more influenced by preexisting structures of feeling about Islam and nativeness. Stereotypical symbols were issues of struggle, as in the overinterpretation of women's public appearance. As time passed and as the new city municipality settled in, new issues came to the fore that could not have been anticipated by either parties of the struggle before or during the time of the elections. No ironic humor, no creative imagination, no unrestrained whispers could foretell what absurdities would become matters of contention in the course of the following months. The domain of the municipalities, in practice, was creating new sites of struggle, new discourses, and possible new prophecies.

The Prophecy

A famous example of how "Western" notions of Islam can generate self-fulfilling prophecies may be found in the Rushdie affair. A particular analysis of the Rushdie affair via prophecy will be instructive for the argument developed here about politics of culture in Turkey. In a 1996 article published in *The Guardian* (UK), Mehdi Mozaffari wrote a disclaimer to the representation of Ayatollah Khomeini's statement after the publication of Salman Rushdie's *Satanic Verses*. The author argued that Khomeini had not, contrary to the claims of Western reporters, declared a "fatwa" against Rushdie. In this article, "The Fatwa that Wasn't," Mozaffari wrote a genealogy for the use of the term "fatwa" in international public discourses during the Rushdie affair:

> It was not the clergy of Iran, nor the Iranians, nor the Muslims who first called Ayatollah Khomeini's death decree against Salman Rushdie a fatwa. Khomeini's office which published the ayatollah's message on Rushdie on February 14, 1989, made no claim that it was a fatwa—an enduring decision by a recognized religious authority.

> Why, then, did this non-fatwa suddenly become a fatwa, and who made it a fatwa? (1996, 16)

According to Mozaffari, the term "fatwa" in characterization of the Muslim world's response to Salman Rushdie, was first used by two young French journalists, Olivier Roy and Gilles Keppel.[28]

> First, Olivier Roy wrote on February 17: "The fatwa decree by Imam Khomeini . . . "; and then came what could be called the real beginning of "the fatwa" usage with Gilles Keppel's article in *Le Monde* on February 25 (16).

The author noted that, in the few months that followed Khomeini's statement against Rushdie, no one in Iran, including high-ranking members of the clergy, spoke of it as a "fatwa." As the term "fundamentalism" was first coined by Western observers, Mozaffari notes, so was "fatwa" (16).

Perhaps one could carry Mozaffari's documentation and argument further to argue that Western reporters who had first (mis)characterized Khomeini's statement as "fatwa" were filling the void of an existing Western structure of feeling or fear about an Islamic order. The story of the fatwa was desired by a Western reading public. The French experts on Islamism delivered it.[29] What followed were major demonstrations on the part of European Muslims against Salman Rushdie's book. British Muslims took to the streets burning Salman Rushdie's book in public. They thought that Khomeini had really declared a fatwa.[30] In this event, the worst fear of the British had been realized. As the British wanted to portray their internal "Muslim other" as scary and threatening, the incidents of book burning confirmed their notions. Here was proof for their worries. I will suggest that the Rushdie affair was the manufacture of a situated Western discourse on Islam. It turned out to be a self-fulfilling prophecy. No one at that particular time had noted, like Mehdi Mozaffari, that the events of burning Rushdie books materialized *after* the Western press represented Khomeini's statement as a fatwa. But events could also have taken a different course. The prophecy of French journalists about the coming of fatwa was there, but it was received by a Muslim immigrant public in Europe within a specific historical contingency rather than as a result of historical determination. For British Muslims who burned *The Satanic Verses*, "the fatwa that wasn't" spoke of something particular. It was an expression of their feelings of being marginalized in contemporary Britain.

My study of the relation between secularists' discourse on Islamists and the subsequent events in Istanbul's municipal domain should be interpreted as such as well. I argue that it is in no way "essential" to Islamism— or to the supporters of the Welfare Party—to segregate men and women by gender or to impose veiling on women. Secularists in Turkey have projected this onto Islamism as part of their own expectations of an Islamic

order. In the process of cross-political relations, Welfarists came to understand themselves in these terms, as well. Secularist discourse, given its
institutional backing in the Turkish state (with the military as the strongest
secularist institution), is still more powerful and effective in Turkey than
Islamism. And, to a certain extent, Welfarists began to know themselves
and to take action upon the world in assuming, internalizing, reversing,
and upholding what secularists had demonized. Islamists were working
within the conditions of possibility of a secularist discourse and structure
of feeling in Turkey's predominant public culture. It is not a coincidence
for them to have picked up the cliché of headscarves and miniskirts as
issues to be worked through in the city's municipal domain. The issues at
stake had been defined as such by secularists in mass media and public
domains. But if the issue of headscarves had not resonated within a structure of feeling that Islamists shared with secularists in the contingency
concerned, headscarves might not have been magnified as a symbol for
Islamist politics.

Public Life and the Construction of "Local Culture"

According to whom is Islam "local culture"? What has turned Islam into a
sign of control of women's public appearance and of public space? By
focusing on the first sites of controversy when Welfare administration became Istanbul's reality, I have argued in this chapter that Islamist politics
takes place within the conditions of possibility yielded by an established
secularist discourse on local culture. I argue that, to a certain extent, Islamist policy was the making of the secularists; it was a relational and
reactive effect of secularists' othering practices. The cases studied in this
chapter display the dilemmas of Islamists working within the parameters
and language of culture set up by a dominant secularist discourse on culture, one that (in time) shifted as secularists realized that it was self-
defeating. The notion of local culture, employed by Islamists in their urban
politics, was construed in the domain of a public culture dominated by
secularists. Indeed, more often than not, Islamists in the first months of
their rule were actualizing the fears of their opponents.

My ethnographic data also reveals that the everyday workings of urban
politics also produced a shift in conditions of possibility. At several moments, Islamists attempted to escape the pigeonholes in which secularists
attempted to lock them, taking actions upon the world in ways that would
disprove secularist projections. At best, Islamists had been straddling the
fence. So is it still today, after having earned a majority in several national
parliaments. Welfarists have been making contradictory strategic moves at
every point, at times fulfilling and at other times countering secularists'

worrisome anticipations. Yet they have always been doing so relationally. As work on identity politics has shown, identity formation and everyday practice is always relational, always in reference to a negative other (Devji 1992).

In the process of inventing their politics in urban space, Welfare administrators had to come to terms with a multiplicity of lifestyles that were customary (or really local) to Istanbul. In other words, the nativeness that they prided themselves on for representing exclusively, did not match the lifestyles of many inhabitants of the city. The process of cross-political interaction in the city, then, opened some possibilities outside a dominant discourse on nativeness. The event of sharing urban, institutional, and public space across cultural, ideological, and religious differences put the very notion of Turkey's culture into question, whether in its secularist or Islamist productions and enactments. This was enhanced, as I suggest, by secularists' shift of discourse, in coming to assert the nativeness of their own life practices to Turkey.

Anthropological sensitivities to local or native culture often overlook the historical dynamism in which cultures take shape, and they tend to leave out of the picture the domain of everyday contestation and debate in which the notion of local culture is implicated. This chapter was an attempt to place power and historical contingency in the center of anthropological inquiries about native culture.

2

The Place of Turkey: Contested Regionalism in an Ambiguous Area

> For us Turkey is not a country that can be
> considered for full membership in the European
> Union. We have to remember that the Union's
> project is for a European civilization.
> —*Wilfried Martens, Head of Christian Democrats in the European
> Parliament, March 1997*

"Turkey" as Sign

On my trip from Istanbul to New York in the fall of 1995, I witnessed a confrontation between a middle-aged Turkish man and an Arabic-speaking couple with two children. As I was leaning back half asleep after a few hours on the flight, I heard a loud man's voice yelling in Turkish, "Get up! Get up! Where do you think you are? On a train? This is Turkish Airlines!" In the space of a couple of seconds, I woke up to what was happening. The father of the Arabic-speaking family sitting in the row of four seats in front of me had been resting length-wise on the floor, underneath the row of seats. The Turkish man, wearing a suit and tie, did not seem very sober. He was trying to kick the man lying on the floor while simultaneously screaming, "Tell him to get up! This is a Turkish plane! You can't lie on the floor like this!" Startled by the event, the mother of the family got up and sought help from the hostesses in English. "Move him away, he is kicking my husband," she said, "and don't give him any more drinks, he is drunk." The Turkish man was forcibly removed by the hostesses of Turkish Airlines, yet, obsessed by what he saw, this man kept returning to check whether the family was sitting in the plane properly. Another Turkish man sitting beside me commented, "He's crazy. But this Arab guy also doesn't know how to behave."

This event, which was brushed aside by the hostesses of Turkish Airlines as a matter of security or explained away by my fellow passengers under the rubric of drunkenness or craziness, actually says a lot about the unique burden of history carried on the shoulders of the ("proper") citizen of Turkey, even (or perhaps especially) on the transatlantic flight. Turkish

Airlines, open to the critical gaze of Westerners (i.e., to the foreigners who mattered), had to portray the best possible image of Turkey. The middle-aged Turkish man, with the half-conscious courage acquired by alcohol, had taken on the role of policing the proper enactment of this image. The figure of the Arabic-speaking man lying on the ground reminded him of a common form of behavior on boats and trains in his own country, in Turkey. Throughout years of socialization in state-controlled schools, he had probably learned to dissociate the ideal of Turkey from this behavior. And on this occasion he had to make the distinction between Turks and Arabs clear. He couldn't restrain himself. He created a scene.

This minor incident on the plane took place at a time when the idea of Turkey was undergoing an intensified rejuggling by clashing social movements and the state. For some years, the Turkish state and army had been under pressure from Kurdish social movements. Feeling economically, culturally, and politically marginalized in the context of Turkish nationalism, Kurds of various persuasions had become more outspoken in their demands for human rights. The PKK, the Kurdish Workers' Party, had intensified its struggle for a separate state, and its attacks on both army and civilian targets throughout the country attracted much public attention and fear. Over the same period, the Islamist movement, with its several branches and offshoots, had made significant gains in strength and popularity, culminating in the wins of the Islamist Welfare Party in nation-wide municipality elections in March 1994. The following eighteen months of Islamist local administration had seen many changes in day-to-day urban life. Meanwhile, faced with economic depression, the Turkish state had for a while been attempting to be accepted as a member of Europe, not to much avail. "The image of Turkey in the eyes of Westerners" was a theme that was much mentioned and magnified in public discourse at that time, and there were many campaigns for selling the virtues of Turkey to the European Union.

In August 1995, a month before the confrontation occurred on the Turkish airbus, there had been a major uproar over the public hanging of some Turkish men in Saudi Arabia on drug charges. Turkish journalists and statespeople had reproached the Saudis for what they called an "uncivilized" manner of resolving a legal matter, something that Turks had supposedly overcome with the abolishment of Islamic law (*seriat*) under the early republic. As if this were not enough, two days before the airbus affair, the government in Turkey had resigned over disagreement between the two parties leading the coalition. The leadership of Turkey was up for grabs. It was at such a time of perceived uncertainty about the future of Turkey that the middle-aged Turkish passenger took on the role of asserting an official notion of Turkey, as he had been disciplined to perceive it through socialization in republican Turkish institutions.

The History of "Region"

The question "where does Turkey belong?" has a long history. Indeed, the concept of region (*bölge*), as an articulated abstraction, has been in the public discourse of inhabitants of what was historically made to be Turkey.[1] "Region" had high resonance in the period between 1994 and 1996 when I did my research. In positioning themselves against one another in conflicts over cultural identity and politics, Islamists and secularists wrote mutual counter-narratives of regional belonging. As potent as it was as a signifier, region was an existential concern for my informants.

Placed between the Black Sea in the north, the Aegean in the west, and the Mediterranean in the south, the bulk of the Turkish nation-state is a peninsula, projecting into the sea from land on the westernmost points of what was historically named "the continent of Asia." Aside from the south-ernmost district of Hatay, the present borders of Turkey were demarcated in the 1920s, after the Turkish "War of Liberation" against invading powers from Europe. In that strategic drawing of the maps, the Armenian Repub-lic of the Soviet Union and Iran were to be Turkey's eastern neighbors; Iraq, under British control, and Syria, under the French, would border the south; Cyprus was still under British mandate; and Greece and Bulgaria would mark Turkey's borders in the west. In 1939, after years of delibera-tion, the district of Hatay in the south, with a large Arabic-speaking popu-lation, was transferred to Turkish administration. If one were tentatively to employ naturalistic geographical categories to designate continents, the area of Turkey in the aftermath of 1939, was spread between a tip of territory on the continent of Europe (what is called Eastern Thrace and what includes one side of the city of Istanbul that is divided by the Bos-phorus strait) and a mass of land in Asia (what, in Greek and in Western archaeological terms was designated "Anatolia" and what, in Turkish lan-guage, was appropriated as "Anadolu").

The area that constituted Turkey after national consolidation was finally very different from what was considered much of the heartland of the Ottoman Empire. The Balkans had been central to the Ottoman polity, entrenching the Ottoman Empire in Europe for most of its life history. Toward the end of the eighteenth century, the Ottomans had begun to lose territory to other European empires and rising Balkan nationalisms. Mas-sive exchanges of population were undertaken on a religious (and not an ethnic) differential, where Muslims (of mixed background) were forced to emigrate eastward and (hybrid) Christians pushed to emigrate to the west of the Aegean sea zone.[2] At the turn of the twentieth century, Muslim populations from Caucasia had emigrated toward what is now Turkey and many Pontic Greeks from Trebizond (now Trabzon) of the eastern Black

Sea region of today's Turkey had to move to Georgia, Ukraine, and Russia (later the Soviet Union), among other places.[3] There was also an extraordinary transformation in the population of the eastern and southern districts of what was constructed as Turkey, brought on by the massacre and forced expulsion of Armenians in 1915.[4] By the end of the nineteenth century, the Ottoman State had lost its territory and power in North Africa as well as the Middle East.

The "Life Knowledge" (*Hayat Bilgisi*) textbooks used in Turkish elementary schools and the history and geography books of secondary and high schools are central institutions in the construction of public knowledge on the territory that was the Ottoman Empire and on that which became Turkey.[5] In the official narrative of the Ottoman rise (from the fifteenth to seventeenth centuries) and decline (during the eighteenth and nineteenth),[6] schoolchildren are given the impression of their ancestors having been driven from territories that they were entitled to, of having compromised on a smaller piece of land after defeat by European powers and rising nationalisms. Fault is implicitly laid, in these ethnocentric accounts of Turkic-to-Ottoman-to-Turkish history, on corrupt sultans of the latter half of the empire's history. So there is an implicit consciousness of "having been imperial" that is instilled in all those children who have attended Ministry of Education schools since the foundation of the republic. A memory of "once broader space and territory" is inculcated in students from an early age. Hence the pronouncement of the former Prime Minister Tansu Çiller against Kurdish separatism in 1995: "Turkey will not give up any more territory." Çiller's statement was emerging from the structure of feeling of a latent postimperial consciousness in Turkey.

After the loss and the displacements and the consequent look of the map in the 1920s and 1930s, representatives of the new state under the authority of Ataturk crafted a new territorial strategy for themselves. In the interests of dissociating themselves from the Ottoman Sultanate and positioning themselves against Balkan and Arab nationalisms, Republicanist politicians and army officers shifted their attention to what came to be called "Anadolu" ("Anatolia"). Anadolu was to form the cultural essence of the Turkish nation. Anatolia was not only imaginatively but also materially constructed as "Turkish" space with forced migrations in which Muslims replaced Christians. Now primarily composed of Muslims, Anatolia was from now on to be identified and constituted as the cradle of Turkish culture and domain of the Turkish state. Anadolu, in the discourse of Republicanists, was "more Turkish" than other areas of the Ottoman Empire that had been lost to other nationalisms. In contradistinction to early-twentieth-century aspirations for connection with Turks of Central Asia as imagined by the early pan-Turkists (such as Ziya Gökalp), Ataturk and other Republicanists began to cultivate the idea of Anadolu as the core of

Turkey. Members of the urban and educated middle classes, idealist men and women, were sent all over Anadolu to perform various functions in fields ranging from education and medicine to government and development. The purpose was to engender a dialogue between the "villagers of Anadolu" (*köylüler*, as they were called) and the "enlightened" (*münevverler*, or later, *aydınlar*) urbanites of Istanbul, Izmir, smaller cities, and the newly emerging Ankara. Teachers were to "educate" villagers. And in attempting to instill more "civilized" (*medeni*) ways and ideas among villagers, the teachers would in turn learn about "Turkish culture" from Anatolian villagers' traditions. An anthropological relationship of sorts was forged in those first two decades of the republic between the urban nationalists and the villagers, in which the former began to collect data and craft cultural inventories about the latter. The habits of Anatolian villagers were studied and interpreted to be representative of a survival of Turkish culture as distinct from the dynastic culture of the Ottoman elites in the former imperial capital, Istanbul.[7]

The material that was collected in those power-laden encounters between the urban middle classes and the villagers found its way into the official textbooks on the Ministry of Education's list. The idea was that Anatolian folklore is the material of Turkish culture.[8] If one can be taught to position one's gaze, consciousness, worldview, and aspirations in a particular geography, the Ministry of Education books attempted to forge links between so-called Turkish Anatolia and the West. Affinities between Turkish culture and European civilization were ascribed and emphasized. And even when the history of the Ottomans' imperial involvement in the Middle East and North Africa was narrated along with chapters on the history of early Islam and the Turks' adoption of the religion, special care was given in these textbooks to differentiate the Turkish from the Arab, the Anatolian from the formerly Ottoman provinces that lay to modern Turkey's south. The project of the Ataturkist revolution was to create a distinct Turkish culture, Muslim-born yet secular, different from Arabs and keen to adopt Western life practices and technologies.[9]

Ministry of Education textbooks in history and geography have undergone some change over the years. Since the late 1940s, when the Republican Peoples' Party (CHP) of Ataturk and his heirs was defeated in national elections, emphasis shifted increasingly from a secular Anatolian culture to what is called the "Turkish-Islamic synthesis."[10] Political parties that received their votes from a more religious electorate alienated by what they called "elite secularism," modified official history to emphasize harmony between Turkish culture and Islamic civilization. Yet there was only so much change that could be brought to the official account under the gaze of entrenched Republicanist institutions, and especially the army. Policy after the military coup of 1980 was much along these lines, the Turkish-

Islamic synthesis in the guise of army secularism. So despite this significant change, there is still considerable continuity between the schooling of the generation of the 1940s and those of the 1970s and 1980s. In other words, as far as public schooling goes, these two generations somehow still belong to the same "imagined community" (Anderson 1991). Despite the incorporation of the religious identity of Turks through the Turkish-Islamic synthesis, there was little that was compromised in the state's official construction of Turkey's region or placement in the world. Until 1995, when the Welfare Party began to increase its constituency and popularity, no affinity between Turkish and Arab cultures of the Middle East was allowed in official accounts of geography and history. That constructed "cultural border" between Turkey and the Arab World was protected in school books, in spite of the dilution of state secularism from the early 1950s onwards.

Throughout the years of Republicanism, many people were brought up to be Turks in republican institutions, whether their ancestors be Abkhazian Muslim immigrants from Georgia, Slavic converts to Islam from Serbia, Armenian-speaking Muslims of the Hemşin region, or Arabs, Kurds, Lazs, Circassians, or other. Turkishness was internalized and adopted to varying extents and in various fashions. Some people had an easier time in assuming Turkishness as an identity than others. Some were willing to assimilate or to assume this identity, while others were not. This was less problematic for Circassians and Albanians, for example, than it has been for Kurds; easier for the Muslim-born and difficult for the willing Jew. With the Lausanne Agreement (signed in 1923), certain non-Muslims (*gayrimüslimler*) were allowed to remain in what became Turkey, under the status of minorities (*azınlık*). These Jews, Istanbul Greeks (all other Greeks had been forced out with the population exchange), and surviving Armenians were to be the officially recognized non-Turks. Otherwise, in the official construction, all Muslims of Turkey were Turks.[11] Muslim-born populations who might have wished to claim minority status and rights, such as the Kurds, could not do so without serious consequences (e.g., war). As Muslims, they were officially designated and categorized as Turks.

Intrinsic to this construction of Turkish nationhood, was a manufactured regional and cultural difference from Arabs. After having lived under Ottoman-Turkish sovereignty for centuries, Arabs, in the official Turkish view, had betrayed their religious brethren to form nationalisms of their own; they had never agreed with a Turkish hold over the Caliphate. To form and preserve itself as a nation-state, Turkey had had to fight with Arabs, as far as official history was concerned. And so "the Arab world," in that constructed total sense, was written out of the narrative of Turkey's regional affiliations.

This regionalist move mapped well onto Republicanists' aspirations for secularism. As much as it was primarily (really) meant for the Muslim-born heirs of the Ottoman Empire (and not for those categorized as non-Muslim minorities), and as much force as the state has maintained over religious institutions, the staunchly secularist early Republicanists wanted Turkey to dissociate itself from religious Islam. Republican cultural reforms had been geared to craft a distinctly Turkish culture that had greater affinities with Europe. Westernization was defined as akin to the culture of Anatolia as well as to that of the Turks' original Central Asia. In this construction, the Middle East was foreign and external to Turkish culture. Indeed, what was called modernization was the project of early republican reformers. And to be modern in this particular historical contingency, one had to have a "nation."[12] The projects of Westernization and Turkish nationalism, then, did not contradict but complemented one another in the official version. Regional affinity with the Arab world was considered an obstacle in the accomplishment of this project.

In the mid-1990s, the question of where does Turkey belong? was once again a public issue. More so, because of the rising popularity of the Islamist movement under the umbrella of the Welfare Party. Welfarists were keen to remake broken relations with the Muslim countries of the Middle East. They were openly critical of secularist attempts to join the European Union and they promised to forge new regional collaborations for Turkey. Welfarists maintained that Turks had original affinities with Muslim Arabs, relations that were abruptly and forcefully broken with the Westernizing agencies of the secularist regimes. If Turkey were to unite with its Muslim brethren, it would be spared the humiliation that came from constant rejection of applications to the European Union. Indeed, the leader of the Welfare Party, Necmettin Erbakan, declared in public, "Instead of 65 million of a Turkish identity detested by all, we prefer a billion of a powerful Islamic identity" (Ekşi 1997, 7).

But Welfare Party leaders and their supporters were to find themselves disappointed in their alternative aspirations for regionalism. When Erbakan assumed the prime ministry in the second half of the 1990s, he made his first trip abroad, on purpose and as a statement, to the Arab world. In Egypt, his trip was not taken seriously by Husnu Mubarek, who missed his appointment with the Turkish delegation. In Libya, Erbakan was criticized by Qaddafi for Turkey's treatment of the Kurds. Nowhere in the Arab world was the Turkish-Islamist team received with the ostentatious welcome that it had expected. Somewhere in the Ottomanist and postimperialist discourse of Turkish-Islamists, the fact that Arabs had mostly been on the receiving (subjected) end of Ottoman imperialism passed unnoticed. Attempts to switch Turkey's regional loyalties and identify with the Muslim or Arab world resulted in embarrassment for Turkish-Islamists.

The issue of Turkey's "region" was highly contested in 1994 and 1995, as it has been throughout Turkey's modern history. From contemporary secularist perspectives, Turkey was and had to remain distinct from the Middle East. Some of my secularist informants suggested that "Turkey is a Mediterranean country." Angry with Europeans for refusing Turkey in the European Union, one of my informants purported that "at least they should accept us as a Mediterranean culture!" She was arguing that there was no big difference between Turkey and Greece or southern Italy. At times of crisis with Islamists, the discourse on region was intense. The more Welfarists attempted to forge cultural and economic links with Saudi Arabia, Iran, and other Muslim countries, the more secularists panicked. The ethnographic sections that follow focus on the contemporary debate over region.

Beheadings in Saudi Arabia

In August 1995, news circulated about the sentencing of forty-one Turks to death in Saudi Arabia, on charges of drug smuggling. The Saudi government had beheaded others previously convicted for the same crime, according to the report. The Foreign Ministry of Turkey was in a state of alarm, threatening Saudi Arabia with the withdrawal of the Turkish embassy.[13] Secular mainstream newspapers and TV channels in Turkey immediately seized on the matter and began to exploit it.

The event in Saudi Arabia was received within an existing secularist-Turkish discourse on Islamic law (şeriat) and the Middle East.[14] Those who wanted to attack the Welfare Party, then the strongest political party in Turkey, found good ammunition in the Saudi Arabian issue. News reports in the papers and on TV were imbued with interpretations of the event. TV screens were flooded with images of decapitation: men kneeling down with arms tightly tied back and eyes covered, submitting bared necks to the cut of the sword. SHOW TV, one of the most popular TV channels at the time, used the clip of a beheading from the movie *Lawrence of Arabia* to illustrate what was going on in Saudi Arabia that week. The report did not indicate that the clips were from a feature film. "We are going to cut them all" was the headline of a widely circulating secular-mainstream newspaper that wanted to represent "the Saudi mentality."[15] Beheading was contrasted with other forms of capital punishment such as the electric chair, the latter represented as "more humane."[16] The image of beheading (kelle kesmek) was employed as a representation of what the Welfare Party would do if it came to power. The Welfare Party advocated Islamic law. And şeriat (Islamic law), in the minds of many a Turkish secularist, was an uncivilized system of justice. Aside from individual authors challenging reversals of discourse,[17] most of the secular mainstream press constructed the

Saudi event as "the savage executions" (vahşi infaz).[18] Columnists spoke of it as "the backward practice" (çağdışı uygulama).[19] Public debates were focused on discussing whether this was şeriat (Islamic law) and whether this was what Welfarists would institute if they attained governmental power in Turkey.

Underneath the sensationalist terms used to discuss the Saudi regime was a discourse of republican Turkish nationalism in its contemporary form. In commenting upon Saudi Arabia, people redrew the boundaries around their imagined community as Turks. They defined what Turkish culture and the Turkish state had to be distinguished from. Not surprisingly, the notion of Saudi Arabia provided an easy contrast for what Turkey was or what secularists wanted it to be. The event, as a chronotope, well fitted the dominant terms of political difference between secularists and Islamists at the time. Secularists wrote of beheading as a practice that was "foreign to Turks and the level of civilization that Turkish culture represented." They likened Islamists to the Saudis and, in doing so, they attempted to write Islamists out of their narrative of Turkey. As Saudi Arabia was ascribed to another region, Turkish-Islamists were interpreted as inauthentic and alien. Those powerful secularists with access to the mainstream of cultural industry, and with avenues for public and publicized expression, were reproducing old republican discursive forms in the present day.

An article by Gülay Göktürk, published during that time of controversy, is emblematic of secularists' drawing of the borders of Turkish culture. In her regular column in the secular-libertarian Yeni Yüzyıl , Göktürk entitled her article, "Bedouin identity":

The landing of the sharp sword of şeriat on the neck of four Turks has put Welfarists and those who long for şeriat in much difficulty. . . . Whatever anybody might say, the Islamic law practiced in Saudi Arabia is part of the identity kimlik of people of that country. Saudis apparently gather around the executioner after the Friday noontime prayer and clap to the savagery [of the beheadings]. Islamic law is part of the culture of a people who are uneducated, unindustrious, and underdeveloped in every aspect. This concept of justice is part of Bedouin identity.

If we believe [as advocates of multiculturalism in Turkey do] that the Arab people should protect this different identity of theirs that comes from their history, culture, and religious particularities and if we argue against the assimilation of different identities, this means that we will also have to respect their law.[20] And we will accept this law as the expression of this identity.

Or, we will counter this identity with universal human identity and its law. We will pray for Arab society to be rid of Arab identity which carries all the primitivism, backwardness, and even savagery that is possible, for this identity to be dissolved and thrown in the waste basket of history. We will encourage every move that the desert Bedouin takes towards becoming a citizen of the world. . . .

What is called "identity," is not a composition of a few folkloric elements, colorful clothes and local foods. "Identity" comprises a peoples' ethics, customs and traditions, and approaches to law. For a Muslim Arab living in Saudi Arabia today, stoning an adulterous woman to death is a legal form of punishment. Likewise, for a Kurd, shooting an adulterous woman after a family decision is a legal form of punishment. This is his approach to justice, his law, it is a part of Kurdish identity.[21]

With such racist language, Göktürk positions herself against Arabs, as well as Turkish-Islamists and Kurds. She uses the grammar of Republican-ist Turkish nationalism in describing this ultimate "other" whom she fears. A fantasy for the Turkish state, which I study in the final chapters of this book, forms the subtext for her imagination, in which Islamists and Kurds are felt to be threats to the unity of Turkey. In wanting to write this threat away, in a single move, Göktürk associates Islamists and Kurds with Arabs. She constructs Arabs to be "other" in time, law, and ethics. As the kernel of an imaginary, with her concept of "Bedouin," she refers to all that mod-ernization theory and her own modernism deplores: lack of education, un-derdevelopment, lack of industry, and attachment to cultural traditions. By way of characterizing the Saudis, Göktürk associates these features with Islamists and Kurds, the wound in her fantasy of Turkey. Inculcated in her representations is fear of those who challenge the Turkish state, specifically the Kurdish and Islamist movements. And as she attempts to distance Saudi Arabia from Turkey's regionality, she also tries to rid Turkey of what she calls "the cultural particularities" of Kurds and Islamists.

What is interesting about Göktürk's account is that it pretends to tran-scend nationalism, to be beyond an ideology or a point of view. Göktürk aligns herself with what she calls "universal humanism." As a secular Turk, she imagines that she is above culture and identity and beyond historical particularity. She is extremely self-assured. She has the sort of confidence that my secular Turkish informants had of feeling at home within the fan-tasy that the Turkish state was created for them. She has, in her words, "a universal identity," as do other secularist Turks like her. In her conception, it is Kurds and Islamists who are "cultural."[22]

The common Turkish-secularist approach to Arabs and the Middle East is evident in another article published in August 1995 by yet another col-umnist. This account bears the mark of the official narrative of Turkish history that was described in the beginning of this chapter. Hasan Pulur writes,

It is true that we are coreligionists [dindaş] with Arabs, but our brotherhood [kardeşlik] is in vain. We wouldn't like to dwell on the past, but our brothers' (!) treachery during the First World War is unforgettable. When the First World War erupted, the Ottoman sultan who was also the Caliph declared a fatwa calling 350 million Muslims to aid the Turkish army which was at war in three continents.

Şerif Hüseyin, the emir of Mecca was the first to respond to this call. He became subservient to the English spy Lawrence and revolted against the Caliph of the Muslims. He walked towards Medina which was being defended by Fahrettin Paşa (the last sultan of the Ottomans).

Those bold children of Anatolia, whose teeth were shed and who caught scurvy from hunger and lack of nutrition, became martyrs, announcing that "we will give our life rather than give the tomb of our Prophet to the infidel." They had defended the Prophet's tomb against "his grandchildren" who had strengthened themselves with English gold.

When we withdrew from Syria, those who shot Ataturk's army in the back were once again our glorious Arab brothers. Wasn't it Nasser who had embraced the Cypriot priest Makarios?

Yes, our coreligionists' accomplishments are extensive. We wouldn't like to open those old notebooks [of history] and to recount those actions. Yet when some speak of "our great religion brothers, the Arabs,"[23] our blood [rushes] to our head.

No, the relation between them and us is not one of "brotherhood," but one of "coreligion" (1995, 3).

In contrast to Göktürk, Hasan Pulur is more direct in his defense of Turkish nationalism and the republic. He does not speak in the language of universal humanism. What he tries to do is to touch Welfarists rhetorically on their sore point. The Welfare Party is not, Pulur knows, a party that would like to work against Turkish nationalism. Welfare Islamism is a child of republican Turkish nationalism, albeit a more religious offspring. Welfarists are Turkish nationalists, too. Many of them have close links with supporters of the pan-Turkist Nationalist Action Party (MHP). So Pulur writes in assuming a common structure of nationalist feeling. "Being a Turk" is the primary loyalty of this secularist. And he challenges Welfarists on account of their Turkishness. He implies that they have no authority in the Turkish republic to act and to believe as they do, let alone to forge regional relations of the sort they advocate. Islamists are confronted with the question of belonging or not belonging in Turkey.

It turned out that Pulur was right in thinking that Welfarists would hesitate before placing Turkishness aside. In the week that followed the event in Saudi Arabia, Islamist intellectuals, religious leaders, and Welfare Party officials were asked whether beheading was a punishment that was prescribed under Islamic law. Islamists were publicly interrogated about their regional loyalties. Where did they stand vis-à-vis Saudi Arabia? In response, Islamists distinguished their understanding of Islamic law from what was reportedly practiced in Saudi Arabia under the name of *"shari'a."*

Abdurrahman Dilipak, one of the most widely read authors of the Islamist intelligentsia, was reported to have said, "The practice [of beheading] in Saudi Arabia is not what is commanded [in Islamic law] for drug smuggling. This is not a direct order of Islamic law. I would expect any sort of evil from the Saudi regime."[24] A parliamentarian of the Welfare Party, Mukadder Başeğmez likewise challenged the Saudi state in saying, "If what is reported [the beheadings] really took place, the state has much fault in this. In Saudi Arabia, desert practices are in operation. These have nothing to do with *seriat*. In *seriat* there is reprisal."[25] A high-ranking Welfare Party official, Abdullah Gül spoke of the incident in similar terms: "The executions in Arabia have nothing to do with the order of *seriat*. That place is a kingdom. I lived in Saudi Arabia. I don't think that country is being ruled by Islamic law."[26]

In the conditions of possibility of the incident, Islamists, too, distanced themselves from Saudi Arabia. Yet, rather than distinguishing themselves as Turks from Arabs, or Turkey as a region from the Middle East, Islamists, including active Welfarists, criticized the Saudi political system for misinterpreting and mispracticing Islamic law. They took issue with the Saudi kingdom and the Saudi power structure; they did not want to erect cultural distinctions between themselves and Arabs. All they did was to distinguish their own reading of Islamic law from that of the Saudi state. This was not, they assured the Turkish public and electorate, what the Welfare Party would do if it came to national power. Islamists found themselves in a dilemma. They wanted to argue their commitment to *seriat* without endangering their position within the Turkish nation. Within Turkish nationalist discourse, it was tricky to relate to Arabs.

Joining the Customs Union

Just about ten days were left before the national elections of December 1995, when the European parliament in Strasbourg voted to accept Turkey in the Customs Union. Since filing away Turkey's application for membership in 1959, the EU had been due to come to a decision on the issue for more than thirty years.[27] The Socialist Group and the Green Group had recently been objecting to a customs union with Turkey, reminding the parliament that human rights conditions in Turkey were still unfavorable and that Turkey was continuing its war against the Kurds and its occupation of northern Cyprus. In spite of these objections, the decision to accept Turkey was passed in the European Parliament on December 13, 1995. Turkey was not being accepted as a member of Europe. It was only agreeing to lift all taxes and tariffs on European goods, a move that the Europeans in turn would have to reciprocate. Moreover, Turkey would have to follow embargo regulations as set by the Customs Union, rules over which it had no control, since it had no representation in the EU. In fact, most Turkish companies (other than the textile industry) would not be able to compete with European multinationals in terms of price. And Turkey, having also lifted tariffs, would be flooded with European commodities. European multinationals would have an easier time, now, in investing in Turkey and in using Turkish labor power. The EU had nothing to lose, only a massive new market to exploit.

The leaders of the coalition government at that time signed the agreement with the EU without asking the Turkish parliament in Ankara to vote on it. Prime minister Tansu Çiller of the right-wing DYP and her social democratic aide Deniz Baykal of the CHP were overjoyed by the event. They were preparing for the imminent national elections. Their campaign managers presented them as "the conquerors of the Customs Union" (*gümrük birliği fatihi*),[28] countering the Welfare Party's use of metaphors of "conquest." The government sent orders to governorships in cities all over the country asking for a "Customs Union Holiday" to be observed in schools and public offices. Schools were asked to display Turkish flags in the spirit of a national holiday.[29] The leaders of government represented themselves as having unified Turkey with one of the strongest regional powers in the world. The symbols of "joining Europe" and "becoming European" were used extensively by these politicians to seduce an electorate who wanted to be European. The content and consequences of the agreement offered little cause for celebration compared to that powerful signifier "Europe."

The Islamist press covered the story with irony. The Welfare Party's mouthpiece *Milli Gazete* made allusions to the Sèvres agreement at the beginning of the century when Ottoman territories were distributed among allied European powers. Making further references back to the Tanzimat, the official date for the beginning of Ottoman-Turkish Westernization in Islamist discourse, *Milli Gazete* likened the event to the Ottoman Empire's "submission" to Europe in the nineteenth century. "The first step for the point we are at was taken with the Tanzimat," according to this report. "The Tanzimat edict was not too different from the Customs Union of today. The edict had given liberties to non-Muslims in the Empire to perform every activity that they pleased. . . . Likewise, the Customs Union wants Turkey not to produce anything. Europeans are saying that they will sell, that they can even come and produce in our country, as long as we orient ourselves to consumption and not to production." Naming the leaders of government as "slaves" and "butlers" of Europe, the Welfare Party's bulletin invited its readers to yet another "War of Liberation."[30] Erbakan, the leader of the Welfare Party, had deplored the event, promising that he would "tear up this rag of an agreement" when he came to

power in eleven days. He noted that Europeans had no intention of allow-
ing Turkey to join the EU, "only to tether Turkey to a pole." "Just as we
tore up the Sèvres agreement and accomplished the War of Liberation,"
Erbakan put forth, "so we will do today."[31] *Milli Gazete* presented the Welfare Party as "the only way out of treachery."[32] Other Islamist newspapers
constructed the event in similar terms. *Zaman*, the newspaper of the sufi
sheyh Fethullah Gülen and a rival to the Welfare Party, suggested that
"the one hundred and fifty years of love of the supporters of the West and
Turkey's thirty-three years of desire was satisfied with the Customs Union."[33]
The newspaper of Islamist intellectuals *Yeni Şafak* wrote against "the latest
signature to surrender."[34] The radical Islamist *akit*, often critical of the
Welfare Party for compromising with the status quo, countered the secularist parties' announcement of "a Customs Union Holiday," speaking of it
as "the holiday of betrayal."[35] Abdurrahman Dilipak, a columnist in *akit*,
entitled his piece "Now we have become Europeans!" with sarcasm. "We
had not yet become Europeans when this piece was being written. But as
you read this article, the tariff barriers between Turkey and Europe will
probably have been lifted and one with the Turkic Republics [of Central
Asia] and Islamic countries will have been erected. From now on, it will be
harder to trade with the Turkic Republics and Islamic countries, and easier
to do so with the West" (1995, 1). Dilipak's Islamism was imbued with
Turkish nationalism. He wrote, "After this, they will come to defend the
[Greek Orthodox] Patriarchate. There is Armenia waiting in line. And we
will have to accept all their [Europeans'] directives with regard to the
Kurdish problem" (9).[36] "This agreement is placing dynamite," he added,
"under the foundation of the Turkish Republic which was built after a War
of Liberation; it is threatening the independence of Turkey." A fantasy for
the Turkish state dominated the imaginary of Islamists, too. They contested only the content of this imaginary.

Another debate over Turkey's region was under way. This time the borders of Turkey with Europe were at stake. It was again by no means obvious in which region Turkey belonged. Just as Turkish culture has been a
historical matter of debate, so has Turkey's region been an unsettled issue.
As in the discord over Saudi Arabia, nationalist discourse formed an underlying structure of feeling in arguments over the Customs Union. When the
time came to discuss Turkey's relation to Europe, Islamists' discourse did
not contradict secularists' nationalism. The terms and the structure were
the same. Once again, Islamists were arguing against secularists by claiming the War of Liberation for themselves. In joining the Customs Union,
Turkey's national independence would be sacrificed, according to Islamist
public personalities. Like secularists, Islamists were fearful of Kurdish
threats to Turkey's unity and they approached the question of Turkey's
region from a nation-state-centered perspective. However, Islamists were

attempting to challenge and reverse the representation of the internal alien in Turkey. In drawing a boundary with Europe, Islamists attempted to undermine the European history of Turkey in order to exclude secularists.

The references and the language were shared. I will argue that the *fantasy for the state* was the same. Actors took up different roles and masks in a shared public drama. In the historical consciousness of both secularists and Islamists was the War of Liberation as declared by the Anatolian defense forces after the Ottoman sultan's signing of the Sèvres agreement of surrender to European powers. The de facto parliament formed in Ankara, in opposition to the sultanate in Istanbul in 1920, had disregarded the Sèvres agreement and declared the continuation of the War of Liberation. In the crisis over the Customs Union, Erbakan, the leader of the Welfare Party who normally shaped his political discourse by criticizing Ataturk and supporting the Ottoman regime, was claiming the mantle of the leaders of the War of Liberation. In Erbakan's opinion, the secular leaders of government had given in to the Customs Union, which intended to exploit Turkey like the sultan who had submitted to the Sèvres agreement. In the issue of the Saudi beheadings, the roles of that emblematic Turkish historical plot had been claimed in the reverse. Then, it was secularists who were claiming the symbols of the War for themselves, likening Islamists to Arabs and writing them off as traitors of the Turkish nation. Region was ardently contested and debated in these eventful encounters. Yet, the Turkish state was not up for grabs. The terms of secularist and Islamist politics of identity were set within a Turkish discourse of state-centered nationalism.

The Place of Turkey

Fatma was born in Ankara in the early 1940s. Her father, like many residents of Ankara in that decade, was a state official. He held an important post in the Ministry of Economics. Her mother had moved to Ankara from Istanbul after marriage and taught elementary school children in one of the capital's schools. In the formative years of the state, theirs was one of Ankara's active Republicanist families. Fatma's parents had a circle of friends among the capital's bureaucrats, teachers, and other state employees. Her parents, she used to say, felt that they had molded the republic with their hands like a statue. Even further, Fatma said that "they felt that they were the state," they embodied it. As Fatma's mother had been involved in the crafting of educational policies, especially for women, so was her father active in the making of the national economy.

The maternal side of the family was from the Balkans and the Caucasus. Fatma's grandfather was from a small town in what is now northern Greece and since this was the area that surrounds Thessaloniki (in Turkish,

Selanik), Fatma would later wonder whether he was of Jewish origin. Thessaloniki, she had come to learn in her later years, had been the center of a heretic Jewish movement in the seventeenth century under the charismatic self-declared messiah Sabbetai Zevi. Zevi had been forced to convert to Islam by Ottoman-Turkish authorities and died Muslim, with many of his followers adopting Islam after him.[37] The descendants of the Sabbateans were known in Turkey as the *dönme*s (the converts). As much as *dönme*s would recognize and know of each other, it was not common for them to discuss the issue publicly even in the 1990s. Fatma suspected that her grandfather was a descendant of converts to Islam. But this was a taboo issue and she had never dared to ask her grandfather's survivors whether it was really so. Fatma's grandmother on her mother's side was from the Caucasus and of Georgian ancestry. This part of the family had settled in Istanbul in the first quarter of the twentieth century.

The paternal side of the family had its background in Iraq. Yet it was never discussed whether the family had any Arab origin. By the late 1940s, most of the father's family had migrated from Iraq to what had become a separate Turkey. The family identified themselves as Turkish and even though the elder members knew Arabic perfectly, they never spoke it. Fatma's father had been brought up in Ottoman-Turkish, but he had tamed his language in the process of becoming active in republican politics, where modernization and Turkification were the policies. The father had made a point of communicating with the younger generation who were being socialized in "modern Turkish."

Fatma had been brought up by parents who dedicated themselves to the Ataturkist revolution. Both her parents had been active in the making of secularist institutions and worldview. In her upbringing, according to Fatma, she was never taught how to do the *namaz*.[38] "They taught us nothing about Islam," she said in bewilderment. We were speaking at that time when conflict between secularists and Islamists in Istanbul was at its height. It was the middle of the 1990s. Nor had she taught herself the *namaz*. This was not a deliberate decision on her part. It wasn't that she was an atheist or that she had spent intellectual energy criticizing religion and God. She had just never been interested, or, had never had to be interested in Islam. The *namaz*, for example, was not something that figured in her everyday life in Ankara or Istanbul where she had mostly lived. Most of the people in her life did not practice the religion either.

After her divorce, Fatma had fallen seriously ill for three years. "In those years," she once said, "I had contemplated turning to religion to find peace. But right after considering this, I became furious with myself and said, 'Fatma, don't even consider it!' Because, when you say 'religion,' I think of covering, I think of immersing one's self in the Kuran. 'Instead of doing that, go to a psychologist,' I said to myself. And so I did."

Fatma had not been taught to practice Islam, yet she remembered being disciplined to believe in something else, the secular republic as founded by Ataturk. "In those years, when I was growing up [the 1940s], when İstiklal Marşı [the national anthem] was played, we would feel a shiver down our spine. Even now on television, when I see a Turkish soccer team being sent to games abroad, I feel like crying. My father was also very nationalist. I remember one evening when my father and I were at home alone. At midnight, the national anthem started to be played on the radio. There was no one around to see what we were doing, but my father told me to get up. And we stood there in the *hazırol* position [of formal respect] in the house by ourselves. It was like that in those days."[39] On the 10th of every November in the 1950s, commemoration dates for Ataturk, Fatma recalled that entertainment was forbidden. When the sirens sounded at 9:05 to commemorate the moment when Ataturk died in 1938, people on the street froze in respect until the sirens finished. "But now," Fatma said, "when the sirens sound, I see lots of people not bother to show respect and just walk by."

Fatma identified more with her mother's side of the family. She had cultivated many Greek friends, had visited Greece a number of times, and was taking lessons in the Greek language from an Istanbul Greek. She knew Greece like the palm of her hand, she used to say, using idiomatic Turkish. But she felt a bit distant from her father. She was not as interested in the history of his Iraqi side of the family.

As I came to know her family, I realized that Fatma used the formal pronoun *siz* in Turkish, instead of the informal *sen*, in addressing her parents and other elder members of the family. This was much in the keeping of upper-class Ottoman rules of manner of the sort that were reproduced among the early republican elite. Fatma was a little more relaxed with her daughter, and they alternated between the formal and informal pronouns in speaking with each other. Fatma's mother, however, was uncompromising. There was not one person in the family, not even the little grandchildren, whom the mother would address in the informal. The word *efendim*, which literally means "sir" and which used to be a title given to literate people, clergymen, or certain members of the army in Ottoman times, was a mark of politeness that followed many of the everyday conversational sentences used by the elderly members of Fatma's family. "We went to the market for shopping, *efendim*." "*Efendim*, we saw our old acquaintance Hasan on the street." Such statements of well-mannered deference were most common in the family circle. Yet, the use of such etiquette did not formalize Fatma's family. This was the way they showed affection to one another.

Fatma had married at a very young age to a businessman from Istanbul whom her parents admired. She has a daughter from this marriage. The husband was of a social background similar to Fatma's own. When she divorced, after ten years of marriage, Fatma's friends recount that her personality underwent important changes. She became a much more humorous person, using Turkish slang to describe people and events in her life, being explicitly forthright and deliberate in her interactions with people. She much enjoyed revealing her feelings, then, unlike the elder members of her family, and liked to move her friends to raucous laughter with stories from her everyday life. She frequented the bars and cafés of Istanbul, especially in the Beyoğlu area and in the Arnavutköy and Bebek environs of the Bosphorus, and most of her friends were artists, filmmakers, writers, or academics. When I met her, Fatma had been involved with an artist for the past six years. She had a joking relationship with him and a flirtatious one with their common male friends, in keeping with the culture of the intellectual community of Istanbul. Fatma was a lecturer in political science in a university in Istanbul.

It was once again in the midst of heightened tension between secularists and Islamists, when I visited Fatma at her family's summer home. Elderly members of the family were politely conversing about the rise of the Islamists and sharing their worries with one another, when the *ezan*, the call to prayer, was sounded from a nearby mosque. One of Fatma's nephews shouted in a joking manner, "Attention! Don't be scared, the *ezan* is being read!" No member of the family went to prayer. It was so much out of their practice that this nephew found it amusing. Later, this same nephew would say that "the reason for the underdevelopment of this country is its Muslimness. If my son were to show interest in Islam, I would prevent him from it; I would send him immediately abroad, to Europe. If he wants to learn music, let him do so, but let him learn Western classical music. If he wants to travel, let him visit Europe first; other places only after that."[40]

Indeed, Fatma and her family wanted to identify Turkey regionally with the West. In response to one of my questions about region, Fatma had said, "I think that Turkey is neither European, nor Middle Eastern, it is a unique country. Actually, it is a country that belongs to Anatolia. Whoever passed through Anatolia has left a trace of his culture." Here Fatma was employing an early republican discourse on Turkey's region. Yet, in a more spontaneous conversation in Fatma's family home, Fatma had wanted to identify Turkey not with Anatolia, but with Europe. She said, "Because of these Islamists, from now on the border between Europe and Asia will be assigned as that between Greece and Turkey. Westerners would no longer count us as part of Europe!"[41]

Even though part of the family had roots in Iraq, this family had much prejudice against Arabs. Fatma told her daughter, Şirin, for example to "marry a foreigner, if you want, but let him not be an Arab." She reproached the wedding of a daughter of one of her friends' to an Egyptian

man. She said that they had played *arabesk* music in the wedding, one of
the most popular genres of music in Turkey, which combines Arabic tunes
with folkloric Turkish music.[42] "But of course," Fatma then snapped, "if she
is marrying an Arab, she has gone out of our hands, of course she will play
arabesk!"

Fatma lived in Elmadağ, a neighborhood close to Beyoğlu, the entertainment and contemporary publishing district. She had moved there a few
years after her divorce and illness in order to be closer to the part of town
inhabited by her artist friends. Previously, during her first marriage, she
had lived in Ulus, one of Istanbul's upper-class neighborhoods, having left
her parents' most recent family home in Nişantaşı, again a posh part of
town. Fatma knew only certain parts of Istanbul, though she considered
herself an Istanbuli (*Istanbullu*). In the district of Beyoğlu, she knew the
main İstiklal street and its side alleys extremely well. She frequented the
bookshops of this district and old book dealers found her all the out-of-
print books that she looked for. All the little savory shops on the street
corners had distinct places in her daydreams and everyday roundabouts.
She made appointments with her lover and friends in the newly established cafés with Parisian decor. The songs of Edith Piaf rang in Fatma's
ears. She ordered cappucino most of the time; these cafés did not serve
Turkish coffee or tea. They had large assortments of herbal teas and served
genres of vegetarian health food. For her clothes shopping, Fatma still
went to her parents' latest neighborhood, Nişantaşı. She bought stylish and
expensive clothes from some of Turkey's established clothing rings. As she
used to wear darker color clothes and more classical styles of skirts, Fatma
said that after her divorce and changes in her life, she had begun to dress
in livelier colors and in loose pants and blouses. She had her hair done at a
particular hairdresser, again in this neighborhood. Her graying black curly
hair was cut in a bob.

There were other neighborhoods that Fatma knew well, as well. On the
weekends especially, she liked to go for walks on the Bosphorus by the sea.
She knew the western coast of the Bosphorus all the way to Rumelihisar
quite well. Sometimes she went to discover the backstreets of Arnavutköy,
here, on her own. The newer upper-class suburbs of Istanbul, the neighborhoods of Etiler, Levent, and Ulus, were in her everyday routine. For
work, she drove over the Bosphorus bridge to the other side to teach at
the university. During the week, most of her time was spent at school. Yet,
she knew little of the environs of the university, except for the suburbs of
Caddebostan, Suadiye, and Göztepe, which were not too different from
the suburb of Ulus, where she used to live when she was married. Apartment houses of several stories were lined beside one another with gardens
in their entrances. Most of the people whom Fatma knew lived in such
apartment flats in Istanbul—this was called the "Istanbul apartment life."

But Fatma rarely went to the old districts of Istanbul across the Golden Horn (Haliç). She did not know the districts of Fatih, Eyüp, and Sultanahmet too well. She of course had brought some of her foreign friends to visit the Süleymaniye and Sultanahmet mosques a number of times on their visits to Turkey. Similarly she enjoyed visiting the Grand Bazaar on organized outings with her friends. And in summers she never missed Western classical music concerts held in the Aya Irini Church by the Topkapı Palace during the Istanbul Festival of Arts. She liked that part of town, yet she went there only on special days out.

Fatma knew that I was doing some of my research in Fatih. She admitted never having passed through that neighborhood. Fatih was known, at the time we were speaking, to be inhabited especially by members of sufi orders (tarikats) and Islamist organizations. Newspapers had been running stories about the lifestyles of the religious in Fatih. Fatma asked, "That place is a separate country, isn't it?" Her daughter asked, "Is everyone veiled there? Do men with turbans and robes appear on the streets? Is there anyone there who wanders around like you without a headscarf? Don't you get scared?" I told them that there were many women on the streets of Fatih who did not veil and who walked on the streets alone wearing jeans and blouses and keeping their hair loose. Yes, there were more women in Fatih who were veiled, in comparison to the districts that Fatma and Şirin knew in Istanbul. But Fatih was a cosmopolitan neighborhood, representing all the facets of Turkey and Istanbul, like so many other districts.

Because she was curious, I brought Fatma with me to Fatih one day. We walked all the way from Beyazıt on the main street to Fatih. Fatma really didn't know this part of the city. "It's as if we have come to a different country," she said, repeating what she had imagined in one of our earlier conversations. She noticed the veiled women on the street with a peculiar curiosity.

As we were walking, four young men with brown and black robes, long beards, and white turbans appeared, walking on the main street with scepters in each of their hands. Fatma did not notice them at first as everyone on the street turned to look at the robed men in bewilderment. This was certainly not common attire in Turkey's public life. People on the street couldn't keep from turning and looking at these turbaned passersby. The turbaned men were waving their scepters forward and back in a manner that caught everyone's attention. As some laughed and as others cast sidelong glances, Fatma saw the men and became terrified. "Are these Turks?" she first asked. "Yes, probably," I said. Other people on the street were asking the same question. "They are probably Turks, but from Central Asia," said one man. "I think they must be from Afghanistan," said another. One person asked the police. "I don't know where they are from," said the policeman, "they also caught my eye." One young boy screamed, "They are coming! They are coming!" "Where could they have come from?" said Fatma, holding tightly onto my arm. "How odd!" said a shopkeeper there. "*Ils sont bizarres*," said a French tourist to her partner. "But they are speaking Turkish!" said someone on the street.[43]

Fatma's fears and projections about Fatih had been to a certain extent realized. Yet, as I drew her to the side streets of Fatih, she came to have more of an idea about the neighborhood. She realized, for example, that it was not a shanty neighborhood (*gecekondu*) of the sort inhabited by the young woman who kept her house. I told her that this was a lower-income neighborhood where, most of the time, only the man of the family worked, and that most of Fatih's residents generally ate well at home, maintained their homes, and tried not to exhibit their poverty. I mentioned that many of Fatih's families had their origins in small Anatolian cities or towns and that a lot of them were believers and that some were conservative. I also told her that not necessarily all women who lived in Fatih veiled, and that, in fact, there was conflict between those who veiled and those who didn't, all neighbors in the same streets.

The apartment houses of Fatih were lower-built than those Fatma was used to in Ulus, Göztepe, and Elmadağ. They were tightly lined beside one another and were clearly made from cheaper materials, by builders rather than engineers or architects. Yet these were not shanty houses either. Unlike most of Istanbul's shanty neighborhoods, Fatih is one of Istanbul's oldest residential areas. Its environs are marked by old fountains, mosques, dervish lodges, saint's tombs, and *medreses* (old schools of Islamic learning that are now closed). Here Fatma saw a number of İmam Hatip schools, which were funded by the Ministry of Religious Affairs to train imams (leaders of prayer) and which were popular among religious families. There were also a good number of Kuranic schools (*Kuran okulları*) for younger children.[44] She saw a number of religious book shops and many clothes shops selling overcoats (*pardösü*) and headscarves (*türban*) for women in many colors, including the black veil (*çarşaf*). This was indeed a different experience for someone who had lived in Istanbul for most of her life.

On our way back, we passed through İstiklal Street in Beyoğlu, that favorite part of Istanbul for Fatma. It was late in the evening. The streets were crowded with people walking around, shopping, going to the movies, or to eat out. There were mostly men on the streets, but also many women, mostly uncovered, some alone and others with their friends, family, lovers, or husbands. Fatma walked in silence and then she began to reflect on what she called "the passing away of Beyoğlu." It was months after the Welfare Party had started to administer the municipality of this district. The Welfarist mayor had ordered restaurant and café owners to remove their tables from the street and to limit the service of alcohol to indoors. Fatma was noticing some important changes in Beyoğlu. She complained that there were fewer women on the streets at night than a couple of years before. She said that "unrecognizable" men had started to frequent İstiklal street; that during the day she noticed more and more veiling women. "The feel of the place is changing," she said, reflecting on our visit to Fatih.

The Contest over "Region"

Region is only to a certain extent determined by geographical location. Indeed, what "region" implies and the shape it ultimately takes is historically relative.[45] In the preceding ethnographic sections, I began to demonstrate the regional trajectory that was set for Turkey in its republican history through the practice of nationalist discourse.

After the War of Liberation (*Kurtuluş Savaşı*)[46] and in the decade that followed, Turkey rid itself of most of its vast Armenian population with the forceful deportations and the massacre in 1915, and evacuated its indigenous Greeks from western Anatolia.[47] If today Islamists and others like to speak of Turkey as "99 percent Muslim," this is the result of several xenophobic events and policies targeted at non-Muslims.[48] Under the terms in which it established itself in the 1920s and 1930s, secular and Westernist Turkey was created mainly for the Muslim inheritors of the Ottoman Empire who were already within or else had migrated to the territories that became Turkey. Only some non-Muslims would be allowed to remain, under minority status.[49]

Yet, despite the violent physical and symbolic erasure of most of the Greek, Armenian, Syriac-Christian, and Jewish presence, the territory of Turkey that remained was still quite cosmopolitan. The early nationalists had to make monoculturalist sense out of a country that was composed of speakers of Kurdish, Laz, Arabic, Azeri, Serbo-Croatian, Ladino, Armenian, Greek, and Turkish, and of people with ancestral roots in Bosnia, Macedonia, Albania, Bulgaria, Greece, the Aegean Islands, Anatolia, the Caucasus, Central Asia, Iraq, Egypt, Lebanon, Palestine, and Syria. A singular "imagined community" (Anderson 1991) had to be composed from the results of war, deportation, diaspora, and immigration. Now primarily composed of Muslims, secular Turkey could not count on a singular category of "belonging." The early nationalists hoped that the Muslim heirs of the empire, diverse as they were, would become assimilated as "Turkish."

As I discussed in an earlier section, on the history of region, Turkey was set up as a nation-state with a structural disposition to Europe.[50] Then, to a certain extent, Turkey's affiliation with Europe as its "region" is the result of the particular history of nationalist discourse and practice. Yet, for many of the heirs of the Ottoman Empire, Muslim and non-Muslim, Turkey had never been external to Europe. Many of Turkey's new citizens were forcefully uprooted from their hometowns to move eastwards to what was determined to be their nation-state. And many of those who did not geographically live in what was called the continent of Europe, had ongoing relations with Europe, to the extent that they could only with difficulty be categorized as "regionally apart."

Fatma's family history is not exceptional among Turkey's so-called Turks. Her preference for her mother's background in the Balkans must, to a certain extent, have been the effect of a Western-affiliated nationalist discourse. Although her father's side of the family had its background in Iraq, Fatma had never cultivated an interest in the Arabic language of the sort that she had developed for Greek. She used to say that she did not feel much different culturally from the urbanites of Athens. She was angered by and argued against the European Union's conception of Europe. It was ludicrous, from her point of view, to suggest that Athens was "more European" than Istanbul. It was only the Europeans' prejudice against Turks that made this false distinction. Fatma was involved in domestic Turkish debates over regionalism. She, like many others in Turkey, had a stake in making Turkey a "European country." She wanted Turkey to be a democracy and a welfare state with good social services. She took West European social democracies as models for what she wanted the condition of human rights in Turkey to look like. She wanted to carry on her own lifestyle and not to have to conceal her femininity as she thought an Islamist state would demand. She wanted to be as she was, have her relationship with her lover while living as a single woman, go out at night, laugh out loud naturally as she did among friends. She worried that she would have to change if Turkey were to become internally conceived as non-European.

The region that secularists and Islamists inhabit is the same, yet the stories about region, as I studied them, were different. Every representation of Turkey's region was situated.[51] In this highly polarized politics of culture, the meaning of region was not stable, set, or evident, but rather indeterminate. What Turkey's region was, then, was to a certain extent an effect of public argument, nationalist discourse, and counter-official narratives of belonging.

If we were to propose that Turkey's "Europeanness" is only the effect of a Westernist nationalist discourse and modernizing disciplinary mechanisms, we would be left with the Eurocentric premise that Turkey is actually "extra-European." As Fatma's life history reveals, Turks were not outside Europe even before nationalism. Insofar as Fatma has turned her back on the other (Arab) side of her heritage, she reproduces nationalist discourse. Yet there is also a historical basis for her feelings of affinity for Europe.

"The Middle Eastern Woman"

It is rare, in scholarly work on Middle Eastern women, to find accounts of the life histories of women who are neither Westernized in the manner of upper-class or highly educated elites (like Fatma), nor Islamicized through following Islamist groups or sufi orders, nor yet villagers who have not urbanized.[52] In the 1980s and 1990s, Islamist women in particular have been perhaps the most popular topic of query in Middle Eastern studies, anthropological and otherwise. Turkish-Islamist women whom I came to know in the mid-1990s often complained of having been turned into objects of study by secular sociologists in Turkey, Western scholars, and local journalists. Indeed, at that stage a whole bibliography of scholarly and journalistic work was being produced on Islamist women, bringing about specialized knowledge concerning them,[53] while ordinary urban women who did not veil were not identified as subjects for social scientific research.[54] A counterpoint to Islamist women as an object of social science, has been oral history of Kemalist women, who survived the early republican reforms.[55] In the search for the "culturally distinct," as in narratives of Islamist, elite Kemalist, Alevi, or rural women, most studies of women in Turkey have ignored the lives of lower-middle-class, working-class, and urban Sunni women who are not religious.

Many scholarly narratives on the relation of Middle Eastern women with the West, have mapped the signifier "European" too easily onto a conventional story of Westernization as imposed by upper-class elites on the rest of the population. An Occidentalism of sorts exists in such studies that look for the subaltern or the Middle Eastern in signifiers and symbols that contradict the Western, as if it were possible to disaggregate the Middle Eastern from the European in life stories, after a long history of relations of power between peoples of these regions. A certain narrative of class structure has guided much scholarly discourse on region and culture in the Middle East, where markers of "Europe" are associated with the elites and those of locality with the subaltern. Such studies which would like to be critical of Orientalism, colonialism, and Westernization, as well as of the class structure in the Middle East, often end up reproducing the assumptions that they set out to deconstruct. The subaltern is once again written out of the history of Europe and a (white West European) purity and identity is (by default) maintained for Europe. The lives of a significant number of Turkish women, undecipherable through the dominant schol-

arly discourses, do not get represented in such studies that keep working
on the premise of "Middle East versus Europe." It is to the story of one
such woman and her narrative of place and region that I now turn.

Unlike Fatma, whose family had been at the center of republican institutions from the beginning, Zeynep's parents had no determinative connections with the state. They were originally from a village of Aydın in what is
geographically western Anatolia and they thought that their ancestors were
yörüks, or nomads from Central Asia. The family did not have a consciousness of being Sunni until Alevi-Sunni conflicts of identity were advertised on
television news. There weren't any Alevi villages in the area that surrounded
the family's village in Aydın, unlike other districts, such as Tokat and Sıvas,
which, until the recent flight of Alevis, were dotted with neighboring Alevi
and Sunni villages in conflict. Zeynep's parents knew that Kurds had migrated to downtown Aydın from southeastern Turkey and occasionally they
made sneering remarks about "the conservative ways of those people from
the East." Zeynep's mother, just about fifty years old, had specifically discouraged Zeynep from marrying "an Easterner" (*Doğulu*) on the grounds that
"Eastern" men were tough and strict with their wives, that they forced them
to cover, and did not let them work outside the home. Zeynep's family had a
shorter life history in Istanbul than Fatma's family. Once farmers with a small
plot of land, the parents had moved from Aydın to Istanbul for better work
when Zeynep was about ten years old. They had been encouraged to do so by
other people from their place of origin (*memleket*) whom they referred to as
their "fellow townsmen" (*hemşeri*).

The twenty years of their life in Istanbul had been spent mainly in one
of the shanty areas of Bakırköy. The father had switched jobs a number of
times, until he found work as an assistant in the shop of an acquaintance.
In Istanbul, the mother had become a housewife. At the end of every
month, Zeynep remembered that they barely made ends meet, yet they
never felt poor. "We are middle class," Zeynep used to say (*orta sınıf*),
though their savings and standard of life were vastly different from that of
the bourgeoisie.

Zeynep had a younger sister and two older brothers who worked as
clerks in the municipality. She was especially close to one of her brothers
and did many things with him. Before she got married, she liked to be
taken out by her brother and his friends for walks by the Marmara Sea or
to go to the movies when they could afford it. She had become friendly
with her brother's circle, had fallen in love with one friend, and asked her
parents for permission to marry this man. He was now her husband. She
had gone out with him ("*konuştuk*," she said, "we talked"; or sometimes
"*çıktık*," "we went out")[56] for two years before telling her father. Her mother
knew the story pretty much from the beginning. Zeynep was twenty-seven
years old when she got married.

Zeynep's mother had long wavy hair tied up in a bun behind her head. She loosely covered her head with a scarf when she went out of the house, leaving a couple of stray locks on the side of her forehead. She wore plain colored skirts that reached below her knees and colorful blouses to match. The mother did not cover her head in the presence of men who weren't relatives and even though she mostly talked to the women when they had visitors at home, the whole company sat together in the living room. The parents did not want their daughters to wear headscarves, not even in the loosely attached newly urbanized style of the mother. On the contrary, they feared that their daughters would be influenced by friends and would take up the veil. Zeynep and her sister did not wear headscarves. They both wore their hair down in public and once in a while went to the hairdressers in Bakırköy to have their hair trimmed and blow-dried. Zeynep liked to wear lipstick every day and she nicely shaded her eyes with black liner and mascara. She took a lot of care to dress prettily. She would wear tight white jeans and a white blouse, for example, with a necklace around her neck. When out with friends, she would sometimes wear a tight skirt. In summer, she liked to wear miniskirts made of denim as well as shorts.

Zeynep's family was not religious. In her adolescence and directly after migrating to Istanbul, Zeynep had become interested in religion, had asked to be bought books of prayer and the Kuran, and used to read and memorize passages by herself at night. She had asked her mother to teach her how to do the *namaz*. And it is then that she had learned how to perform ablutions (*abdest*) and to pray five times a day. Yet Zeynep had lost interest in religion after a couple of years. No one in her family was devout. Her parents would do the *namaz* only once a year on the Sacrifice Holiday (*Kurban Bayramı*), for which they attempted to buy a sheep, at least once every couple of years, to sacrifice. The father would participate in funeral *namaz*s, in the event of an acquaintance's death.

But Zeynep, her mother, sister, girlfriends, and women neighbors were very much into fortune telling. The mother was known in the community for making successful predictions from the grinds in Turkish coffee cups. There was not a single day in Zeynep's family home when coffee cups wouldn't be turned over to be read by the mother or other friends who also told fortunes. Zeynep would frequently refer to such readings of her life and its prospects. Love, work, home, and money were topics to ponder. Zeynep and her mother had also learned about the tombs of several of Istanbul's mystical saints (*evliyalar*). They went once in a while to Eyüp, one of Istanbul's most sacred neighborhoods,[57] and made wishes by the tombs of specific saints recommended by close friends. Zeynep and her women friends believed in the evil eye (*nazar*). Zeynep always wore a bracelet of blue beads that were said to protect the wearer from the cast of envious gazes. Zeynep's mother and other women in their neighborhood also believed in magic (*büyü*). The mother thought, for example, that her unmarried younger daughter had been jinxed by a jealous relative. Zeynep laughed at her mother's stories of magic. "Just listen to these amazing stories," she used to say. Feeling more "educated" and "conscious" than her mother, Zeynep once in a while tried to dissuade her from believing in magic. Yet she always listened to the stories attentively.

After finishing elementary school and a few years of middle school in Aydın, Zeynep continued her studies in Istanbul, where she graduated from a normal lycée for boys and girls.[58] She had lots of friends in high school, most of them girls. But she befriended boys as well and had gone out with a couple of boys from her school. After highschool, Zeynep had studied to enroll in the University, but did not succeed in the exams. She then decided to attend a Public Learning center (*Açık Öğretim*) to learn computer programming and English. She wanted to have good skills to become a secretary. She had regularly attended the courses there, while continuing to work, yet she felt that she wasn't taught very much in the center. After working as a lower-level secretary in a couple of small businesses close to her family home, Zeynep had taken a temporary job as shop assistant alongside a friend of hers who worked in the district of Fatih. That is what she was doing when I met her. She took the commuter train from Bakırköy, where she lived, all the way to Sirkeci. She walked up to the bus station, and took a bus to Fatih.

Zeynep had taken up this job in Fatih so as not to be unemployed in that period after she was laid off from the company she used to work for. The friend who found her the job lived in Fatih and Zeynep had visited this neighborhood several times before. Yet she strongly disliked the area. "It's a terrible place," she said. She wished to find a job in another district of Istanbul, less dominated by religion. The shop where Zeynep worked sold a selection of women's urban clothes, blue jeans, blouses, T-shirts, sweaters, and skirts of many sizes. Zeynep was there to show customers around, along with two men and two other women shop assistants. Working in Fatih, Zeynep exchanged many stories about Islamists with her coworkers. One day she recounted the story of a veiled woman who entered the shop to try on a skirt, but had to ask the male shop attendants to leave the room before she would put on any shop items. Zeynep found this hilarious. The shop where Zeynep worked stood out among numerous shops for veils and overcoats for religious women. Zeynep said that she wanted her boss to hang a portrait of Ataturk up in the shop. Yet she said that "no one in this district would buy from us if we were to exhibit a portrait of Ataturk." She was perplexed by the activity of buying and selling that went on in the shops for veiled women (*tesettür giyim dükkânları*).[59]

Zeynep liked to tell stories of the "insincerity" or "hypocrisy" of veiled women. She constructed Islamist women as morally corrupt since they pretended to be virtuous through their clothes and public manners. She recounted, for example, a story that she overheard from a cab driver of a veiled woman who took her veil off on her way from Fatih to another neighborhood of Istanbul. "She apparently appeared, under her veil, with lots of makeup, a miniskirt, and well-dressed hair," Zeynep said. "Now, is this honor?" she exclaimed. She thought Islamist women were "fake" (*sahte*). On one of our lunches in the little sandwich shop close to her work, Zeynep and her boss exchanged views about the veiled women who sat close by. While one of these women was dressed in a black veil that revealed only her eyes and nose, two of the women who accompanied her were dressed in overcoats and scarves (*türban*) in pastel colors, and one had loosely tied a scarf around her hair. Zeynep's boss snapped while giving side glances to the women and asked Zeynep, "For God's sake, did your grandmother dress up in this way? The veil is not worn like this in our traditions. She has even covered her mouth! They are copying this from the Arabs. Do they think they are going to sell snails in a Muslim neighborhood?"[60] Zeynep agreed and said, "These women are fake!" The boss's little son had come to eat out with us. He pointed at the veiled woman and asked in a loud voice, "Mother! Are you talking about that woman with black clothes?" Zeynep and her boss burst out laughing as everyone turned and looked at our table. "Shut up!" the boss whispered to her son, "that sort would chop us into little pieces!"

In Zeynep's everyday conversations about Islamists (one of her favorite topics of discussion at the time), she constructed them to be "greedy" and "out for money and personal interest." "I am also Muslim," she said. "Everyone should care only for their own religion. These types are all sold out. Erbakan has apparently been distributing golden bracelets, money, and apartment flats to those who veil and who promise to vote for Welfare. All these women are doing it for the money!" She liked to tell stories about a woman who took up the veil in her neighborhood close to Bakırköy. "This woman, until a few months ago, cried every day about her debts. After she covered, there is no sound. Why do you think? And now she tries to convince everyone to vote for Erbakan." At the time of our conversation, mainstream TV stations were also producing news about Welfare's gifts to potential voters. This strategy of the Welfare Party was circulated, at the time, in public secularist discourse.

"I asked this woman," Zeynep continued, referring to her neighbor who veiled, "Whose state do you think you are living in? Not Ataturk's?" Zeynep was conscious of being member of a particular kind of state. And veiled women contradicted the portrait of what she conceived Turkey to be. "These people," she said, objectifying Islamists with othering language, "return to their village, having earned lots of money. They then begin to brainwash their fellow villagers. Now, you have come from village to city. Instead of modernizing and leaving village mentality behind, instead of progressing a little bit, go and remain that way, go backwards. Turn to the past instead of taking the opportunity to develop." Zeynep's narrative of modernity was that of a first generation immigrant to Istanbul who had been encouraged by parents to adapt to the city's ways. "I told the Welfarist woman: 'It would serve you right if your husband took ten extra wives!'" Zeynep was referring to a common secular notion that Islamist men had four wives. "In the hands of such people," Zeynep said, "we would not be able to stand up for our rights in front of our husbands. This freedom of ours would be taken from our hands." Zeynep distinguished her family from Islamists. "My father," she said, "encouraged me and my sister to practice everyting that befits a civilized (*medeni*) life. When our proper age had come, for example, both me and my sister applied for driving licenses. I know how to drive." Yet Zeynep's family did not own a car.

In that period of heightened tension between secularists and Islamists, Zeynep had started to attend secularist public events and demonstrations. On the sensationalized celebration of Republic Day 1994,[61] for example, Zeynep and her husband had gone to Taksim Square to attend the ceremony and have a pleasant day out on the street listening to popular music. By 1996, she began to participate in women's marches against Islamic law. She shouted slogans along with thousands of women on the street, crying "Turkey will not become Iran!" She sang along to old Ataturkist marches. She participated in the daily "turning off lights for one minute" resistance in protest of the government's corruption and the Welfare Party's rule in the beginning of 1997. By 1996, Zeynep had defined her position in politics of identity and region between secularists and Islamists. She was out on the streets shouting for the return of Ataturk's state model.

Zeynep's Istanbul was quite different from the Istanbul of Fatma. The neighborhood in Bakırköy where she spent most of her evenings and weekends was central to her life. Her home was frequented by neighbors and friends. Most of her and her husband's relatives lived close by, where casual visits back and forth were quite ordinary. Zeynep and her husband went out for walks on weekends to the Yıldız Park and by the Marmara Sea. They very rarely ate in a restaurant and did so only on special occasions. On the street, they ate mostly fast food sold in little booths, sandwiches of *döner* or tripe, *lahmacun*.[62] Lately she had developed a taste for baked potatoes stuffed with American or Italian salad that were sold relatively cheaply in little booths all over Istanbul's entertainment districts.

Zeynep enjoyed herself enormously on her walks with her husband. She felt overjoyed when he suggested going to a part of Istanbul she did not know. But she also went out regularly with her mother, sister, or women friends. She would go to Mahmutpaşa behind the spice bazaar in Eminönü for cheap houseware and clothes. When she wanted to buy something special, she went to the clothing shops in downtown Bakırköy. She rarely went to Beyoğlu, that favorite neighborhood of Fatma's. And she did not remember whether she had ever been to Nişantaşı, the posh neighborhood of Fatma's parents. She did not know the downtown areas of the upper class Levent and Ulus where Fatma had lived as a married woman, but only the shanty towns such as Gültepe, which bordered the suburbs of the rich. During holidays, Zeynep and her family would alternate between Gültepe and Alibeyköy to visit relatives from their village of origin.

Undoing Area Studies

The issues of contemporary Istanbul's politics of culture can be compared instructively with contemporary debates in metropolitan anthropology.[63] As the subjects of the Turkish state debate "Turkey's proper region" among themselves, the question of "place" is central to contemporary anthropological theory. Institutionalized as a formal discipline in the social sciences, anthropology had the task of accumulating and delivering intensive firsthand knowledge about specific places, regions, or localities. Certain kinds of knowledge could be attained from the study of particular geographical areas against others. The anthropologist was the specialist who related regional specificity to theoretical debates in metropolitan anthropology. Regional specialization has been a central characteristic sought in anthropologists who assume authority through expert knowledge on the minutae of the culture of specific places. Locally based and small-scale field research has been associated in disciplinary anthropological discourse with knowledge of a region, whether this be South Asia, the Middle East, or Latin America. Anthropology's regionalism has not yet been undone, in spite of recent theoretical critiques of its fetishism of place (Gupta and Ferguson 1992, 1997).

Until very recently, regions were fundamental to the study of specific questions and theoretical issues by anthropologists. To study kinship, one had to do fieldwork in Africa; gift exchange, Melanesia; hierarchy, South Asia; segmentation, Middle East; and honor and shame, the Mediterranean. Excellent critiques have been written about these iconized regional specializations in anthropology (Strathern 1990, Fardon 1990, Appadurai 1986, Abu-Lughod 1990, and Herzfeld 1984). And reviewers of regional bibliographies in anthropology have attempted to direct inquiry away from theoretical pigeonholes in the study of cultural areas. Identifying classical issues in the anthropology of the Arab World (segmentation, the harem, and Islam), Lila Abu-Lughod has encouraged students of the Middle East to ask new questions, ones that address "state violence and repression, military occupation, poverty, migration, and cultural imperialism, to name just a few" (1990, 118). Such valuable recent critiques have served to diversify the questions posed by anthropologists about specific regions, charting new avenues for cross-regional comparison. And yet, most of these recent critiques still take region for granted, as if there were a "cultural area" that preceded its construction as such. Region creeps in through the back door in many anthropological attempts to deconstruct it. The fantasy of region remains.

Abu-Lughod's review of the anthropology of the Arab World, for example, aims to nudge scholarship on the Middle East toward more theoretical sophistication. Her article introduces the Foucauldian notion of "discourse" to studies of the Middle East via Edward Said, inviting anthropologists of this region to be attentive to "representation" instead of seeking "truth" (1990, 83–85).[64] However, Abu-Lughod ends up only advocating better representations in place of Orientalist misrepresentations in anthropology.[65] For example, nowhere in the article that charts a new agenda for the anthropology of the Middle East, does Abu-Lughod question the notion of "the Arab world," itself. Abu-Lughod questions all other categories. But nowhere in her incorporation of post-structuralist theory does she argue for an inquiry into nationalist discourses in Arab states. Her suggestion to study "state violence and repression" does not question the notion of "the Arab" as a central organizing category of contemporary state power in the Middle East. Therefore, in her attempts to transcend the limits of area studies, Abu-Lughod ends up with an essentialist reconstruction of the cultural region under study.

The category "Arab world" reifies "Arabness" to the detriment of other sorts of identifications, hybrid identities, diasporic existences, minorities, and marginal communities in this region. It also assumes and reconstructs a necessary difference with Iran, Turkey, Sudan, Israel, and Europe, among other important spaces in the region. It therefore reproduces the barriers of difference among these populations as if they were natural rather than products of specific histories, agencies, or colonial and nationalist discourses and practices. Arabness is lived as real, one could indeed argue, by those who identify with this cultural category against others. Yet it is another thing for the anthropologist to reproduce such categories in analysis, as if they were ahistorical, extra-discursive, straightforward, or essential.

Much recent critical scholarship on the Middle East or the Arab world defines the area as composed primarily of Arab Muslims. That is the picture of the Middle East that is significantly available for us in newly institutionalized (post-Orientalist) studies of the region. Yet, like Turkey, which was rendered predominantly Turkish and Muslim only through distinctive historical events such as the forceful exchange of populations with Greece,

the Arab world reached its present composition through historical processes, too. Palestinian Arabs were driven from their homeland, to be replaced by immigrant Jews and settlers. Soon after, Middle Eastern Jews
were pressured to associate themselves with what was constructed as their
nation-state, to leave their homelands for Israel and other parts of the
world.[66] There is a distinct historical precedence to the contemporary composition of Arab nation-states. The notion of the Arab world, however,
implies that the picture of the region was always essentially the same.

In the same way that Jews in general fall outside the notion of the Arab
world—as if the Arab / Jewish conflict, national identifications, and nationalist distinctions had always (since time immemorial) been the case—so
do Copts, Berbers, Druzes, Greeks, Maronites, Turks, Armenians, Kurds,
Lazs, Alevites, Circassians, Georgians, Azeris, and Iranians.[67] Much of the
historiography of the Middle East has interpreted non-Muslims to be
"comprador" merchants who worked as handmaidens to colonialism. Inter-
faith marriages, conversions, complex cultural backgrounds, class conflict,
diaspora and immigration, and already existing relations with Europe do
not have much place in such characterizations of the region. In contrast,
Abdellah Hammoudi's *Master and Disciple* (1997) studies and critically
engages with power in whatever cultural baggage it might present itself,
whether it be Arab, Berber, Muslim, Moroccan, or French.

Following Hammoudi's ethnographic trajectory, this book, written
against the grain of the notions of Turkey, Turkish culture, Turks, and the
Turkish state, attempts to approach region differently. Region is still taken
for granted in studies that have not attended to the internally contested
aspect of regionalism. Turkey's region is not that obvious, as I would assume it shouldn't be in certain Arab nation-states from the point of view of
their subjects. There are competing local narratives for what it was, what it
is, and what it ought to be. The context of secularist / Islamist politics of
culture has further intensified such debates. Region, then, is not obvious
but socially constructed and historically situated.

In contrast to the anthropological study of the Arab World, the anthropology of the Mediterranean has been relatively more (self-)critical of the
relevant nationalist discourses and regional essentialisms. The internally
indeterminate and contested quality of regional affiliation has been addressed by a number of ethnographers, especially those studying Greece.[68]
Possible complicities between nationalisms on the one hand and area- or
nation-based anthropologies on the other have been questioned as well
(Herzfeld 1982, 1984, 1995). Michael Herzfeld has attempted to illustrate
the historical construction of difference between Greeks and Turks in that
overly symbolic and highly interpreted border in the Thrace and the Aegean Sea, which has discursively been taken to represent the distinction
between "Europe" and "the East."[69]

So curiously, within contemporary anthropological writing, the difference between Turks and Greeks is now easier to breach than that between Turks and Arabs. In other words, in the anthropology of the Middle East, defining itself as centrally Muslim and Arab and reproducing a discourse about its regional otherness to Europe, the life histories that I narrate in this ethnography would find no space for articulation. From this rubric, Fatma would probably be read as a cultural hybrid who had sold out and become a Westernized elite. Zeynep's life and worldview, on the other hand, would be incomprehensible. Perhaps only Islamist women—as they attempt to bridge the gap between the past and the present, Islam and Turkey, Turkey and the Arab World—would find a place in the anthropology of the Middle East, as conceived and theorized by anthropologists to date. Because of what has been written as its history of Westernization, Turkey has been studied as a peculiar deviation from the norm of the ("real") Middle East. I would like, through this ethnography, to begin a project of thinking Europe as well as the Middle East anew. From an existential gaze situated in Turkey, that of Zeynep for example, both of these constructed categories actually appear rather problematic.

From the standpoint of post-Orientalist scholarship and politics, it is politically correct to conceive of Turkey as Middle Eastern. From the same point of view, it is deemed problematic to argue that Turkey is (even also) European. To suggest this is to reproduce the modernism of Ataturkist elites. Indeed, this new academic discourse has the tendency to reproduce what it had set up to deconstruct: Orientalism. The European Union, one of the contemporary world's central loci of power, would like to keep regional authenticities intact, to understand Turkey to be culturally "other" to Europe (unless the contrary is demonstrated), to write the histories of the Ottoman Empire, Andalusia, as well as the history of Muslim Europeans and Muslim immigrants to Europe, out of the concept of Europe. And yet, as I mentioned before, Turks, Arabs, and Jews were never outside Europe. Turks have been intrinsic to European history from the fourteenth century, to the point where it is problematic to try to impose categorical distinctions between the study of Turks and the study of Europeans. Anthropology's disciplinary attempts to move beyond Western categories of analysis to grasp better "the native's point of view" is still interesting only insofar as it does not construct a drift, in this case, in the native's historical involvement with Europe. Specifically in the ethnography of contemporary Turkey, it is a problematic exercise to try to distinguish the native from the Western, or the Turkish from the European. Is the headscarf (*türban*) and the overcoat (*pardösü*) worn by Islamist women in contemporary Turkey, for example, more Turkish, Islamic, Middle Eastern, or native than the blue jeans and tight-fitting T-shirts worn by Zeynep?

Conversely, one could ask whether the life history of Zeynep is not Middle Eastern. I will suggest that such regionalist queries and specifications cannot avoid becoming a quest for reified markers of native culture. The discursive categories of academic area studies and of anthropological regions are not useful if they have the consequence of reproducing already existing terms of difference in state societies.

3

The Market for Identities: Buying and Selling Secularity and Islam

> In the 1980s and 1990s, every issue has been
> politicized in the medium of consumable style,
> regardless of its ideological orientation: from
> antiracism, antisexism, and antihomophobia, to
> evangelism, antiabortion, and right-wing
> antigovernment stances.
> —*George Yudice, 1995*

Consuming "Culture"

"Culture" has too often been conceptualized as distinct from the domain of commodification.[1] Anthropologists have written numerous ethnographies of the disruption or transformation of culture through the incoming forces of capitalism. Like the concepts of structure and change (products of binarism), the categories of "culture" and "economy," too, have been pit against each other in ways that overlook their inherency. While culture has been too easily mapped onto "what is local," economy, even after centuries of worldwide capitalism, has been associated with "what is Western" and therefore with what is "external" to and what supposedly contradicts "local culture."

From a perspective that would separate "culture" and "economy" into different disciplines in the social sciences (anthropology and political economy, respectively), into different historical periods (tradition versus capitalist modernity), and into different places (the Middle East, for example, versus the West), it would be possible simply to study Islamists in contemporary Turkey as representative of culture and secular Westernists as the handmaidens of capitalist economy. This would be a perspective that imagines "culture" to be manifested originally outside political economy, or, that perceives economy to be an ensuing appendage upon or an interruption of a formerly pristine domain of culture.

This ethnography of consumerism and contemporary politics of culture in Turkey questions such binarist approaches to society and history that end up reproducing, sometimes by default, positivist notions of culture.

This chapter presents a social history of the political economy of culture. Political economy, focused upon through the medium of commodification, is studied as a domain of construction. Constructionists have too often studied the imagination of nations, cultures, and identities in idealist terms, as if these categories materialized in our consciousnesses and were then applied to produce historical events. Construction, however, is also about political economy, or, to put it differently, political economy is intrinsic to the construction of cultures. For, as easy as it seems to raise our consciousness about the constructedness of our political categories, it is difficult to change the political economic conditions of such construction.

This chapter studies the manufacture of the veil and of the portrait of Ataturk as central commodities and symbols of cultural identity in contemporary Turkey. I use the term "manufacture" to refer not only to abstract imagination, but also, literally, to production in real and tangible terms. In following the work of Stuart Hall (1993), I offer an ethnography of the production of culture. I argue that secularist and Islamist identities in contemporary Turkey are products of manufacture. They are not original and essential, even though they are experienced as such. In other words, they are not reflections of some primordial "Turkishness." Drawing upon fieldwork conducted in the Islamist veiling sector, in marketplaces for religious commodities, in public centers for the manifestation of politics of identity, and among secularists, I ask: If the "veil" and "Ataturk" became central symbols in contemporary politics of identity, what is the social history of their manufacture?

Politics of culture between secularists and Islamists in Turkey in the 1980s and 1990s developed in the context of a consumer market influenced by globalization. So central was consumerism to the social life of this period that political conflicts were organized, expressed, and mediated through this medium. Islamist movements have mostly represented themselves in reaction to commodity cultures, which spread Western lifestyles and values. Therefore certain scholars of Islamism have studied the movement as an expression of a "critique of modernity." My observations of the mainstream Islamist movement in Turkey have been otherwise. Commodification proved to be a context and activity that was historically shared by Islamists and secularists alike, rather than a domain that divided them. There certainly were variations within secularist and Islamist modes of consumerist practice. And yet, it would be ethnographically inaccurate to associate commodification with Westernization, as if it were necessarily antithetical to local practices of Islam or to a movement that organizes itself around the theme of the sacred.

Commodification had a central role in the shaping of this particular politics of culture. I argue that the realm of Islamist and secularist public cultures was already commodified. It is not that commodification disturbed formerly genuine identities. Rather, Islamists and secularists consumed *and* they felt that their identities were genuine, making the very opposition "genuine / false" obsolete. Commodification had much to do with the reification of certain symbols, like the veil and Ataturk, as emblems of identity. Pitting consumable signifiers against one another, commodification had a role in transforming politics of culture into a war over symbols.

In the 1980s, cultural identities were packaged to be assumed in commodity form. Battles over political difference were waged over manners of consumption. As Islamists came to forge identities in distinction from secularists, they thought about their habits of use and modified or radically changed the sorts of things that they bought and sold. They wore different clothes, they ate only certain kinds of food, they frequented particular shops, they started special businesses of their own, and so forth. The rise of the Islamist movement in popularity and power is indissoluble from the development of specialized businesses for "Islamic goods" and the formation of market networks for believers. Islamists came to define themselves as having an "identity" (*kimlik*) in acquiring and using new things that in their minds represented "the lost Islamic past." The creativity poured into the making of political activism went hand in hand with market innovation.

When Turgut Özal came to power in the mid 1980s, he did so in addressing the secular bourgeoisie in the metropolises as well as the believing businesspeople of small-town Anatolia. Özal set Turkey's course for privatization, for a massive intrusion by multinational companies, a free market, and foreign goods. Things that were never found in shops in Turkey until then became quickly commonplace. Turkey's economy grew into what was later called "the boom time." As television was privatized, the advertising industry took a new shape, having found an invaluable resource for publicity. New businesses started in turn, introducing further new products to the consumer market.

Özal's economics had followed three years of martial law under a military government. This was the first elected government to follow the coup of 1980, and Özal had ambiguous relations with the generals who disapproved of his connections with Sufi orders and religious communities and were skeptical of his bold moves toward economic and political liberalization. Yet Özal managed his relations with the army so that the army would keep the law and order that was needed for the economic reforms.

Public life was transformed in the Özal period with the emergence of young urban professionals. In the aftermath of the coup, when most of the student leaders of the left were still in prison, a new culture of learning developed in universities, where students predominantly opted to study business administration, economics, or marketing. "Success" was readvertised to be the greatest value, and making lots of money was highly prized. Opening one's own business, getting married, owning a house, a car, and home appliances, traveling on holidays, and being financially comfortable came to be *the* aspiration. TV ads featured families who had "made it." Happiness was measured on a scale of buying and easily consuming. Young people who "successfully" completed their studies in business or related subjects went on to work in the newly privatized media companies and in the increasing number of advertising agencies, banks, and businesses. Restaurants, cinemas, clothing chains, bars, and cafés in the city multiplied dramatically. Istanbul was quickly remade in this period to serve a lifestyle of expanding consumption.

Yet changes did not take place in the lives of the secular urbanites only. The state's economy under Özal was also (and especially) geared to the advantage of the businesses of the religious in smaller cities of Anatolia. Özal himself came of a conservative religious family from Malatya. His family had strong ties with a branch of the Nakshibendi Sufi order and he had formerly been a member of the National Salvation Party, which was later to be transformed into the Welfare Party. Özal's aim was to channel resources to *this* category of Turkish capital as well, to revive the market by bringing Muslim capitalists, businesspeople, and small traders to compete with the secular bourgeoisie, who had longer enduring ties with Western-centered capitalism. While the advertising and culture industries of the secular mainstream grew in that period, an extensive market also developed under the management of religious businesspeople, some of whom were Islamists. The culture and values of the Özal period also influenced those who identified with Islamists.

Turkish businesses were now engaged in a massive export drive, even though, due to the free-market policies of the new government, the import of foreign goods always exceeded export. And businesses were not only involved in trading with foreign countries, but also in investing as multinationals abroad. Muslim capitalists,[2] as specially encouraged by the Özal government, were forming their own conglomerates as well. The Kuralkan company group, for example, and İhlas Ltd. produced all sorts of items from cars to biscuits. In time, Muslim capital came to compete in almost all the sectors of the economy, producing paint, ceramics, timber, soap, detergents, and petroleum, along with almost everything else that was marketable. When advertising certain products, such as food and clothing, these new or expanded companies introduced themselves as moral from an Islamic point of view. That was what differentiated them, in their preferred representation, from the companies of secularists. Some "Muslim companies" presented themselves in the market by claiming higher values: following the dietary prescriptions of Islam, not investing in interest, not serving food to employees during Ramazan (the month of fasting), reserving money for charity (*zekât*),[3] producing good quality products, and earning "just" profits. Ülker biscuits, for example, were claimed to contain no lard, leaving the older Eti brand in the cold. Many of these "Muslim companies" in time turned into self-managed multinationals.

What was significant about the consumer culture of this period was its close links with politics of identity. As conservative small-town capital holders grew to become small urban shop owners or founders of bigger companies in the metropolis, they created a market for their lifestyle and ideology. They developed their capital in following the logic of contemporary capitalism. Yet they also geared their energy to the production of an alternative market of goods for those who felt alienated from the religiously forbidden (*haram*) or the Westernized goods that had dominated the arenas of consumption. As they leaned on the financial strength gained from investing in all areas, these companies also made sure that all the needs of a Muslim, as they defined him or her, were specially met.

The Veil as a Commodity

The veil was considered one of the most important goods to have been put in the trading circuit by Muslim businesspeople in Turkey.[4] Compared to other consumer items that were produced in Muslim companies, there was an overload of symbolic interpretation around the veil and its many versions. In the 1980s, Turkey's textile industry had grown to be highly competitive in the world market, selling Europeans what they liked to wear in good style and at a cheaper price. But clothing businesses also developed in the Muslim sector of the economy. The rise of the Islamist movement in the 1980s and 1990s in Turkey was integral to the creation of a market for headscarves, overcoats, and veils for women. Several companies sprang up, then, for the production and sale of all sorts of clothing items for women who "covered."[5]

There were certain clothing shops that were cheap and geared to the basic needs of women of low or average income. Such shops would be placed in the side or back streets of neighborhoods inhabited by Islamists rather than on the main promenade. Here, the colors of overcoats would generally be plain—dark blue, dark green, black, or brown. The cloth used in such variations would be either cotton or polyester.

However, most shop owners whom I interviewed said that women who wore Muslim dress did not prefer cheap veils and overcoats, that they especially bought good quality things and paid the price since they considered these to be the most important apparel that they would be investing in. Young Islamist women, especially those who attended university or who held jobs outside the home, liked to dress not from such side street shops, but from those that had more stylish selections of headscarves and coats. In the mid-1990s, specific colors were in fashion among "covered" university students: light pink and lavender, all shades of purple, pastel blue, green, yellow, and gray. Students carefully matched the color of their *türbans* (as one version of headscarf came to be called after the 1980s) to that of their overcoats, in the fashion that they took out to the streets at that time.

Islamist women students had also developed a liking for a special kind of cloth for overcoats, that which was made of stoned silk. These particular *pardösüs* (overcoat, from the French *pardessus*) as they were called, were not cheap. In 1994, when I did a survey of veil shops in the Fatih and Unkapanı districts of Istanbul, overcoats in stoned silk were 3.5 million Turkish liras (about $50 (U.S.) at the time), expensive for the average budget in Turkey. Those made of pure silk were 4.5 million. One could also find cheaper coats for 2 million liras made of cotton and others that were partly made of wool for 3 to 4 million. Those *pardösüs* of stoned silk that were the fashion among Islamist women students were not made of locally produced cloth. Stoned silk was promoted in Islamist shops as a "foreign product" (*yabancı mal*) with the intent of signifying better quality. The veils and overcoats that were in fashion among Islamist women students, and that were defended as representative of local culture, the local past, and local values, were made of English cloth.

Veil shops introduced their products as heirs of "the past." A woman who worked in a headscarf company in 1994 said that they had started trading in headscarves twenty years ago. "The headscarf's past lies in Ottoman times," she said, arguing that there had been a break in the use of this item in the republican period until it was picked up again in the 1980s. She read an Islamist narrative of Turkish history into the veiling apparel in her shop window. This particular headscarf shop was one among thirty in a bazaar of covered women's clothing (*tesettür giyim*) in Unkapanı, Istanbul. Some of the headscarf and overcoat companies had brand names that evoked Islam: "Tevhid," for example, referring to unity under one God, "Ihvan," signifying Muslim brotherhood, or "Hak," using one of the names for God.

A shop attendant here recounted the history of the market for veils in Istanbul. He noted that he and his boss had started their own particular business twenty-five years ago, when such brands as Mesture or Tekbir in veiling were not yet around. They used to sew veil models to special order at that time. They had very few customers and they produced overcoats on request. Most of the time, they prepared other sorts of clothing. Later, the shop attendant said, when they saw that there was a developing market for religious women's clothes, they went straight into that business. By that time, the conglomerates Mesture and Tekbir had started to mass produce headscarves and overcoats, and people were buying ready-made goods on the market. In time, "covered" women even began to show care about the brand (*marka*) of what they bought, exchanging information with one another in comparing quality and style. "In the end," the shop attendant said,

we had to modify our styles to match those that were being invented by the big veiling companies. We had to do that in order to remain in the market. We try to reproduce those popularized designs with less cloth so that our prices can still be competitive beside the monopolies' price cuts. Plus, clothing is not like food. You have to change things in order to keep getting customers, in order not to have them bored. For example, silk was in fashion last year. Everyone wore that until they had enough of silk. Then, one of the big companies put the stoned silk models on the market. That is what is in fashion this year. We now have to produce that, too.

This merchant's story is illustrative of the commodified quality of covered women's clothes.

Another trader of Islamic clothing in the Unkapanı marketplace had his own understanding of proper "covering." "There can be no such thing as 'fashion' (*moda*) in Islamic covering," he said.

If you are covering, you will not pay attention to showing off or ostentation. Aren't there those who do? There are, of course. The Tekbir company for example has created a fashion for veiling. They saw that there was demand and they started to do the trade. Of course, you will dress beautifully. The other one [the secularist] is dressing pretty. Aren't you going to dress pretty? In Islam, there is the commandment to cover, but to cover in a pretty way. The condition in covering is to conceal the contours of the body. You have to wear wide and loose-fitting clothes, in other words, and never tightly trimmed ones in public. Sometimes I get customers who request tight models in overcoats. But the one who covers with knowledge and good conscience would not do that.

Producers and sellers of "Muslim women's clothes" had agency, say, and role in the shaping of what proper covering was about. Trading and the economy were not compartments apart from the making of contemporary Islamist identities.

The market for headscarves, overcoats, and veils had extensions all over Turkey, as in parts of Western Europe. The shops in Unkapanı sent most of their products to cities and towns especially in Eastern Anatolia. There was less demand for headscarves and overcoats of this sort, shop keepers noted, in the Aegean region of Turkey. On the other hand, a great demand for veils came from Germany. Many Turkish workers and immigrants there had taken up the headscarf, looking for the specific brands that they liked from Turkey.[6]

One of the contexts for the rising Islamist movement in Turkey of the 1980s and 1990s was the free market of commodities. As a culture of excessive consumption developed among the mainstream secular middle class, especially in the metropolises, Islamists of small-city Anatolian background defined their difference by organizing other strategies of use. Companies and shops of people of differing cultural and social backgrounds came to compete with one another in the same capitalist market. And distinction, quality, and morality in goods were now defined around the terms of politics of identity. Secularists were ultimately "different" from Islamists because they consumed different things. Habits of consumption became central markers of internal cultural difference in Turkey.

Secularist Commodities

Until the market for "Muslim identities" developed, secular mainstream textile companies did not accentuate the cultural symbolism of what they exhibited in their shop windows. There were buttoned shirts, sweaters, short skirts, stylish long skirts with vents up to above the knees, low-cut and tight-fitting T-shirts that were introduced as "badi" (Turkish transliteration for the English word "body"), and all sorts and colors of jeans, long dresses, and short dresses. In the 1980s, Turkey's mainstream textile companies came to compete with Italian and French trademarks in producing "European" clothing. A number of big clothing companies, such as Mudo and Yargıcı, began to hire their own designers. Some became world renowned, like Zeki Triko, which advertised its women's bathing suits and bikinis by paying the world's top models (e.g., Cindy Crawford) to pose for its internationally distributed brochures. As certain European multinationals began to use cheap Turkish labor to produce their goods, simultaneously these Turkish-owned textile companies were beginning to teach Europeans what they ought to wear.

But, initially, these widening Turkish textile companies introduced their goods as the norm for "what is worn in the modern world." Until the Islamist market for clothes developed, Turkey's secular mainstream companies did not overinterpret the culture that they in fact produced. The clothes exhibited in the chic boutiques of posh neighborhoods in Istanbul, as well as their variations and copies sold in smaller and more modest shops in other parts of town, were introduced to be "standard" clothing or what was habitually worn "in contemporary times" contrary to the advent of Islamic textiles. The associations of "culturalism" were objectified only onto the clothing practices of Islamists, when the ways of secularists were constructed to be neutral or devoid of symbolism and history.[7]

In the mid-1990s, the established secular companies had started to define themselves as producers of a "secular lifestyle" (*laik yaşam tarzı*) and a "civilized identity" (*çağdaş kimlik*).[8] They were the followers of Ataturk's Hat Law that had been put in order in 1925, as they wanted to be repre-

sented. They were those to carry Ataturk's values to the present. If secularist women in Ataturk's time wore suits (*tayyör*),[9] their granddaughters
would wear the clothes produced by these companies: jeans, dresses,
blouses, and skirts. In symbolically attacking the Muslim companies, these
secular companies began to present their items as the apparel of "modernity." To be modern (in Turkish secularist language, *çağdaş* or *modern*), one
had to dress in the ways advised by the mainstream and central textile
industry. Some companies even attempted to appropriate the meaning of
the headscarf. The "modern" way of wearing a scarf was around the neck
and not over the head. Photos of women with stylish scarves around their
shoulders were sent to the press. That was "the modern look." "The modern woman" was to be distinguished from "the backward Islamist woman,"
in the discourse of the secular mainstream textile companies, according to
what she consumed and especially what she wore.

Women's clothes were most highly symbolic in a market war over identities. Yet there were other items, too, that were crafted by secular mainstream businesses and shops in reaction to Islamist consumer goods. At the
height of conflict with Islamists, Ataturk paraphernalia was put on the market. In 1994, after the Welfare Party's election victory in municipalities,
one could find all sorts of things on the market with Ataturk's figure on
them. There were pins of Ataturk to be attached to one's coat, sweater, or
blouse as brooches. Ataturkist women and men began to wear these en
masse to be even more visibly distinguishable from Islamists. There were
silver-colored pins with Ataturk's portrait as well as gold-coated ones. One
could find these in most little shops, now, on the market. Traders in Istanbul's informal market, with their makeshift little counters on sidewalks,
now sold Ataturk pins along with pins of the grey wolf that was the symbol
of pan-Turkism. There were new commodities to label every "identity." As
the well-advertised celebrations of Republic Day 1994 drew to a close,
other sorts of Ataturk paraphernalia also appeared in shops. There were
posters, framed portraits, postcards, and pictures of Ataturk to be found in
every style, shape, and color. One image of Ataturk was especially popular,
one in which he was presented in white shirt and black suit-and-tie looking
up to the sky, and therefore to "progress." On important secularist public
commemoration dates, such as Republic Day (October 29) and Ataturk's
death (November 10), mainstream secular newspapers such as *Sabah*,
Hürriyet, and *Milliyet* distributed free posters of Ataturk to their readers
(see figure 1). Framed copies of the texts of Ataturk's "Sermon to Youth"
(*Gençliğe Hitabe*) were up for sale, as were those of the "Tenth Year of the
Republic March" (*Onuncu Yıl Marşı*).

In time, wearing Ataturk paraphernalia became quite widespread in society. State employees, for example, who were angered by the rise of Islamism in public institutions attached pins to their suits or uniforms to

Tüm vatandaşlarımızın
Cumhuriyet Bayramını kutlar,
birlik ve **beraberlik** içinde
daha nice mutlu bayramlar temenni ederiz.

Lebensmittel-Handelsgesellschaft mbH

Figure 1. Newspaper advertisement that ran on Republic Day, 1994, featuring the portrait of Ataturk.

Figure 2. This giant statue of Ataturk in army uniform is an original made by Mehmet İnci, when he first founded his studio in the 1930s. The statue is strikingly visible from the busy highway that links the industrial city of İzmit with Istanbul.

show their reaction to the Welfare Party. School teachers, working women, businesswomen and men wore Ataturk pins, semiotically defending their lifestyles against the one professed and practiced by veiling Islamist women. Secularists began to decorate excessively their offices, their homes, and themselves with images (in object form) of Ataturk: a small bust of Ataturk with one of his sayings inscribed underneath, along with one of his characteristic portraits in the background, a flag of Turkey on the side, and an Ataturk pin on one's suit became an ordinary way to surround one's space with material culture.

Ataturk paraphernalia has a history that predates politics of secularist and Islamist identities of the 1980s and 1990s. In the 1930s, when Ataturk was head of state, foreign sculptors had been hired to make and erect big Ataturk statues in the newly constructed boulevards of Ankara as well as in Taksim Square, Istanbul. In time Turkish artisans had also taken up the trade, sculpting Ataturk statues out of marble or cement for all the schools and public offices of the country. Today the statue that is most frequently encountered all over Turkey is still that of Ataturk.

Mehmet İnci was among the first Turks to produce statues of Ataturk in the period between 1936 and 1940. His son, Necati, who still practices his father's profession in a studio originally built in 1942, in the Maltepe district of Istanbul, recounts, "That standard look that you are accustomed to see[ing] in Ataturk statues was first created in my father's studio as a mold." Indeed the İnci statue studio had produced images of Ataturk in army uniform, as found in front of military institutions; teaching the Latin alphabet to Turkish youth, as encountered in front of many schools; on top of a rearing horse, as in public squares; dressed in bowler hat, tailcoat, and cloak by cultural institutions; and taking his first footstep in Samsun to start the War of Liberation, as seen on mountain or hill tops all over Turkey and northern Cyprus (figure 2). There were hundreds of Ataturk statue studios in Turkey, but İnci's was one of the first. According to Necati İnci, until the Welfare Party took hold of Istanbul's municipalities, the main demand for Ataturk statues came from municipal leaders. "Welfarists are not erecting statues of Ataturk in every public site as the old municipalities used to," İnci said. At the time of my interview with him, he was still sending statues to schools and public offices, but he noted that there had been increased interest from the private sector. More and more Ataturkist organizations and secular-minded owners of companies and shops were demanding Ataturk statues. The molds in İnci's father's studio shop had lived through almost all of Turkey's republican history. Statues had been produced in an artisanal way to be funded mostly by institutions of the state. Yet what was happening in 1994 was different. There was now an excess of demand for Ataturk statues on the part of private industries eager to reproduce Turkey's secularist history into the future. This shop was not fit for that mass production that the new politics of identity required. The market for Ataturk figures was slowly shifting to be encompassed by commodification.

There is now a full-fledged commodity market for both Islamist and secularist identities in Turkey. Any study that isolates politics of culture from the consumerist context in which it was produced in the 1980s and 1990s would be significantly misguided.[10] As new goods were put on the market by companies that wanted to lure their customers to innovation, new forms of "being" or "identity" were shaped as well. Businesses began to craft and sell "Turkish nativity" whether it be in "secularist" or "Islamist" garb. Consumers assumed what they wore and ate was "authentic," when it was market produced.

Istanbul's New Marketplaces

In the 1980s, a new kind of market was introduced to Istanbul. Modeled on the multistoried shopping malls of the United States and their West European versions, major marketing centers were constructed in the heart of the city. Placed in the Bakırköy district of Istanbul, Galleria was the first such structure to be erected. The shopping mall targeted the newly rich inhabitants of the luxury apartment complexes in the Ataköy neighborhood. Other customers would be able to reach "Galleria" by car and conveniently park in the vast underground garages.

When it first opened its sliding doors to customers, thousands flocked to Galleria to check it out. One floor of the shopping mall, as window-shoppers were to observe, had been reserved for chic boutiques that mostly had "Western" sounding brand names exhibiting fashionable European-style clothes. There was a shop for socks and stockings of all sorts and one for expensive lingerie. High-heeled shoes in all their variations were lined up on the stalls of one shop window by women's dresses, pants, and accessories that were displayed and presented as "fashionable."

The mall's newest visitors were shocked to see the price tags attached to the merchandise. Many of them could not afford the items on display. Indeed, in the beginning, lots of people only went to Galleria to look. They were curious to see what was advertised as "the modern way of shopping." Families of four, five, or more from shanty neighborhoods that bordered Bakırköy walked all the way to Galleria, some women in the headscarves that they had taken up after having migrated to the city, to browse in the new department stores. One floor of Galleria was most crowded of all. American-style fast food from Mexico, China, and Italy was served to those who wanted to get a taste of "modernity." Young waiters and waitresses who had been hired for their "European looks," tall and slim with blue-green eyes and light-colored hair, served hamburgers and fries in their flashy uniforms of phosporescent colors.

In time, Istanbul's middle and upper classes integrated Galleria into their shopping habits. More structures of this kind were put up in other sides of the city. In the center of the upper-class neighborhoods of Levent, Akatlar, Etiler, and Ulus was erected the imposing Akmerkez, with more than forty glossy stories mirroring back the rays of the sun, standing out in Istanbul's otherwise lower-built silhouette. A similar mall of this kind was built, finally, on the Anatolian side of the Bosphorus, under the name "Capitol," to attract the well-to-do of the districts of Kadıköy and Erenköy.

The vast shopping arcades were presented as emblems of "a modern and civilized life." Spending time in such spaces, riding on escalators, walking past glittery shop windows, and being served in the indoor cafés of clothing companies, people would come to sense what it felt like "to be in the West" or "to live like a Westerner." "Europe has come to Istanbul," many shoppers said in appreciation. The malls were advertised with temporal symbolisms. They were promoted as belonging to "the new times," as "contemporary" and "up-to-date." These were the spaces that would lead Turkey into a future of "civilization and prosperity."

In 1994, the mainstream secular newpaper *Hürriyet* published a series of articles describing Istanbul's shopping malls. Akmerkez was promoted as "an up-with-the-times (*çağdaş*) shopping center that extends into the next century." "Since it opened ten months ago, the center has attracted people like a magnet, has become part of life," the article in the newspaper read, concluding that "people are experiencing civilization in these spaces."[11] The advocates of the new malls spoke through a discourse of progress that they assumed made sense to their target customers. These shops, "like Europe," looked to the future. And there was nothing, from this point of view, that could be better than moving Turkey "ahead."

Islamist publications represented the new shopping malls in a different way. The Welfare Party's press organ *Milli Gazete* filled the caption of a photograph of the Capitol mall in writing:

> Turkey has two faces: the rich and the poor. . . . The rich shop in giant shopping centers and spend loads of money. They easily waste the money that they easily earn. . . . These people who are obsessed with trademarks pay twice, thrice, or five times as much money for things of the same sort and quality that they could buy elsewhere for less. . . . In Turkey, which is claimed to have jumped a century ahead, the rich [get] richer and the poor [are] further crushed, more impoverished.[12]

The new shopping centers were compared, in this article, with the informal market of the Topkapı district of Istanbul. By contrast, in Topkapı, the writer noted, "You cannot find people who have fetishized trademarks.

Those who shop here give priority to covering and cleanliness. This is what befits civilized (*medeni*) people."[13] Another Islamist publication, the *Aksiyon* news weekly of the *Zaman* newspaper, likened Capitol to a "temple for consumption." The author of this piece headed his critique of the new consumerism with a social history of the market in the Ottoman Empire. He was interested in nostalgic comparison. When the doors of the Grand Bazaar used to open in the morning, a prayer would be read against trickery, he recounted, citing *The Encyclopedia of Old Monuments* as reference:

> For many centuries, the ethical values of our bazaars comprised of disinterest in profit, of contentedness, and of sufficing with little. The trader who had gotten his first customer for the day [*siftah*] would send the next to his neighbor who hadn't. The richness of our spiritual and moral lives used to extend from our homes and temples to our bazaars. Until the second half of the nineteenth century, our bazaars had been through times when the customer was not harassed by sellers and when the word for stealing was not in dictionaries.
>
> Customers were also different in that period. It was considered detestable to buy something that exceeded one's need. People knew their accounts in that period and there was no such thing as credit cards. In those times when quality products could be found for cheap, bargaining was first in the list of deplored manners. In those times when there weren't fast-food stalls, bowling rings, or cafés, local tastes and traditional values were observed in marketplaces.
>
> Not too much time, only a century, has passed since. People learned about export and import and got caught in the magic of the free market. Globalization and transformation started to give shape to peoples' lives. And giant shopping centers took the place of covered bazaars.[14]

In such Islamist ethnographies of Istanbul's new markets, the secularist public's narratives of progress were countered with nostalgia for Ottoman times. Islamists identified themselves with "a previous time," which they idealized as morally superior. Those who critiqued the "rise of consumerism," as they called it, professed to keep a distance from the values of the "new times" that were idealized by the beneficiaries of the economic boom. And Islamists differentiated themselves, in their public discourses, from what they constructed as "the Westernized secularists" not only in temporal affiliation but also in social status. As the *Milli Gazete*'s juxtaposition of "the rich and the poor" illustrates, certain Islamists associated the shopping centers with the economic power of the wealthy.

The shopping malls were received in Turkey through the prism of a polarized politics of culture between secularists and Islamists, as played out in the domain of public life. Those secularists who might otherwise have criticized the advent of a new style of consumerism found themselves defending the malls vis-à-vis an Islamist culturalist critique. Likewise, well-off Islamists who wanted to arrange their life habits to include the new malls ended up taking positions against them in their public discourses. At the level of public statement, secularists and Islamists appeared to be polarized over the shopping malls. And in time, those malls that did not at first use secularist symbolism in their packaging and advertisements, started to exhibit pictures of Ataturk in their hallways and among their products.

In December 1995, right before the national elections, the entrance corridor of the Akmerkez shopping mall looked different. Behind a glossy glass curtain were lined up black and white portraits of Ataturk blown-up to four times his life size. The Welfare Party was due to win in the upcoming elections and almost everyone who followed polls was aware of this. The managers of Akmerkez advertised where they stood in politics of identity: secularism. While Ataturk in his own time had built the state-owned clothing industry to be supported by the public Sümerbank, in 1995, the supporters of Turkey's participation in the free market were reinscribing the definition of "Ataturk" into the definition of conspicuous consumption. Yet the pictures of Ataturk at the mall's entrance did not appear peculiar to most shoppers. Here they were living a "modern lifestyle" as Ataturk had determined, they thought. Fearing an Islamist discipline of the everyday, many secularists domesticated at least the semiotics of Akmerkez and its likes as part of "their identity," even if they could not afford to shop at this mall. The mall came to represent the epitomy of secularist versus to Islamist ways of carrying on with everyday practices of life.

Yet as over interpreted as they have been, shopping malls have not yet swallowed up the whole market domain of Istanbul, as they seem to have done in parts of the United States. Different kinds of shopping are still available in Istanbul's many neighborhoods. I could, at this point, direct my ethnography straight out of the mall and into the lower key sector of small trading in Islamic goods. As the writer of *Milli Gazete* had done, I could move to contrast Akmerkez with the simplicity and modesty of shops of religious commodities in the district of Eyüp, for example, where religious shop owners expose prayer mats, turbans, robes, nonalcoholic perfumes, rose water, and the like in makeshift counters on the sidewalk.[15] Certain cultural critics of Istanbul have taken up such rhetorical comparisons, characterizing Istanbul as a "dual city, *alaturka*," with posh suburbs on the one hand, inhabited by the rich, and shanty neighborhoods on the other, occupied by the poor. But this portrayal of Istanbul's residential panorama in relation to class is too simplistic. It glosses over the realities of life of those who live in cheap apartment housing, in old urban neighborhoods, and in well-settled shanties. A dualistic narrative of Istanbul's history of class relations is problematic because it produces a tendency to interpret every political conflict flatly within the distinction between the very wealthy and the very poor. Asu Aksoy and Kevin Robins have been mapping the secularist / Islamist distinction too easily onto such a dualistic narrative of class, whereby the former are written to represent the economically privileged to the disadvantage of the latter.[16] Class difference is central to Istanbul's urban politics, but it is not an accurate representation of the secularist / Islamist conflict. The narrative of class difference used as analysis by Aksoy and Robins is quite common to the populist political discourse of Islamists. Many Islamists represent themselves as the economically disadvantaged. The Welfare Party got most of its votes from Istanbul's shanty residents in municipality elections and, like other populisms, has been presenting itself as "the voice of the poor." But, as my account in this chapter has begun to illustrate, the Islamist movement is implicated as well in a politics of capital, wealth, and consumerism. The Welfare Party gained in strength through investments by Muslim capitalists. So rather than going to Eyüp to visit the little shops on the side street of the mosque, as a dualistic narrative of shops and identities would do, I will move my narrative of Istanbul's markets to the shop windows of Islamism, the wave of consumerism to which the Eyüp shops are now connected.

The Islamist Department Store

Right beside the Fatih branch of Benetton is the shop of Turkey's now biggest company for Muslim apparel: Tekbir, Inc. Centrally located on the main street of Fatih (a neighborhood preferred by religious families) and right across the Fatih mosque (one of Istanbul's biggest), the Tekbir company has its shop window. *Tekbir* is the Islamic word for a call to cry "God is great" (*Allahüekber*). The *tekbir* precedes the call to prayer (the *ezan*) and the performance of the *namaz*. During their demonstrations in the 1990s in protest of secularist institutional measures against religious life and politics, Turkish-Islamists had taken up the habit of calling *tekbir* after every public pronouncement. Like other shops for "covered" women's clothing, and like Islamist publishing houses, this particular company had taken up a name of God as its brand. As the word *tekbir* asks all believers to pronounce the greatness of God, so would the dresses and apparel sold in this company's shops. Above the two shop windows, open to the gaze of pedestrians, was the emblem of the company, reading "Tekbir, Inc." (*Tekbir, A.Ş.*).

The two exhibition windows of Tekbir, Inc. contained TV screens that constantly played a video of models wearing the company's tailored scarves and overcoats. Beside the televisions stood several mannequins displaying the clothes. They had been positioned with their backs turned against the shop's windows and heads down to look at the floor, in indication of Islamic modesty. Every one of these mannequins had been dressed in a sample of the Tekbir company's line of veils. The colors of the overcoats varied in their rich maroons and light greens; the headscarves were colorful as well. On Fatih's main street, women came to view the exhibition as put up by the managers of this most popular company for veils.

In November 1994, I interviewed one of the owners of Tekbir, Inc. at its Fatih branch. Mustafa Karaduman, head of the company group, was born in 1957 in a village of Malatya. He was a fellow townsman of the late president Turgut Özal. As he recounted his life story, he moved to Istanbul in 1969 after finishing elementary school, with only 100 liras that his father had borrowed from a neighbor. He entered the textile industry as middle ironer, but quickly advanced to become final ironer, machinist, and tailor. After some years, he started a sewing studio with his brothers, where they sometimes styled veils to order. Tekbir, Inc. was now owned by these eight brothers. The company had donated 200 million Turkish liras in alms (*zekât*) that year, had payed 15 billion liras of tax to the state, but did not work with any banks, refraining from dealing with interest, as commanded by Islam.

Karaduman sat behind the cashier counter of the Fatih shop as we were talking. His shop attendants, all covered women, came and went, asking him questions and bringing him things to show. They addressed him in the familiarized "Mustafa brother" (*Mustafa abi*) and some were his relatives. Customers interrupted our conversation as they came to pay. Mustafa Karaduman was the owner of a multinational company, yet, unlike the secularist owners of conglomerates of the same size and capital, he sat as cashier in one of his shops. Tekbir employees knew their boss personally.

Karaduman narrated his world and vision in the following way:

We started our business before the community of believers had expanded. In the years when we began, there was no market sector for "covered women's clothes" [*tesettür giyim*]. We created the sector. It hadn't an infrastructure or market at the time. "Since we are Muslim, let us produce what befits our beliefs," we said. We started the business in 1978. Within three years we were organizing fashion shows [*defile*]. In the Turkish market, we were the first to introduce the ready-to-wear black veil [*çarşaf*].[17] In the beginning, demand was not obvious; shops were not used to this business. In the 1970s, there were traditional firms who made dresses for those who "covered." But these were very limited.

There were women who decided to cover after seeing the styles in our exhibition. We worked on this concept in our advertisements: we used the images of covered women as doctors, students, and business executives. Women thought that they would be forced to enter a sack if they practiced Islam. We broke this conception. All organs of the media had to admit that "covering" is beautiful. What preachers could not accomplish through their sermons, we were able to communicate through our shops and fashion shows.

We do not only aspire to influence fashion [*moda*] in Turkey. We would like to make a mark on world fashion. We believe that Turkish people can give a direction to the world, too. If all people in the world are creative, so are we. We are going to spread all over Europe. We are going to change the flow of the world. How did the miniskirt spread worldwide? Likewise, we will spread covering to all of the world.

Mustafa Karaduman was very ambitious. His rivals were not other veil companies that his company had largely out-competed, but the clothing companies of secular Turkish businesspeople. Like them, he would speak to the fashion world of the West. Tekbir, Inc.'s styles would be liked so much that they would be preferred to those of Yves Saint-Laurent, he said, expressing his perspective. And he professed to have achieved this. His company had shops in nine cities of Germany and one each in the Netherlands, Belgium, Denmark, France, Australia, the United States, Lebanon, and Saudi Arabia. Karaduman accomplished his neo-Ottomanist aspirations through the medium of multinational capitalism. He said,

> In Europe, they think "Tekbir" is the word for "covering " (*tesettür*). When you go to buy gas in Turkey, you do not ask for "gas" but for "Aygaz," don't you?[18] And likewise, when you ask your grocer for butter, you say that you want "Sana."[19] Like this, in Europe they say that they want "Tekbir" when they are looking for covered women's clothes.

One could be skeptical of Karaduman, with the tone of bragging in his account. Yet, it should be clear from these excerpts how much Karaduman's Islamist aspirations are accompanied by a version of capitalism with a look to the West.

Karaduman professed to be doing business in accordance with the prescriptions of Islam. Like this, he liked to differentiate himself from secular businesspeople. He said, for example, that his company did not invest in interest. Interest, the profit that one receives in return for lending money for a period of time, was forbidden in Islam, according to Karaduman. He spoke of practicing commerce through a higher order of ethics and maintained that his company had distinguished itself from the rules of the world market. He claimed, also, to be paying wages in excess of minimum wage to his workers on the shop floor. Above all, his self-declared mission was to put apparel for a higher ethic of life on the market.

As the manager of the most popular veiling company in Turkey, Karaduman had a specific definition of the proper dress and manners of "the Muslim woman":

> In Egypt and Algeria, the veiling sector remains amateur. When Arabs come to visit Turkey, you see the shape of their bodies. The purpose of "covering" is to keep the garment long enough to reach your ankles and your wrists. The shape of the back or of the breasts should not be obvious. The headscarf will cover all

the hair and the neck. The Egyptians order cloth and overcoat models from France. The Frenchman does not know what covering is. He sends the narrowest style of overcoat. Now the Egyptians are demanding products from us.

When you are developing a style for veils, you have to think about the culture and climate of the country you are designing it for. Plus, everyone has to abide by fluctuations in fashion. As European clothing styles are not designed for covering women, we cannot benefit that much from them. But we do follow yearly fashions in color. You can do anything you want with color as long as you do not compromise on the precepts of Islam with regard to proper "covering." The framework put forward in the Kuran is this: the contours of the body will not be visible.

The owner of Tekbir, Inc. closely followed the waves of fashion as produced and reproduced by Turkey's secularist clothing companies that were sought after in Europe. He envisioned himself to be no less in worldwide prestige or personal capital and he had no less of a modern capitalist practice and outlook. Yet he wanted to achieve these aims through the alternative road of "Islam" in the way that he and his partners defined it. He understood, he said, that women refrained from the veil because it was not beautiful. Women preferred to wear "open" (açık) clothes because they felt that that is how they looked pretty.[20] Tekbir, Inc. had set out to show, however, that veiling could be more beautiful than wearing ordinary "open" clothes. Women could look nice and fashionable, and, most importantly, modern and upper class as they simultaneously followed the orders of Islam, in Tekbir's understanding.

Karaduman claimed to have had a role in fashioning the popularization of "covering" among Turkish women. He outspokenly took a political position in support of "covered" students who were being ousted from university classrooms and were organizing demonstrations in protest. He had agency in the making of politics of culture between secularists and Islamists. "Covering" women students had become the center of focus in this politics. He said,

We are with the "covered" girl students with all our hearts. If they want to "cover" as their belief demands, they should be able to. These girls are not "covering" out of force; they are doing this because they want to. You cannot force anyone to "cover" or to do the namaz. When headscarves were outlawed in universities for the first time, some "open" girls (açık kızlar) were standing beside their "covered" sisters in coalition. When we saw this, we gave them gifts of headscarves (türban) as a spiritual gesture. They said that no one else had shown them support of the sort.

Indeed, I had observed in other Islamist demonstrations, too, that companies for Muslim apparel were distributing headscarves to the demonstrating students for free. That Tekbir, Inc. had influenced the construction of the modern "Muslim woman's look" had already been suggested to me by owners of smaller veiling businesses. Tekbir, Inc. had indeed paved the way for a market for headscarves. Over time turning into the most popular outlet for "covered women's clothing," this company's managers had had agency and say in the constitution of "Muslim womanhood" in contemporary Turkey.

In the 1980s, the Institute of Higher Education (YÖK) had formally forbidden the wearing of the headscarf in university classrooms. Veiled woman students had taken to the streets in widespread demonstrations of protest. In return, the Institute that is attached to the state's Ministry of Education had had to modify its definition of the sort of "covering" that was to be disallowed. Black veils (*kara çarşaf*) would be unquestionably forbidden in classrooms. However, the *türban* would be permissible. In this construction, the *türban*, which was colorful, bright, and stylish in the model of scarves that European women threw around their shoulders, would be tolerated as it presented students who wanted to cover in relatively more "civilized" (*çağdaş*, in its Turkish modernist sense) gear. And it indeed was Tekbir, Inc. of Mustafa Karaduman and his brothers (along with other producers of headscarves) who had realized the ministry's definition of "modern covering" in commodity form. Tekbir, Inc. produced ready-to-buy *türban*s that would befit the requirements of the state's Institute of Higher Education. The image of the modern covered woman would be available, now, for consumers. In fact, producers of the *türban* were actualizing the Kemalist state's modernist aspirations. Women were to be modern even if they wanted to veil. Or, women could veil *and* be modern if they used the *türban*. This would be a specific (religious) kind of modernity, but modernity (and capitalism) it would be, none the less.

And yet, the owner of Tekbir, Inc. still claimed to have received inspiration from "the past." He proposed that the clothes that his company put on the market were "authentically Islamic," that they were versions of the clothes worn by Turkey's Ottoman predecessors before the institution of Ataturk's Clothing Reforms in the mid-1920s. Karaduman used all contemporary means to present his dress styles as replications of "the original Islamic way of covering." He was, in fact, creating images that could satisfy the quest for "authenticity" among covering women who wanted to be "modern."

The Trademark of Islam

Tekbir, Inc. reached its clients through well-advertised fashion shows (*de-file*). Indeed, the company to a certain extent modeled its practice on the business of textile companies owned by secularists in Turkey. The exhibition was central to the making of fashion and the creation of a clientele, as

Karaduman had observed. After our meeting, he gave me an invitation for one of Tekbir's fashion shows.

The fashion show was held in November 1994 at the entrance floor of the Tekbir Department Store in Merter, an industrial district of Istanbul reserved for textile companies. The space was quite small, not enough for the number of people who had come to watch the show. The organizers had attempted to segregate seating and standing room by gender (*harem-selamlık*). They had tried to construe a proper Islamic way of watching a show, men on one side and women on the other.

Yet, even before the show began, it turned out to be difficult to carry this separation out in practice. There were more women in the audience and not enough space in the women's section. So some of us were sent to stand behind the men. Girls ran to talk to their fathers, women who had forgotten to mention something to their husbands or male friends walked right into the men's section, children ran back and forth. The segregation was only theoretically in place.

Most of the women in the audience were covered, although none of them wore the black veil. Few women were "open," sitting beside their covered woman relatives or friends. There were older as well as young women. It seemed that women had come to the show as an outing for the weekend.

In the middle of the fashion hall was a T-shaped stage for the exhibition. The seats on the right-hand side of the stage had been reserved for journalists and indeed there were reporters from a number of TV stations, including those of the secular mainstream. Cameras were focused first at the audience and then at the models who took to the stage. The other side of the stage was the place for honored male guests.

Above the well-lit stage was inscribed the much-advertised brand "Tekbir." The company's logo read: "The World's Trademark in Covered Women's Clothing" (*Tesettürde Dünya Markası*). The brand and its matching logo were lit up by the projecting lights and then the show began.

Through the mist of artificially produced clouds appeared a couple of professional models on the stage. Both were dressed in extravagant clothes covering their bodies from head to toe. As the poignant rhythm of the music from the film *1492* was sounded in the background, the models began to trot, discretely moving their hips from left to right on their column-like legs supported by high-heeled shoes. The audience applauded with much amazement and enthusiasm. Silken covered-wear of flashy colors with well-dressed headgear, leaving only a blue-eyed and made-up face uncovered. Models who normally exhibited underwear, bathing suits, and Westernized clothes to the secular bourgeoisie in big hotels around the city had now come to exhibit covered women's clothes to those who wanted to follow an "alternative fashion" (see figure 3).

Figure 3. Model on runway in the Tekbir fashion show, November 1994.

"*Mashallah! Mashallah!*" cried old people in the audience, "God has blessed you!" At first, the eyes of the viewers beside me were directed at the faces of the professional models, big blue eyes etched with mascara, lip-lined mouths, thin and small noses, carefully plucked eyebrows. And then, "Look at that waist," one young woman beside me gasped, "I will throw myself over a flight of eleven stairs," she exclaimed. She was expressing her sense of feeling "little" beside the majestic-looking models. "Wow! Look at that face! I am looking only at the faces, not at the clothes," another covered woman remarked. And, "These women are seducing me," one woman declared amidst repressed laughter.

"Black and White" announced the male voice on the loudspeaker that introduced the next selection of the company's fashionable clothes. And again through artificial vapor appeared well-covered models, this time in combinations of black-and-white headscarf and overcoat. The last show was an exhibition of "Inspiration from the Ottoman Palace." Models, whose faces were covered to reveal only their light-colored eyes, strutted on the stage in glitzy clothes. "This is how women dressed in the Ottoman harem," the program announcer cried through the microphone. Richness emanated from the embroidered pieces of cloth, decorated with pearls and gold, which draped the bodies of the models. Tall, thin, blue-eyed women's beauty, as institutionalized in Turkey's mainstream fashion industry, grinned through the *türbans* that were exhibited as morally appropriate. During the show, the model who received the most enthusiatic applause was one who wore a silken black veil that covered all the body including the nose and the mouth. The facial section of the veil had been decorated with gold spangles, causing the model's blue eyes to stand out (see figure 4).[21] Those blue eyes, which represented "modernity" to Turks, were employed not only in the secularist fashion industry, but also in Islamist sectors that aspired to be Muslim and modern. One could be blue-eyed and wear a black veil, in this form of image-making that addressed itself to the public world of symbols in contemporary Turkey.

As the models walked by, I noticed that much of their body shapes could be discerned through the clothes that they were exhibiting. Their full breasts, slender waists, and thin columns of legs imposed themselves through the clothes that they wore which were marked "Islamic." "Is this fitting with Islam?" I asked a covered woman who was standing and watching beside me, "these tightly-sewn, narrow gowns that disclose the contours of one's body?" "Well," said the perplexed-looking woman, noticing my uncovered head and for a while unable to find an answer. "This is homewear, you know, only to be worn beside one's husband and relatives." "But all these men are watching these models here," I said. "Doesn't that contradict Islamic law?" One covered woman who heard my question nodded in agreement with my stated confusion. The first woman, again

Figure 4. News clip on the Tekbir fashion show; in the middle is the much-applauded model wearing the black veil (source: *Sabah* newspaper).

perplexed, said: "They are doing this now to introduce the clothes. Normally people wouldn't wear these clothes in public. I am also a trader, you know. And a trader has to exhibit his products. This man is doing this and he is doing it well."

After the show was over, the models quickly dressed back into their normal clothes: tights, miniskirts, and high-heeled boots. They then sprang out of their dressing room, tossing their dyed raw blonde hair about as they mingled with the "covered" audience that was helping itself to lemonade and cookies. "How do you feel about appearing in a show like this?" I asked one of the models in the dressing room. "I did this once last year and I could not keep back my tears as I walked on the runway," she said. "I am an Ataturkist, you know. But it is undeniable that people are wearing these things. And I am a professional, so I am doing this."

Outside, in the reception room, I spoke to three older women who had watched the show. "The models looked so much prettier under covers than they did in their tights and miniskirts when they came out," one of these women said. "This is the gist of the matter. Take it that way," she said. Another of the women said, "My daughters are not covered. At a time like this, it is hard to tempt young women to cover themselves. This sort of show proves to young women that they can be beautiful, and perhaps even more beautiful, when they cover themselves in the Islamic way." She continued,

> Poor girls in the midwifery section of the Medical School are not being allowed to enter the laboratories. They are discriminating against us. You know, I covered myself when I was thirty-nine years old. Until then, I had lived my life in night clubs with *saz*, play, and drinks.[22] One day, I decided that enough is enough. I would go on the haj and really transform myself.[23] After I wore the headscarf, one day I went to the clothing store where I always used to shop. The woman who always helped me there did not recognize me and treated me like someone who wouldn't be able to afford anything in that store. Only because of my scarf! No one can know anyone's money or belief. They are always discriminating against us like this.

This woman was probably quite well off, given that she used to spend her life in night clubs, that she could afford going on the haj, that she shops in expensive stores, and is disturbed when mistaken for a lower-class person. What shook her the most was the loss of a visible class identity upon assuming the headscarf. She liked the Tekbir fashion show because the styles exhibited by the models allowed her to maintain her middle-class identity as she turned to religion. Unlike radical Islamist critics of consumerism and materialism, this woman had no qualms about revealing her status in the way she spent. She was content, now that she could reconcile her social position with her identity as a believer. This was an attempt to turn the veil into a symbol of high class, to rejuggle the available symbols of class and distinction (Bourdieu 1984).

"It was very beautiful, spectacular!" one of the three women said. When I querried about the compatibility of the veiling exhibition with Islam, one of them was taken aback, saying, "You are not disturbed by such shows when uncovered women do it and you are when we do it! Why shouldn't we, the believing community, benefit from the good things (*nimet*) of the world?"A young woman whom I spoke to after the show also seemed very appreciative of it. "We have to keep afoot with our times," she said. "If our grandmothers wore black veils, we cannot do that today. Perhaps we need to compromise a little. But, no, in fact I don't think we are compromising anything." As we were chatting, one of the models, dressed back in her own clothes, appeared on the stage in tights, high-heeled boots, and a black-leather jacket. The flashy model jumped over the stage steps, made her way through the crowd of covered women, and walked out to wait for a cab. The young woman I was talking to curiously glanced at the nonchalant attitude of this model. After all her appreciative comments on the whole event, she couldn't withhold herself from making a side remark, "I don't think they should come out like this in these clothes."

There was a mixed feeling among the women audience of the show about the value of the enterprise. Many of the women enjoyed what they saw in the exhibition very much. They liked the idea that they could look pretty, rich, modern, and fashionable as they practiced their belief. They watched, as they compared their own figures with those of the models who had been put on a pedestal. Women gazed attentively, scrutinizing the models' looks, clothes, and mincing manners. There were some women who wondered whether the exhibition as an event was fitting of Islamic morality. And there were others yet, who turned the exhibition into fruitful context for political activism: During the reception that followed the show, some women were campaigning for the midwifery students who had been expelled from university classrooms for being covered. They were collecting signatures in support of the students and in protest of the administration of the state university. The fashion show for veils was one important site in public life for the manifestation and shaping of politics of culture.

In Islamist periodicals, the reception of the Tekbir show was mixed, once again. Some newspapers, especially those that were affiliated with the Welfare Party, like *Milli Gazete* and *Yeni Şafak*, published appreciative reports on the exhibition, citing references about "the increasing number of women who cover." But there were others from the more radical Islamist press, represented through the newspapers *Vakit* and *Selam*, who wrote brutal critiques of the Tekbir enterprise.[24] Atilla Özdür, columnist in *Vakit*, drew attention to the fact that the Welfare Party's youth organization (*Milli Gençlik Vakfı*) had also been organizing fashion shows of this sort for "covered" women.[25] This radical Islamist author was associating Tekbir, Inc. with the Welfare Party and the mainstream of Islamism in Turkey. He was arguing that, for the most part, Turkish-Islamists were integrating Islam with the capitalist system. Mustafa Karaduman had asked several religious leaders (*hocaefendiler*) to give *fetvas* (to pronounce their religious opinion) on the clothes produced by Tekbir. The columnist in *Vakit* called those preachers to stand forward and repeat whether such models and behavior were fitting of Islam. Özdür's piece was foregrounded by a critique of capitalism, as a system that solicited growth in market goods in order to prevent crisis. This analysis was followed by an exegesis of Tekbir:

> Turkey, as part of the capitalist world, has entered that atmosphere. Whatever their religion may be, people are unable to keep from adapting to the rules of capitalism in their trading relations. This is a reality. . . .
>
> The Tekbir Clothing Company has been organizing fashion shows for the last three or four years. These were followed by much discussion, for and against, in public. In these fashion shows, models were dressed to cover and were sent to walk in mincing manners to the curious gaze of onlookers; women and men in the audience sat together in rooms that turned into the hot cubicle of public baths [*halvet*]; hundreds of millions [of Turkish liras] were given to luxury hotels, the cost of which was cut from tax statements; and prices on covered women's clothing rose as a result.
>
> We analyzed the event as an enterprise in favor of enhancing consumerism and resolving the crisis of marketing in capitalism. We opposed these fashion shows on the grounds that they eroded a thrifty philosophy of life and the Islamic principles of modesty, asceticism, and abstention from worldly pleasures.[26]
>
> These fashion shows were approved by Muslims who submitted to the hegemony of capitalist relations of business. . . . In democracies, the majority is deemed right. We have remained in the minority. We have been defeated in front of the reality that one cannot be Muslim without being a capitalist.
>
> What is the solution? There is no solution for this. For a lifestyle that befits a Muslim, one that foregrounds abstention from worldly pleasures, would paralyze all the market. If you were to knock over the consumerist practice of fashion shows, the capitalistic building would be destroyed.
>
> We are either, once and for God, going to remain under this wreck or we are going to, as long as we live, be entrapped in imperialism's vicious circle of debt in continuing to sell Islam to one another (Özdür 1994, 4).[27]

The text of this critic's review of the Tekbir fashion shows was imbued with references to Marxist language on capitalism. This radical Islamist was lamenting the incorporation of Muslim ethics into the logic of a consumer market. There were others, however, who argued against Tekbir, Inc. by comparing the manager Karaduman's justifications of his shows with Islamic sources. In a reader's letter published in *Vakit* and *Selam*, Ismail

Uzun (1994) argued against Tekbir's definition of Islamic propriety. No religious leader, according to this reader, would sanction the show of some modeling women to be watched by a joint assembly of men and women. This author, in turn, had his own definition of "proper Islamic covering," which he set against that of Tekbir:

> The principal purpose of covered women's clothing is the prevention of moral degeneration. It is meant to keep women from arousing carnal sentiments in men. When this is the situation, it should not be appropriate for professional models who normally pose in bathing suits to exhibit covered women's clothes.[28]

Mustafa Karaduman, in an interview on an Islamist radio station, had made a reference to Ayşe's life as wife to Prophet Muhammad. He noted that Ayşe had watched a sword-and-shield display in the company of the Prophet. He wanted to legitimize the Tekbir shows on this ground of *sünnet*, of following the lifestyle of personalities in the first centuries of Islam, the era that was called "the Time of Bliss" (*Asr-ı Saadet*) by Islamists. The writer of the open letter in *Vakit* argued against Karaduman's interpretation of Ayşe's act. According to Uzun, "Ayşe had watched a sword-and-shield display through a window beside the great prayer room standing behind the Prophet and leaning her head on his shoulder." As in the case of the fashion show scenario argued by the owners of Tekbir, the text of this author was full of references to sections of the Kuran and to sources on life in "the Time of Bliss." Accordingly, what Tekbir did in the name of Islam contradicted the sources. Tekbir's clothes and manners of trading were inappropriate from the standpoint of the Islamic observance of the lifeways of the Prophet.

Thus, there was dispute within the Islamist community itself about the value of veiling exhibitions. Some radical critics distinguished their understanding of Islam and covered women's clothing from that promoted by Tekbir. Yet on a wider scale, as suggested by one of these critics, it appeared that Tekbir had a greater ground of success than its opponents. Its clothes were extremely popular among Islamist women. Covered students attended the exhibitions as ground for their political cause. Tekbir had an important hold over the market.

It was not only Islamists, of course, who were using the mode of exhibition in the interests of a politics of identity. In fact, in that very week in November 1994, when Tekbir held its fashion show in Merter, another exhibition took place at the Cultural Center in the Harbiye neighborhood of Istanbul, this time for secularist politics. It was November 10, the commemoration date for Ataturk's death. And two secularist organizations, the Culture and Arts Foundation and the Mustafa Kemal Organization, had organized a show, narrating the history of the bowler hat as introduced by Ataturk for Turkish wear in the first decade of the republic.[29] Through this fashion show, entitled "The Hat is a Tale," the secularist organizers wanted to revive the spirit of the Hat Law as instituted in 1925 against the wearing of the fez and the turban. Under this Law, Ataturk had also discouraged the wearing of the veil by women. Turkish men no longer wear the bowler hat introduced by Ataturk, but the organizers of the "hat show" were using the hat as symbol of civilization, in their terms, to counteract Islamist women's headscarves. The hat, in this exhibition, when worn by models on display, represented "being up with the times," whereas "the veil" was a sign of "backwardness." On this catwalk, too, politics of identity was at play. Producers of new versions of the classical bowler hat and long gowns constructed these as contemporary and modern clothing (*çağdaş*, in secularist language), in an attempt to make a bold statement against Islamists. They simultaneously were introducing and advertising their companies' styles as available in Istanbul's fashionable boutiques and department stores.

The fashion exhibition has a longer history in Ataturkist institutions, predating Islamist ones. In fact, fashion shows, as such, were started in Turkey under the auspices of the Girls' Institutes, which had been founded in the 1920s and 1930s to promote European-style dress among Turkish women. Students in the Girls' Institutes would produce the sort of clothing that was fashionable in Europe at that time, integrating it with Turkish motifs and embroidery.[30] The institutes, of course, were there to help enforce the Hat Law and no clothing style produced there included headscarves of any sort for women. Students who designed and sewed the dresses under the supervision of their European-trained instructors would then exhibit their products in front of their mothers, fathers, and relatives, as well as the Republicanist bureaucratic elite of the 1920s and 1930s. Girls' Institute tailored clothes were in vogue, then, among the wives and daughters of bureaucrats. However, the mode of exhibition, as practiced in early republican years in the institutes, was qualitatively different from those undertaken in 1994 by secularist or Islamist fashion companies. The latter is in a different context, that of the free market for commodities at the end of the twentieth century.

The Force of Symbols

The claim to be representative of a "past Ottoman and Islamic reality" was what gave the Tekbir exhibition its legitimacy and force. Indeed, the exhibition of veils and headcovers would not have had claim to morality were it not for the argument for revivalism. The announcer of the fashionable headcovers presented the company's models under such titles as "Inspiration from the Ottoman Palace." The manager of the Tekbir company had called religious leaders (*hocas*) to pronounce their opinion on the propriety of the veils produced by the company. Karaduman and his brothers wanted to do business in the Islamic way. And when they spoke about their enterprise, they made references to the lifestyle of the Prophet Muhammad and to relevant Islamic sources. Yes, the organizers of the exhibition wanted it to stand for Islamic morality and to be representative of the Islamic past. The ambience of the exhibition hall was also preplanned to be "moral" from an Islamic point of view, whereby women would be segregated from men in the audience. There was an attempt, then, to authenticize (in this case, "Islamicize") the viewer's space too. Unlike much of the world outside the exhibition room, Tekbir's architecture of space would be closer to "what befitted Muslims."

And yet the exhibition also raised problems in representation. Despite the efforts of the managers of Tekbir to package the space and activity of the exhibition, nothing turned out to be so neat and orderly. The space of the audience was separated by gender as demanded by Islam in the manager's politics and belief. However, in the practice of the exhibition, women and men kept visiting one another in the spaces reserved for the other gender. Children kept running back and forth. When there wasn't enough space for women, women were directed to stand behind a row of men's seats. People were unused, in their everyday lives, to such segregation. The managers of Tekbir had attempted to create a representation of Islamic authenticity even in the audience's space within the exhibition. Yet, it turned out to be difficult to maintain this representation's unity between referent and referred.

Things were likewise "messy" on the stage. The manager of Tekbir had likened his setup to the story of Ayşe, the Prophet Muhammad's wife who had watched a show while leaning on the Prophet's shoulder behind a window. He did not want his fashion show to be distinguished from the real life of the Prophet and his wives. The models who were presenting the clothes were all dressed to conceal their body-shapes, leaving only the face or eyes and the hands in the open. The manager of Tekbir had his own understanding of proper Islamic gear for women. And he proposed that what his company was producing was "it." Women who watched the show wanted to share his thinking. Indeed, many of them showed enthusiasm in applause and they defended the show, the event, the company, and the specific clothing models in the name of Islam. They had enjoyed themselves and they wanted to think that this was indeed "true," that they could dress up beautifully like this and be Muslims.

However, women also expressed reservations in private. They felt intimidated by the tall, slender models and their poses. They weren't sure whether it was right for the men in the audience to be watching the models who were exhibiting Islamic homewear. At the end of the show, the fashion models, who had dressed back into their own clothes—black leather jackets, miniskirts, boots—and exposed their wavy blond hair, walked from the backstage onto the stage and through the reception room where the audience was helping itself to refreshments, and departed through the front door of the department store. Covered women who were chatting there did not like the appearance of the models in such explicit gear after just having displayed "modest" Islamic clothing. The models who had walked on the podium to "represent Islam" had complained backstage about being Ataturkists and had trotted through the exhibition hall in the end in their own clothes. The problems with the representation were obvious even to the women in the audience who wanted to hold onto it. Radical Islamist critics in the press made more direct references to the problems with the Tekbir affair.

The Tekbir Fashion Show had claims to authenticity. The managers were presenting their clothing styles to be "alternatives to the world of fashion." Unlike the "open" clothes worn by unbelieving Turkish women, Tekbir clothes were modeled on the so-called "real" that was Islam. Tekbir's motto was "the trademark of Islam." The company was attempting to monopolize the representation of the religion.

And it was certainly successful. Despite a number of critical reviews of the Tekbir fashion shows in radical Islamist newspapers and radios, Tekbir clothes were indeed extremely popular among covered women, and more so than any other brand or style of covered women's clothing. And like the women who had watched the fashion show, many of the company's customers wanted to believe in the representation. The confusion of the women in the audience was compounded by their ardent desire to hold onto the representation as a symbol of "reality."

This happened in spite of the women's at least partial awareness of problems with the Tekbir representation of Islamic clothes. People in the audience questioned the certainty of Tekbir's representations and there were significant critics who queried the validity and legitimacy of the whole enterprise. Islamist women were not totally immersed in a discourse that works through mechanisms of representation. They expressed confusion, they reflected on what they watched, they thought it through and elaborated.

However, there was still an effort to secure the representation, despite ambiguity and questioning. As noted above, Tekbir products are extremely popular and the company has been making huge profits. Moreover, there was immense effort and goodwill on the part of covered women to defend Tekbir clothes and the like. That the representation was not so neat and orderly, and that there was awareness of the mess, did not result in a popular rejection of Tekbir products. On the contrary, there was mass consumption. There was something else, then, that maintained the force of the representation even when its viewers and consumers thought that it wasn't really real. The representation kept stumbling over itself, but it was still effective. How?

It was difficult for Islamists to put the world that they were nostalgic about on display. At every turn, it was too obvious that representation did not match reality and that the representation had taken a life of its own as symbol. Yet there was reluctance among the audience, despite at least partial consciousness about the fakery of representation, to admit that the representation was problematic. Women in the audience mostly wanted to hold onto the representation as if it stood for a greater reality of Islam and Turkish authenticity. They wanted to believe in the representation even if it was difficult, in practice, to uphold the representation with perfect equanimity.

What was happening here was quite complex. The signifier "veil" had taken up such meaning and power that it no longer mattered too much for consumers of Tekbir products whether the representation, as such, was a construction. As a construction, no less, the signifier had power, potency, and a life of its own. Now women consumed veils in-and-of-themselves, rather than for what such apparel stood for. Tekbir veils did not have to represent Islamic morality in an unproblematic way for them to be popularly worn. A politics of identity had become a politics over symbols in the context of consumerism.

To elaborate on this point, let me turn to the work of Jean Baudrillard. In "The System of Objects" (1996), Baudrillard writes about the phenomenon of the "pure signifier, without a signified, signifying itself." He develops this concept in order to distinguish his approach to "the commodity" from that of Marxist philosophers of "need." Marxists critiqued advertising for producing "artificial needs." They differentiated these from needs that they deemed "authentic" (41). In contrast, Baudrillard argues that "in the logic of signs," or in the consumer society that he studies in the late twentieth century, "as in the logic of symbols, objects are no longer tied to a function or to a *defined* need" (44, his emphasis). And there is consumption nevertheless.

The headscarf has been interpreted by Islamists as a representation of Islamic chastity, the holy past, and Turkish local culture. That the representation does not neatly pair up with the ideal is obvious to many women who cover. It appears that in Baudrillard's terms, the signifier "headscarf" has hereby taken on a life of its own, living by itself even beyond its problematic representation. The veil has a "social life,"[31] a different one, now, as signifier. It does not simply refer to female religiosity or belief. Now the veil has gained meaning in-and-of-itself and almost independently of belief. It symbolizes itself, and in itself, it refers to politics of identity in relation to secularists and the secularist state.

It is not the labor value congealed in the veil-as-commodity that disturbs radical Islamist critics of commodification. It is rather the supernatural value—the sacred, religious value. So, the veil for Islamists is the apparel of a religious fetish. The problem arises when it is turned into another kind of (commodity) fetish, from the point of view of radical Islamists. However, that perhaps is precisely the point: in the age of commodification, the veil takes on a different meaning, rather than remaining as apparel of belief. It takes on added significance in itself: "it," rather than belief, becomes the fetish; or, rather than remaining as symbol of belief, "it", the symbol itself, becomes significant (the signifier in-and-of-itself) in cases where politics is waged over the symbol more than on its content.

The Market for Identities

Through the ethnographic material presented in this chapter, I have attempted to show how the politics of identity of secularists and Islamists in the 1980s and 1990s is implicated in a history of commodification. In every development of political activism, "identities" have been expressed through the means of consumer goods.[32] The creativity and innovation that goes into bringing new goods into the free market leaves an imprint on the politics of culture. Identities are, to an important extent, produced in the context of a marketplace. This does not diminish their personal or existential meaning and potency. Rather, through an analysis of "the market for identities," I am interested in challenging claims over "authenticity."

What is most curious is that as market production continues, activists for both secularism and Islamism argue for the respective "authenticity" of their habits of life and use. Secularists and Islamists have been countering one another with contradictory narratives of Turkish authenticity. Two versions of nationalism, both with claims to primordiality and close affinity to the culture of Turkey, run alongside each other. The words used by activists in describing "identity" have force because there is a claim to originality. In the 1980s and 1990s, the market had power in determining the shape of authenticity. Identities are not "real" in the essentialist sense of secularists and Islamists, but are constructions. And one important site for the manufacture of our contemporary notions of "self" and "culture" is the market.

The writing by Turkish-Islamist intellectuals on Turkish identity is a critique of Westernization that could be compared instructively with anthropologies that reify "native culture." In their public discourse, radical Islamist intellectuals have tended to associate consumerism with the culture of Westernists in Turkish society. In much contemporary Islamist writing, secularists are portrayed as "fake" or "simulations of the West." In contrast,

Islamists struggle with one another over the meaning of properly "being one's self" as a Muslim and a Turk. In this reading, secularists are not "authentic." They have mutated to repress their former true selves in adopting Western ways of living. Central to Islamists' critique of "secularists' inauthenticity" is the latter's habits of consumption. Islamists reproach secularists for using "foreign" and religiously forbidden things.

A habitus of consumption is thus part of the everyday life not only of Turkey's secularists but also, to a determining extent, that of Islamists. Islamists have come to identify themselves as such by buying and using things "distinct" from those used by secularists. There is a claim to rectitude here in the consumption of things that are closer to the Turkish Muslim's "true self." The overcoats made of English silk were only one example of an "Islamist good" in which it is hard to distinguish between the Western and the local, the foreign and the Islamic. The *türban* in itself is the best example of the Islamist use of modernist measures in following the prescriptions of a Kemalist state. When Orientalizing themselves and when attempting to present themselves as "modern," Islamists have taken more inspiration from secularists and from the West than they have from the Islamic and Ottoman past. Similar ambiguities exist in products that are emblematized as "secularist."

Islamist social critique too easily maps the lifestyle of Islamists onto that of Turkey's poor or Turkey's economically underpriviledged. The associations of wearing Western clothes and leading Westernized lifestyles are too easily conflated with "Turkey's wealthy" in this political discourse. Accordingly, Westernization was imposed on Turkish society by elites. And, even though the elites developed a lifestyle "foreign" to Turkey, "the rest of Turkey" (also referred to by Islamists as "the other Turkey") kept to its values or since found its true conscience. Islamists have relegated all sorts of lifestyles that they defined to be "improper from an Islamic point of view" to Turkey's rich. "The real Turkey," as Islamist intellectuals often said, or "the culture of the people," was not about using Western things. A binarist discourse on class went hand in hand with Islamists' politics of identity.

This chapter has contested Turkish-Islamists' attempts to map a specific construction of Islamic authenticity onto Turkey's subaltern. A certain popular and mainstream branch of Turkish-Islamism (incorporating the core group of the Welfare Party and its supporters) is interested not in overturning class distinctions per se, but in expanding the domain of middle-class taste and lifestyle to include norms expected of the devout Muslim.

The symbols of modernity have indeed been associated with high class in Turkey (Kandiyoti 1997). Yet, mainstream Islamists are not countering class stratification or the class system, but the symbolic references of high class (Bourdieu 1984). They counter not modernity per se, but its symbols.

They would like "modernity," as a marker of class, to encapsulate the signs of Islamic life, too, for a woman wearing a veil to be perceived as upper class as well.

As I have tried to show, a believing Muslim class of capitalists has developed in Turkey and the Islamist movement has taken its shape in conjunction with the activities of this group. The class of Muslim capitalists is different in many ways from the secularist bourgeoisie. The latter have longer life histories in Turkey's urban centers, more entrenched ties with sources of Western capital, and are descendants of a longer lineage of wealth. Most Muslim capitalists come from the conservative established families of small towns or cities across Anatolia and if they now live in the metropolis, they do so only for the first or second generation. Yet this is a class of capitalists, no less, even though, as I showed in my description of the Islamic marketplace and the Islamist company, the specificities of their business practices differ to a certain extent. Muslim capitalists have created a market for consumption, as well, and a prolific one at that.

Secularists and Islamists in contemporary Turkey are implicated in the same capitalist market of consumption. The politics of identity between these communities developed in the shared context of Turkey's unification with a worldwide free market of commodities and goods. And what is significant now is that Islamists are as active as secularists in the making and shaping of this market.[33]

Part II

STATE FANTASIES

4

Rituals for the State: Public Statism and the Production of "Civil Society"

> Might it turn out, then, that not the basic truths,
> not the Being nor the ideologies of the center, but
> the fantasies of the marginated concerning the
> center are what is most politically important to
> the State idea and hence State fetishism?
> —*Michael Taussig, 1992*

The Soldier's Farewell

Every night, toward nine, ten, or eleven o'clock when buses were scheduled to leave for different parts of Anatolia, groups of people from shantytowns in Istanbul would head toward the central bus station in Taksim to bid farewell to their soldiers-to-be. The new soldier, eighteen years old, would be put in the passenger seat of a car, his close male friends would squeeze themselves in the back seat, and the car would take off toward the bus station. A whole convoy of relatives in a few other cars would follow behind. The young men would stand up inside the cars, thrusting their heads and chests through the open windows, waving Turkish flags while chanting nationalist slogans. The sound of rhythmic announcements of "Turkey is the greatest!" would blend with the noise of violently blown horns. Pedestrians would hasten onto the sidewalks so as not to get hit, accidentally, by the speeding convoy.

There could be no mistake for the onlookers. Here was another new soldier being sent off for a year and a half of military service. "He is now a soldier" read stickers in the back windows of the convoy. He might have been going to the east where the army was warring with the PKK (Kurdish Workers' Party). Enlisting in the Turkish army was a matter of life or death especially for those soldiers assigned to serve in the southeast. It was compulsory for these young men to enter a situation where they would be trained to kill PKK supporters or be killed in turn. Little information about the war was publicly available. What one knew about conditions of life in the east was learned through channels, broadcast or print, subject to strict state censorship. It was within a hazy network of communication, created by a state power that deprived people of knowledge, that most people in Turkey have had to distinguish between fact and fiction. Soldiers who served in the east were upheld by state officials, much applauded on state TV and other cultural organs of the state. Mothers of the deceased (or "the martyrs," *şehitler*, in the language of statist discourses) were publicly honored, sometimes with pension awards. For many young men, coming of age in downtrodden shantytowns of the big cities or in villages across the country, the army has been a vessel of hope. Becoming a soldier gives them the sort of communal respect, show of affection, and high regard of the kind they in no way otherwise could hope to obtain in their young adult lives. It has been a rite of secular statist initiation to masculine adulthood. A number of low-ranking soldiers whom I encountered on assignment in the geographical west of Turkey complained of their ill luck in not having been assigned to the war zone. They envied the sort of attention and respect that their cousins and friends who were sent to the east had been receiving. From their point of view, "there was nothing honorable in being posted in the west."

The convoy of the soldiers' friends and relatives would arrive in the bus station early enough to hold the farewell party. They came to send off the soldier with drum and pipe, two musical instruments commonly used in Turkey for celebration. A couple of men would beat and play as the hearts of the half excited and half nervous soldiers and that of their sad and worried mothers and fathers pounded. Young men, the friends of the soldier, clasped their arms around one another's shoulders, all in a small circle, and folk danced at high tempo. Women with loosely attached scarves (usually not the Islamist veil) stood by each other on the other side of the street or in another corner of the bus station watching the dancers and soothing one another, especially the mother, about the departing soldier, her son. The soldier was thrown up in the air and down, falling in the arms of his friends, up and down again, with festive shouts. The group of young men thrusted their arms up making the "sign of the wolf" with their fingers.

The grey wolf is the symbol of the pan-Turkist, far right-wing Nationalist Action party (MHP) of one of Turkey's most outspoken fascists, Alparslan Türkeş. In the 1990s, farewell rituals for departing soldiers were colonized by the signs, symbols, ways, and slogans of supporters of the MHP who called themselves "the Idealists" (*ülkücüler*). The Idealists reified the "Turkic heritage of Turkey," constructing racial, linguistic, and cultural links between themselves and what they called the Turks of Central Asia. They dreamt of a greater Turkey that spread beyond the borders of eastern Thrace and Anatolia, a "Turkish Turkey" cleansed of other cultural threats and components, especially the Kurdish. The Idealists ideologically defended the state's war against the Kurds, yet they often found the state's measures too mild or insufficient in curbing the PKK.[1] The MHP had concentrated much of its recruiting on youth.

So the group of young men in the bus station chanted "Down with the PKK!" There was no room in the men's section of the farewell for motherly or sisterly sobs. The soldier was sent off with cries for more violent war against Kurds.

The realm of what some have called "civil society" in contemporary Turkey[2] is marked by many scenes, more statist than the state, of the sort I have just narrated. Farewell parties for soldiers-to-be are not officially organized by statespeople or by any state institution. Nor are they compulsory. It is a matter of informally planning a show of support for a friend or a relative. There is a history behind public farewells in the Turkish military. In recent years, however, rituals that might formerly have held other sorts of meanings, have become influenced by a statist ideology of power. The language, symbols, and feeling, the whole experience of the soldier's farewell has been transformed, at least to a certain extent, into a show of veneration for the state. The state is exalted, celebrated, and reified in the soldiers' farewells. The fate of the soldier is uncertain; there is an element of unknowing about what awaits the soldier once he steps off the bus, at his destination. In performing the ritual of separation, the soldier, his friends, and relatives—and even those among them who have already served their army dues—blow up the image of the army in even greater proportion for themselves and others who remain in its periphery of power.

The MHP, a political party that has received between 8 and 18 percent of votes in nationwide elections of the past decade, has injected statism into an arena of what some theorists might still identify as "the separate realm of society."[3] Statist rituals organized by the state for itself are no longer as convincing or as moving as informal ones organized by the people for the state. In Turkey, it has recently proven more effective for state power to reproduce itself, not by enforcing narcissistic rituals, but by enabling certain groups, outside the center of state practice, to produce in-and-of-themselves, in Foucault's sense of the term, rituals of thralldom for the state.

Supporters of the MHP have a high record of crime and violence, yet they have faced relatively little restraint by police, unlike activists on varying degrees of the socialist left. The state of the 1990s, a secular democracy, demanded a realm of civil society in favor of itself. The MHP has served the function of mobilizing so-called members of civil society around nationalism and militarism. The MHP's rise to governmental power in 1999, based on the large proportion of votes that it won in the elections, reflects its increased popularity in the peripheries of the state.[4] Today's soldiers' farewells are *as if* spontaneous. They are one of the central sites in which the Turkish state has attempted to produce an idea of itself as an irreducible and eternal power. The bus station has become a crucial locus for a statist discourse's productive technique of power. In this instance, governmentality is not repressive or enforcing, but self-generating. Here, elements of civil society, as they have so far been defined, take initiative and (actively) resubjugate themselves to "the state," as though it were of their own will.

One could ponder and ask, what alternative is available to these young men and their relatives? Enlisting in the army is compulsory and the statist narrative for departing soldiers is a way of putting meaning into a possibly eternal separation from friends and family. There has to be a point, a basic sense of understanding, about the emotional turmoil that comes from leaving loved ones and enlisting in one of the harshest of disciplinary regimes, one that minutely orders and organizes as it simultaneously produces violence and death. If they were not to cling on to the concept of the state in this moment of danger, it would be harder for mothers and fathers of the soldiers to explain the situation to themselves. Sending their son off to danger: for what? "For the state" is the ultimate and convenient explanation. This makes more sense than sending one's child into a void, into nothingness. The notion of the state is a primary category of "the common-sense" of the world we inhabit at present. It has been normalized. What is interesting in these rituals for the departing soldiers is the element of statist ceremonial in them. For the emotional separation to make sense, extra or excessive meaning has been ascribed to the state on the part of those in the periphery of institutions of state power.

In the context of the 1990s, the notion of Turkey was more popular and powerful than any other symbol of sociality appeared or could have claimed to be. Even though the Islamist movement had gained in strength and following, with offshoots among the pan-Turkist nationalists, belief in God did not move as many people as did a commitment to Turkey. Loyalty to the country (*ülke*) or the motherland (*vatan*) was expressed in many fashions in the domain of public life. Ceremonies for soldiers-to-be were one such site of public performance for and celebration of the Turkish state. Such public events were ordinary in the 1990s, so commonplace that one could regularly encounter such scenes in the everyday of neighborhoods and central public squares of Istanbul. At night, in the narrow streets of a shantytown, in speeding cars along the Bosphorus, or on the main streets of the city, it was no surprise for passersby to encounter young men with the trappings of "Turkey" marching along with slogans in thralldom for the Turkish state. "Turkey is the greatest!" the young men would chant, sometimes accompanied by young women. They would beat drums through the neighborhoods. People would run to their windows to see the Turkish flags held on poles or hung over the young mens' shoul-

ders. The Turkish flag was a central component of such shows of nationalism on the street.[5]

Turkey, then, was a dominant chronotope that people had to engage
with. Yet, nationalism of this sort was not simply enforced by state and
army elites. At the site of the soldier's farewell, as at other sites of celebration for Turkey, there was a significant element of spontaneity. The young
men were making use of a certain agency in gathering around the symbols
of the state. Implicated in a statist discourse that prevailed in public culture and underwrote the very idea of conscription, these young men were
obliged to deal with the state. But, at another level, they were also employing the chronotope of Turkey for their personal interests and identifications. Publicly exhibiting enthusiasm for Turkey had become an aspect of
young masculinity here, particularly in the margins of social and political
power. Young men were enhancing their masculinity vis-à-vis one another
and in relation to women around them, in employing the terms of a state
culture. The accentuated meanings of state and country were deployed in
the reproduction of masculine identities. In those particular individualized
senses, then, the state was not only an abstract and distant idea. For these
men who participated in public rituals for Turkey, the word "Turkey"
spoke to something deeper. It encapsulated their utopic wishes as individuals struggling to get by in the world. "The good of Turkey" was metaphor
for heroic narratives of socio-economic hardship. Through the symbols and
paraphernalia of Turkey, young men told the stories of their experiences in
this world. Upholding the country as ultimate value gave these young men
a sense of collective purpose. In this time of an international culture of
statism, no other chronotope but the state was able to deliver the signifying functions that were needed by these young men. When unemployed,
out of money and means, confused emotionally, growing up, struggling to
survive in a vicious urban world, young men in Istanbul's shantytowns took
to the streets at night, particularly on special occasions such as army con-
scriptions and soccer games, and they shouted for Turkey. They walked
through the broken streets of the poor shanty areas, their homes, and
through the city's public squares while vigorously waving Turkish flags, red
and white, all about.

The soldier's farewell was one scene in which ordinary people in Turkey
appeared to be involved in the making and reproduction of one face of a
statist discourse in their everyday public life. Throughout this chapter and
the next, I will describe many other such scenes, involving people from
diverse segments of society in Turkey—secularist activists, consumers of
popular culture, leftists, as well as cynical critics of the state. The focus will
be on mundane practices of everyday life, ordinary habits of discussing
politics, watching TV, or following sports events, all central sites in the
production and reproduction of public life and culture in contemporary

Turkey. In ethnographically describing specific sites of popular interaction with the idea of state, I will study the manner in which the constructed notion of state is invented and reinvented through ordinary life practices and processes. I agree with Michael Taussig who has argued that it is in the lives and beliefs of ordinary people that the idea of a state takes its shape (1992, 132).

The driving question of this chapter is what makes "the idea of the state" (*devlet*) tick for people in Turkey?[6] What place does the state have in the habits of everyday life? Or, is that precisely the very space on which the idea of state is ideologically constructed (where the state is really located), rather than in the hallways of public institutions or the postures of official personalities? What sort of need does the notion of the state address in ordinary people that something else doesn't seem to satisfy at this historical conjuncture? What makes a constructed idea of state so convincing across ideologies and social differences?

In the middle of the 1990s, there were a number of sites where the notion of Turkey, the Turkish state, and its symbols appeared to have existential significance for people. And yet this very period has been predominantly studied, by social scientists of Turkey, as marker for "the development of civil society" (e.g., Göle 1994). The ethnographic material that informs the theoretical concerns of this chapter helps us reflect upon the analysis of civil society and the state. Are these analytical categories really useful? Here, I would like to propose that before wishfully jumping to conclusions about the development of civil society and the public sphere in Turkey in the 1980s and 1990s, as a doxa of contemporary social science has done, we should attend to the persistent meaning that the Turkish state still holds for actors in society who, in various ways, have fetishized it.[7] In this trip through the extra-official ethnographic loci of statism, I ask, why does the state appear to be an insurmountable reality?

The Wrestler as Leviathan

On August 3, 1996, a little after 7 P.M., the second channel of Turkish state television (TRT2),[8] broke the news of "Turkey's success" in the Olympics. Wrestler Mahmut Demir from Turkey had won the gold medal. "It is the fourth time that Turkey wins a medal in the Olympics," said the reporter. As the image of the well-built Mahmut Demir was shown on the screen, wrestling with his rival in the finals, the breathless voice of the reporter was heard in the background. "Bravo Mahmut!" cried the state-employed speaker. He took a loud and deep breath that gave the impression that he could choke or faint from excitement. "Mahmut, the champion of the Olympics!" said he, in the middle of a gasp. Mahmut appeared on the screen, this time in his awards ceremony. The flag of Turkey had been raised on a pole and a medaled Mahmut, with eyes directed toward the flag and arms straight on either side, sang to the playing of the Turkish national anthem.[9] His eyes were full of tears. The television clip ended as Mahmut was shown wiping his eyes with a handkerchief. His big figure almost disappeared behind a Turkish flag, with its bright red background and its white star-and-crescent. It was not really Mahmut who had won the medal in this representation. As his tearful eyes, which reflected the red-and-white flag, suggested, it was Turkey that had won the medal. Mahmut had to appear proud not for having performed well, but for having earned an honor for his country.

In the 1980s and 1990s, sports became a central site for the production and enhancement of public veneration for the Turkish state. There is, of course, a longer history to the intricate links between sports and nationalism in Turkey. As in Italy and Germany of the 1930s, in Turkey's first decade of national formation, the scout movements for both boys and girls were instituted to promote a feeling of national unity under the state. The 19th of every May was reserved for the celebration of Youth and Sports Day, when young people performed gymnastics in large public stadiums.[10] The development of a culture of disciplining one's body for aesthetics or strength is indistinguishable in Turkey from the process of nation-state formation. Yet, in certain periods, more than others, sports became a particularly fruitful arena for the perpetuation and popularization of the idea of Turkey as the ultimate good for which all ought to strive. This was the case in the 1980s and 1990s.[11]

After the military coup of 1980 and the supression of certain (mainly leftist) sorts of political activity, politicians found that they had to create new strategies for maintaining the idea of the state. Three years later, the army permitted "free" elections (only those parties that were sanctioned by the army could participate), and what in Turkey is "secular democracy" was reestablished.[12] A medium was required, something that would not diminish from the state's facade of democracy, whereby the idea of one state could popularly (in itself) be produced and reproduced. Nothing proved to be a more promising arena than sports for the development of new sites for the self-generation of state power. From the middle of the 1980s, when Turgut Özal was in power with his economic (or neo-) liberalism, massive state funding was reserved for sports. Politicians outspokenly hoped that youth would divert their attentions from politics (of the sort that flourished in the 1970s with a strong socialist movement that almost toppled the state) to the more amicable and apolitical activity of sports. What was presented as apolitical, neutral, and almost child-like was, of course, highly politicized, in that sports in the 1980s and 1990s was once again turned into a crucial domain for the public exhibition of thralldom for the state.

Collective support for national teams in foreign competitions could be represented by the state as a spontaneous feeling generated by society. One form of politics had been substituted for another, this time a politics of the status quo in the garb of fun or popular culture. No other site would prove to be more fruitful for the production of the semblance of support for the Turkish state, than the mundane and popular habit of following sports on TV.

What cricket is for India, soccer and wrestling turned out to be for Turkey. In the development of the culture of sport in the twentieth century, soccer and wrestling distinguished themselves as the most popular and most promising in the incitement of nationalist fervor. They were construed as Turkey's national games. In the 1980s, wrestling, with a history that preceded the building of the republic, was symbolically associated with a tradition of Turkish power: Turkic-to-Ottoman-to-Turkish statecraft personified in the image of the wrestler as Leviathan. The government and presidency of Özal, with its Ottomanist revivalism combined with a version of laissez-faire Westernism, provided special support to the sport of wrestling. Wrestlers were trained not only in strength and physical strategy, but also in an understanding of a Turkish-Islamic tradition of statecraft. The truth effect on the subjectivity of wrestlers was that many of them became practicing Muslims. So much state support was provided for this sport in the 1980s and 1990s that it is not surprising that a Turkish wrestler won in the Olympic games. When Mahmut Demir obtained the gold in the last Olympics, the headlines in the pan-Ottomanist and Islamist *Zaman* newspaper were as follows: "Mahmut's success enabled us to lift our heads from the midst of bad news to take a fresh breath of air."[13] Wins by national teams in foreign competitions have had this sort of effect on a majority of men, as well as women, in Turkey. Games with international, and particularly with European, teams have been more than mundane exhibitions of physical discipline. Beyond the fascination with bodily strength and tactics or with the excitement of betting, what is now at stake for consumers of sports is what media and state organs have termed "the image of Turkey."[14] Sports, like politics, warfare, economics, and beauty contests, have been transformed into an important arena for the Turkish state to test itself against global powers-that-be (invariably Europe or the West). That was the meaning of the *Zaman* newspaper headlines: in the middle of negative stories about the condition of Turkey, Mahmut brought the gift of relief. With his rival's back flat on the mattress, Mahmut caressed the wound of the Turkish state and its fetishists.

Popular interest in wrestling rose as a new domain for a culture of statism in the 1980s. Yet, in this period, no other practice but soccer (*futbol*) proved to be more promising for the production of a popularized notion of state. In Turkey, the activity of watching soccer was historically turned into

an important component of boys' socialization into manhood. A major pastime for a large majority of men, enjoying soccer as spectator, if not as
player, is an important marker of gender. There are many soccer teams,
mostly identified with particular regions of the country or particular neighborhoods of big cities. Early on in their lives, boys are taught to support a
certain team. Many are encouraged to cheer for their father's favorite team
or the one that represents their town of origin. Soccer consumes so much
of a significant proportion of men's lives that the team they favor becomes
part of their identity. Young boys are asked what team they support, after
being questioned about their name and age. Men make and break bonds
with one another over soccer. What is called a fanaticism for soccer is
respected in men as marker of proper masculinity. Girls and women are
not completely excluded from the activity of cheering for soccer teams, yet
when they do so they do it with more of a sense of humor than men. Men
approach soccer more seriously, as something more than plain entertainment. They abandon many other priorities when an important game is on
TV; they structure their days according to game hours; they silence everyone around the screen when critical plays are about to take place. Many
men take the success or failure of the teams they support personally; they
fear being a source of ridicule in front of peers who support rivaling teams.
Soccer, in this period, has been a central medium for the expression and
deployment of gender relations in Turkish society.

In the mid-1990s, soccer games excited physical violence among rivaling
fans. At the end of a number of important games, some people were
beaten up while others were accidentally killed by bullets fired into the air
by festive fans. Supporters of leading teams in Turkey (such as Galatasaray,
Fenerbahçe, Beşiktaş, and Trabzon) have formed "socceric" (as in "ethnic") groupisms for themselves, to the point where the presence of rival-
team fans during moments of excitement or desperation has led to violence. Gender, class, and regionally based divisions have come to be
constructed in the tribunes of soccer stadiums, in front of TV screens at
home, or in neighborhood coffeehouses for men.

To counteract the symbolic effect of intranational sports—that which
accentuates conflict internal to the circumference of Turkey—politicians,
journalists, and advertisers have created a good deal of hype around Turkey's participation in international sports. In the 1980s and 1990s, leading
soccer teams hired foreign trainers to push their players to the World Cup.
And Turkey's national team indeed turned out to be successful in developing itself to compete, and sometimes to win, internationally. The games of
the national team in foreign, and specifically European, stadiums have
been presented in mass media and in cultural organs of the state as a good
chance to create a sense of common (national) purpose among a social
diversity of soccer fans. And during times of desperation about the future

of the integrity (singularity) of Turkey, gatekeepers of the idea of the Turkish state have resorted to the enthusiasm that is generated by Turkish soccer abroad.

Before one of the national team's games with a European rival in the summer of 1996, the daily newspaper *Yeni Yüzyıl* published a front-page editorial that put a heavy symbolic burden on the result of the game. *Yeni Yüzyıl* is one of contemporary Turkey's most liberal newspapers, in the West European social democratic sense, taking individual rights vis-à-vis the state and its commitment to democracy as its litmus test of politics. In its short history of publication, the newspaper has taken a stance against authoritarianism in various institutions and social movements. For example, its journalists have exposed the violent actions of police in suppressing reporters and political activists. Yet when the time came to represent the national team's game in Europe, *Yeni Yüzyıl's* editorial was what I call statist. Like many other organs of what would still be identified as the domain of civil society by certain scholars (e.g., the press), *Yeni Yüzyıl* transformed the activity of supporting the national team into a matter of reflex or common sense, normalizing support for the idea of Turkey. "We hope that the team will be successful enough to elevate a feeling of national unity after all the recent calamities we have had to experience," read the editorial. The games were to be played in the aftermath of politicians' long-lasting struggles with one another and their inability to form government.

The habitus of soccer viewing, when properly constructed, indeed proved to be a productive arena for the perpetuation of Turkey as a common cause. It had the power of *as if* surpassing cultural, ideological, as well as class- or ethnic-based conflicts (if not those of gender) in society. The truth effect of the contemporary activity of following soccer was revealed to me at the time of the national team's game, when I heard the following lines chanted bombastically on the streets of Istanbul:

Europe Europe hear our voice
This is the sound of the footsteps of the Turks
Noone can deal with the Turks
Europe Europe guard yourself!

A statist discourse operating through the discipline of rallying for soccer teams was expressed in this march, *as if* overcoming differences in class, ethnicity, and experience. The national games, more than other sites of stately power, proved to be most effective in creating a façade of egalitarianism and common purpose, an "imagined community" (Anderson 1991), under the Turkish state: if not a state for all its citizens, a state for all who rally for it.

When a national team won a game against a European team (a highly symbolic one in Turkey), hundreds of people took to the streets at night, mostly young men, but also many young women. Central parts of Istanbul, such as Taksim Square, were crowded with people waving Turkish flags, jumping up and down to the steps of the *halay* (a version of Turkish folk dancing), rejoicing, and singing nationalist tunes. The aftermath of such wins was marked by expressions of utter enjoyment and emotional outbursts. Excessive drinking, high speeding in cars, and firing guns randomly in the air were common to the peculiar sense of victory on these occasions. Streets were filled with the wild sound of car horns. The pan-Turkists and Islamists among the soccer fans were heard chanting "God is the greatest" (*Allahüekber!*) in these events, interpreting the defeat of the European team as the bowing down of Christianity (or Europe) to (Turkish-) Islam. Many soccer fans in the crowd waved the three-crescented red flag of the pan-Turkist MHP in the air. If young women did not thrill to viewing soccer on TV or if they argued with their male relatives over the commotion of watching the games in the house, they seemed overjoyed with the show of excitement over Turkey's success once the game was over and it was time to go out into the street with friends and brothers in a spirit of festivity.[15]

What is the meaning of rallying for the idea of Turkey? What is it that has turned a vague notion of the good of the country into a value of second nature to such a majority of people who are from the geographical area that has historically been constructed as Turkey? What is it that gives the notion of this state the sort of potency it maintains, over and above other social, communal, or ideological associations for such a significant majority of people? How is it that in the domain of a diversity of social movements, public critique, and political agendas—including that of the Welfare Party—that the idea of the state is, up to this point, irrecoverable? The almost spontaneous support that it generates among its subjects must be one of the ways in which the Turkish state, in spite of trials and tribulations, remains intact.

The Flag Campaign

In June of 1996, the People's Democracy Party (HADEP), a political party founded by Kurdish intellectuals and activists, held a public meeting in the city of Diyarbakır in southeastern Turkey. The meeting site was decorated with flags of the PKK, at war with the Turkish army for a separate state. But as Turkish political disciplines demand, a flag of Turkey was also maintained, spread over a couple of poles. At the time, HADEP was a political party legally recognized by the Turkish state, hence it was bound to follow certain rituals of Turkish statecraft. HADEP is an offshoot of a former Kurdish party, the DEP (the Democracy Party), which had been banned from parliament on charges of having links with the PKK.[16] HADEP was founded while DEP parliamentarians were still in prison or on trial. The new party had participated in the national elections of December 1995, receiving only about 4 percent of countrywide votes, at least according to formal poll results.[17]

In June, HADEP leaders were attempting to revive their constituency. In that well-attended meeting, a young man climbed up to the pole where the Turkish flag was hanging; he untied the flag and pulled it down, all in front of a huge audience listening to the talks of HADEP leaders. The scene was recorded on the cameras of public and private TV stations. Journalists quickly took note of the young man's act, getting ready to blow it up on the next day's front page. On the following morning, the event was represented as a national scandal in Turkey's mainstream media. The image of the young man tearing down the Turkish flag was constructed as the main issue or the major public event at the time. Culture industries, as often directed by versions of statespeople, capitalized upon this image, enough to have it produce a significant effect on the public culture.

On the week after the scandal of the HADEP meeting, the most popular media companies (in particular, interStar TV, SHOWTV, and the *Hürriyet* newspaper, all privately owned), announced "a flag campaign" (*bayrak kampanyası*) calling on citizens of Turkey to hang Turkish flags on the street-facing windows of their shops and homes. The campaign was introduced by the media giants as a spontaneous protest "of the people (*halk*) against those who want to divide the country." Indeed, on the evening of the declaration of the campaign, Turkish flags appeared on windows all over Istanbul. The whole city was spotted with red-and-white (see figure 5). Not even on national holidays, when it was customary to hang up flags, would one have encountered such a massive display of this symbol of state. There had been no formal pressure on the part of public officials or police to have people join the campaign. That would have defeated the point of the contemporary Turkish state's governmentality in operation. The point was to create an appearance of spontaneity. That it was the press and not the state that had organized the campaign was officially deemed significant. The press, according to the official discourse on democracy, was an organ of civil society, a representation of the people. It was an entity outside the state. That the press and the people in-and-of-themselves collaborated to defend the Turkish flag against Kurdism was taken as symbol of the popular base for Turkey and the Turkish state. Visually, the masses of red-and-white and star-and-crescent, in side streets, local shops, and private homes all over the country, could give the impression of a public support for the idea of a singular Turkish state against that of a separate Kurdish state; of society, of its own will, standing up for the status quo or the Turkish state.

Not every house or shop around the city had a flag hung up, and that

Figure 5. Neighborhood shop in Istanbul, selling nationalist trinkets and paraphernalia, including Turkish flags (in all shapes and sizes), flags of the pan-Turkist Nationalist Action Party (the MHP) with the three crescents, and flags of the soccer team Galatasaray.

information is as important as the apparent participation in the campaign. But I do want to draw attention to what was the more widespread phenomenon of joining the campaign. The ethnographic gaze has often been turned to what is today called resistance in anthropological accounts: resistance to power, to colonialism, to the nation-state.[18] What has been little studied, however, is the more significant, peculiar yet extremely commonplace, practice of active support for the state on the part of the people, or participation in nationalism. As the ethnographic passages in this chapter show, there is significant public support for the idea of the state in Turkey. Much personal and collective meaning has been loaded onto the chronotopes of state and country. Domains that have been analyzed to be outside the state (civil society, the press, social movements) have on these important and widespread occasions operated as sites for the veneration of the state. I am more interested, therefore, in studying public *participation* in and *perpetuation* of, rather than resistance to, state power.

Private TV channels had a crucial role in announcing the Turkish flag campaign. Much scholarship has been devoted to explaining the flourishing of private TV channels in the 1980s (against state monopoly over public broadcasting) as an element of "the development of civil society against the state," or as a test case for a free market of ideas. Journalists employed by private TV companies, many coming from formerly socialist backgrounds, take pride in working for the private as opposed to the public channels, almost as if they are accomplishing their activist political missions. Some of these journalists characterize the rise of privatization in Turkey's TV industry in the 1980s as a time when formerly censored information was made more widely available. Such journalists have channeled their energy to exposing corruption rings involving politicians and violence committed by police. Characters and opinions that had no place on the screens of the state-run TRT—Kurdish leaders, Islamists, and socialists—found slots reserved for themselves in forums organized by the new and private TV stations.

Private TV channels have indeed brought significant change to the circle of publicly available information. This has been a significant development. But another dimension of the mainstream TV channels remains unstudied or overlooked by those scholars who have easily classified such channels as elements of civil society. The most popular TV channels (those heralded by journalists who support freedom of speech) have also been central to the production and reproduction of thralldom for the Turkish state. Their hands-on organization of the flag campaign was one such concrete example.[19]

Does "Civil Society" Exist?

A significant body of social science literature focusing on Turkey in the 1980s and 1990s characterizes the period as one of progressive and favorable democratization and demilitarization, of a decentralization of statecraft, and, most importantly, of a development of "civil society" and a certain sort of pluralism and multiculturalism in Turkish society. Prominent scholars have contributed to creating this picture of the period that followed the coup of 1980.[20] Pivotal in this regard has been the relativist approach of certain of these scholars to the Islamist movement as it rose in popularity. Indeed, the period that these scholars presented as an example of "democratization" and "the development of civil society" was the very period in which Islamisms were developing their constituency. Furthermore, these scholars explicitly interpreted Islamicization in Turkey as "the awakening of civil society against the state" after seventy or more years of slumber. The rise of formerly banned religious orders (*tarikats*) in popularity, the flourishing market for Islamic publications, the opening of numerous Islamist foundations, the adoption of the headscarf (*türban*) and veil by an increasing number of women, were all cited as evidence for "the return of the repressed" by such post-Kemalist social scientists.[21]

Nilüfer Göle's sociology of the 1980s and 1990s is one highly influential example of a post-Kemalist perspective on contemporary social formations in Turkey. In an article titled "Towards an Autonomization of Politics and Civil Society in Turkey," Göle writes,

> In terms of the state-society relationship, the post-1980 era has been a turning point in Turkish political development. During the 1980s, the autonomization of civil societal elements from the grip of the center—a process that started in the 1950s—became even more pronounced.... Only in the 1980s did future-oriented revolutionary political utopias lose their appeal, a change that permitted a more diverse spectrum of political participants. Women, ecologists, veiled students, and homosexuals and transsexuals appeared on the political scene and brought to the agenda such themes as environmental protection, female identity, and individual freedom.... Unprecedented kinds of political action followed to further the new causes: women marching to protest being battered by men, people joining ecologists in demonstrations to save turtles, Islamicist women students resorting to hunger strikes against university dress codes that banned the "Islamic outfit" in the classroom, and homosexuals and transsexuals making public demands for protection of their civil liberties. These new protest movements and their proponents were neither written off as ridiculous, reactionary, or decadent nor considered trivial by the public at large.... Once in power, the ANAP [Motherland Party], began dismantling the state by its policies of decentralization of government, privatization of the state economic enterprises, and reorientation toward a market economy. The development of liberal, Muslim, and leftist movements demonstrated the basic dimensions of the autonomization of civil society. The liberal discourse, which was rediscovered and became fashionable after 1983, developed simultaneously with a market economy.... If the liberal movement represented the economic dimension of the autonomization of civil society, the Islamicist movement represented the cultural dimension. (1994, 213–22).

Central to Göle's analysis of the period is a comparison with the 1970s. As she characterizes the 1970s as period of violent utopian strife between leftist and rightist groups, Göle portrays the 1980s as a context within which public discourse was rationalized, social movements diverted their attention from counter-state politics to constructive searches for new policy under the dominion of the state, people of opposing political leanings could begin to listen to one another in a harmoniously shared social space (212–22). When one reads this sociological account, one may be left thinking that flourishing, diverse civic formations from environmentalists to

Islamicist women's groups, feminists to gays, have evolved to coexist peacefully as elements of a liberated public sphere in Turkey in the aftermath of the military coup of 1980.

However, in seeking to isolate an almost ideal-typical picture of an "autonomous" public sphere, this account overlooks the ongoing presence and power of representatives of the state—city governor, police, riot police, traffic police, municipal police, secret service, soldier, military officer, mafia, judge, university professor, dean, clerk—in the same public sphere. The 1980s, the period that Göle analyzes, was a period of tension-ridden struggles between diverse organs of the state (sometimes in disjuncture with one another) on the one hand, and members of social movements (also in collision) on the other. What has been left out of this account of the public sphere is the effect that martial law and war in the southeast has had on public culture all over Turkey after the military coup, as well as the prevailing repressive, controlling, and intervening power of various organs of the state, in such diverse places as prisons, courtrooms, airport checkpoints, streets, universities, neighborhoods, or through media and other means in one's home. Various representatives and defenders of the state have had an enduring and at times violent presence in the public sphere in the very period that has been defined as one of "democratization" and "the autonomization of the societal sphere."

One may perhaps ask whether it is empirically possible to identify state and society as separate domains. Perhaps there is no autonomization to be observed, but rather what may be called a changing enmeshed relationship. Organs and factions of "the state" have had enduring *repressive* power, in Foucault's sense of the term; however, there has been a simultaneous attempt on the part of "statesmen" to practice power *productively*.[22] The means of enforcement of the state no longer appears sufficient to maintain the idea of the Turkish state, without the independent support of spheres of society. In the 1980s and 1990s, there was extensive effort on the part of statespeople to mobilize "self-generating" or "spontaneous" sites within society in order to reproduce and enhance state power. This is a historically specific and contingent synthesis of Foucault's *repressive* and *productive* hypotheses, developed within the Turkish context. Perhaps Göle and others who read "the development of civil society" into their analyses of contemporary Turkey have confused a changing discourse or technique of state power with an autonomous rise of civil society. Indeed, statesmen have liked to make it seem, especially in the period that Göle describes, that their rule is contingent upon "the progressive development of civil society in Turkey of the 1980s." The idea of a separate realm of society was used by politicians seeking legitimacy, more in this particular historical period in Turkey than any before. The technique of democratic power was the issue.[23] This was no simple and linear development of civil society.

Göle's account can be instructively compared and contrasted with the work of Jürgen Habermas on prospects for the future development of the public sphere. Habermas's theory explores possibilities for the temporal development of the public sphere, or in his terms, of informed and rational communicative interaction about matters of common concern to the public (1989). Göle reads the 1980s as period of progress, in a certain Habermasian sense, that is, of the formation of a public context for reasoned agreement and disagreement, addressing taboo issues in the spirit of cool-minded discussion. What distinguishes Göle from Habermas is perhaps what could be read as her critique of Habermas's Eurocentrism. A crucial component of Göle's account of what she calls "an autonomous societal sphere" (1994, 221) in Turkey of the 1980s is the advent of Islamic values and the Islamicization of politics. Habermas, a secular humanist who takes secularization to be the necessary companion of democratization, would not interpret Islamicist movements as elements of a developing public sphere. For him, as for other Western philosophers in the Marxian and Weberian tradition, Islam, in particular, would fall outside an understanding of rationalization. Göle's work is valuable as a challenge to this sort of Orientalism, a version of which is also prevalent among a significant segment of Turkey's contemporary Kemalists.[24]

The work of such post-Kemalist scholars of Turkey can be studied and situated within a wider conceptual shift in scholarship on the Middle East. For postwar studies of the Middle East, the state was the object of study. Karl Wittfogel's *Oriental Despotism* (1978) was perhaps a bit of a caricature of what was the predominant approach to Muslim societies, where an absolutist, all-seeing, and all-controlling state was constructed as definitive of Islam. Whole institutions of area studies were devoted to demonstrating what was imagined to be the intrinsic incompatibility between Islam and democracy, Islam and civil society.

In turn, in the late 1970s and early 1980s, the publication of critiques of Orientalism by Edward Said and others (e.g., Maxime Rodinson, Samir Amin, Talal Asad), led scholars of the Middle East to reflect on the relation between the analytical categories that they used on the one hand and European power on the other. Concepts that had formerly been assumed to be part-and-parcel of an exclusive European heritage (e.g., capitalism, rationalization, democracy, secularism, and civil society) were deemed relevant in this new generation of studies of Muslim societies. Focus was shifted *from the state to society*, as scholars began to describe forms of public resistance to the state, upheavals, social movements, and civic formations. While previous research tended to deny the existence of society in the Middle East, juxtaposing it with its flourishing counterpart in western Europe, post-Orientalists began to identify elements of civil society, or the authentic political and cultural activity of the people as undirected by the state. There is now a whole body of literature on civil society in the Middle East. The collection edited by Augustus Richard Norton (1995), has been so influential in this regard (see also Turner 1984; Sadowski 1993) that academic journals have organized special issues around this theme, panels have been formed to discuss this subject, and anthologies on the topic have been published. Anthropologists, in particular, have directed their energy to "challenging Western models of civil society," writing ethnographies of alternative, non-Western forms of public coalition beyond the state. They have identified many new domains—Islamicist welfare networks, for example, or working women's informal neighborhood coalitions— as elements of what could be called civil society (see Hann and Dunn 1996). So much attention has been geared to the unearthing of forms of civil society in the Middle East that one could now speak of a new orthodoxy in the discipline. With this conceptual shift, we have moved from Eurocentric studies of domination and power to culturally relative studies of resistance. The work of post-Kemalist Turkish scholars has to be placed within the context of this wider transformation in metropolitan studies of Islam.

While acknowledging the critique of Orientalism and Kemalism advanced by such scholars, I nevertheless remain as unsure of the value of the terms "civil society" or "public sphere" for ethnographic study, as I am about "resistance," a concept that has been overused to explain almost every minor act of social dissent around the world.[25] Significant studies take the state / civil society distinction to be real. There is an attempt to base this distinction empirically on historical and social grounds, as if the state and society were tangible things to be pinpointed and distinguished objectively from one another. The following questions, however, ought to be asked: Where does the state end and society begin? Could one ever locate such divisions empirically? Is resistance an arena that transcends the effects of power? How does one decide sociologically which social group or phenomenon is a representation of civil society and which is not?

The ethnographic events that I studied in the first sections of this chapter reveal a different sort of dynamics in the arena identified by many recent scholars as civil society. In many, if not most instances, public, civil, or popular activities have been shown to enhance a statist ideology of power, one that makes it difficult to imagine sorts of worldly existence that can transcend the state. Recently in Turkey, the idea of the state has been significantly sustained through the everyday life practices of people outside the centers of official power. In life rituals of bidding farewell to soldiers, in the mundane activity of watching national soccer games on TV, in hanging flags up in private quarters in anxiety or festivity, and in many other daily life practices, ordinary people in Turkey reproduce an idea of the Turkish state. Many (now) commonplace events in public culture in Turkey—the matter of everyday life—enhance and normalize, rather than challenge the construction of the Turkish state. Significant groups of people in the last decade in Turkey have voluntarily been organizing ways to uphold the state. There are independent civil movements that, in various ways, rally around and organize for the state. A certain sort of statism, in other words, in various fashions persists in an important segment of what scholars too easily identify as the domain of society. Groups of people in society have had a peculiar existential need for the idea of a strong and unified Turkish state. Through their everyday practices, these actors in society have also been reifying and reinstating the state.

In greater theoretical detail, I will argue in a later section of this and the following chapter that if statism were not produced and reproduced in the everyday practices of ordinary people, the state, as material reality, would have less effect. Public veneration for the state reerects mechanisms of state power, even when they show the potential to disintegrate. Therefore, instead of looking for the state in tangible social institutions or stately persona, the sites of everyday life, where people attempt to produce meaning for themselves by appropriating the political, ought to be studied as a central domain for the production and reproduction of the state. There is an everyday life, an ordinariness to the notion of the state. It is through a certain mundanity and banality that the state achieves its effects. The notion of the state acquires its power not only through ideological enforcement in real social institutions such as the army and the school, but also through quotidian, and seemingly spontaneous events and occasions, among them bidding farewell to soldiers' and watching soccer. The state, then, is also generated from within the agencies of what is called (and reified as) society.

Drawing on Timothy Mitchell's critique of the state-society paradigm (1990, 1991), I approach the distinction as a discursive construction of politics and the social sciences. Mitchell (1990) has argued that binary distinctions commonly used by social scientists for analysis (e.g., state and society, power and resistance, meaning and reality, mind and matter) are the effects of a new discourse of power.[26] In other words, what social scientists claim to study empirically is a construction. These abstractions are the tools of a new form of governmentality. In Mitchell's words, "the apparent existence of such unphysical frameworks or structures is precisely the effect introduced by modern mechanisms of power and it is through this elusive yet powerful effect that modern systems of domination are maintained" (1990, 561). Mitchell terms this mode of power "enframing," or "a variety of modern practices that seem to resolve the world's shifting complexity into two simple distinct dimensions" (566). Mitchell further argues that the use of such concepts regenerates resources of power. The state-society distinction produces the effect of a state that is self-contained and that does not meddle, more than its due, in the affairs of society.

In Turkey, specifically since 1983, with the supposed changeover of government from the military to civil politicians, state officials have needed the constructed distinction between state and society to secure a democratic legitimacy and longevity for the restructured Turkish state. The international community looked for at least a facade (or an image) of attentiveness to democracy and human rights in Turkey. In the 1980s, Turkish statespeople, eager to maintain democratic legitimacy internally and to remake their image internationally (especially vis-à-vis the European Union), realized that the Turkish state, in order to endure, needed the idea of a society in its favor. Turkish officials appropriated the term "civil society" as ideology, in realizing that the state, after martial law, could legitimize itself only if it could demonstrate that there is a separate realm of society unperturbed by it. So Turkish officials began to employ an abstract notion of society in their discourse; it was useful for them to argue that the state had little hold over most of public life and that their power was a reflection of unmanipulated public will. Procedural democracy asked for this sort of a refashioned mechanism of power.

In what follows, I demonstrate that the construction "state-versus-society," as used by social scientists, forms the basis of new ideologies of power in Turkey in struggle with one another for influence over the state. The concept of civil society was employed in various ways in the discourse of Islamists and secularists. Indeed, I show that in the 1990s a discourse of civil society became instrumental in claims for legitimate ownership of state power. So enmeshed are discourses of civil society and state on the ethnographic ground that the analytical distinction is obsolete.

A discourse of state versus society was appropriated in different and culturally specific ways by both Islamist and secularist bureaucrats in the late 1980s and 1990s. In the two following sections of this chapter, I will complicate the narrative of post-Kemalist scholars of civil society in Turkey, with further ethnographic descriptions that come from my fieldwork. First, I will focus on Welfare Party officials' uses and abuses of the terms "state" and "society." In the 1980s, Welfare Party officials incorporated the notion of civil society into their discourse in a specific manner. In fact, they obtained political power, initially in municipalities and eventually in the central government, by arguing that they were not representatives of the state, but of civil society (using the Turkish phrase *sivil toplum*). After assuming state offices, Welfare officials whom I studied still insisted that they were outside of and against the state. Even when it was leading a governing coalition in Turkey, the Welfare Party presented itself as an entity outside the state. Indeed, antistate rhetoric has proven to be part-and-parcel of a contemporary democratic practice of obtaining and maintaining state power in Turkey. And up to this point, Welfarists have shown themselves able to obtain, maintain, and practice modern statecraft quite efficiently.

A following section of the chapter will focus on the incorporation of the notion of civil society into secularist officials' practice of statecraft and secularist women's activism. In the last few years, secularists have had to resort to the notion of civil society in their attempts to defend a secularist establishment. They have wanted to illustrate that secularism is not about the state, but about the will of the people, that it was not an imposition from above, but a reflection of society. The question is, how do the following ethnographic readings modify our approach to civil society in Turkey?

"The Transparent Reflection of Society"

When the Welfare Party assumed state power in the mid-1990s, the practices of its officials were largely represented as antidemocratic by their opponents. Yet, Welfarists' practice of statecraft in the municipalities where I did my research was more attuned to the disciplines of modern statecraft that the officers inherited than to those of the medieval polity that they claimed to reinvent.[27] More accurately, the language of Welfare Party officers was imbued with an interesting combination of the terms of modern statecraft on the one hand and those of the Prophetic Islamic polity on the other. Yet, the present historically prevailed over the past, in that Welfarists kept reading old Islamic forms of statecraft through the lens of modern political categories.

An examination of the language used by Welfare Party officials in the period between 1994 and 1996, when they campaigned for and obtained a form of state power, reveals a proficiency in employing the terms of modern statecraft. Welfarist mayors and officials who were my informants called for "better democracy" in Turkey. As they acquired political power in the mid-1990s, Welfarists did so with a demand for more "social justice" in Turkish statecraft. In protest of the denial of higher education to veiling women students, they called for "human rights." Moreover, while female supporters of the party characterized the veil as a requisite of Islamic practice, they particularly emphasized it as a matter of "human rights" (*insan hakları*). When they were banned from the university for wearing the headscarf, a group of Islamist women filed a complaint to the European Union's court of justice and not to legal authorities in Saudi Arabia or Iran. Indeed, Welfarists spoke in a culturally specific translation of the popular terms of contemporary West European politics of citizenship. They knew

the language of modern statecraft well. Mayors whom I interviewed promised to bring a more "pluralist" (*çoğulcu*) order of statecraft to a society
that was "multicultural" (*çok kültürlü*). They claimed that their party represented the real diversity of cultural life in Turkey, in opposition to the
culture of secular elites represented in entrenched and monist state
institutions.

Most significantly, Welfare Party activists argued that only they, among
all other political parties, were the representatives of civil society in Turkey. The new municipal employees talked about the lives of people who
had been independently gathering around religious orders for decades despite legal obstacles, of those who had been seeking religious knowledge,
and, more recently, of those who had been attending Islamist foundations
and charity organizations. Welfare officials partook in such social networks
and they argued that these sorts of gatherings were what civil society in
Turkey was all about, against the authoritarianism of secular elites and the
state.

Implicit in this version of the state-versus-society distinction was a particular historical consciousness or reading of republican Turkish history.
Welfarist activists whom I came to know understood modernization and
secularism to have been, in their expression, "impositions from above" on
the part of privileged Ottoman and Turkish elites. The ethics of the republican Turkish state, in this reading, had nothing organically or primordially
to do with the life practices, values, and wishes of the majority of the
people (*halk*) and of society (*toplum*). "For seventy years," one Welfare
Party activist would repetitively suggest, "we have been governed in a direction that contradicts the desires of the people." Another Welfare Party
employee in the municipality reflected that "while 98 percent of this country is composed of Muslims, the state functions with laws that punish the
religious." Welfarists defined (Sunni) Islam as "the real culture of the people" and attempted to write the secularist and modernist history of the
republican Turkish state out of the narrative of the Turkish nation. In their
historical consciousness, the state, as far as it had existed until the Welfare
Party's victories, was alien to the nation. And the Welfare Party was democratically to carry "the true values of society" to state offices where they
were overdue.

The account of an official in the Welfare Party's metropolitan municipality in Istanbul appears below. In an interview I conducted with him
during 1994, after the Welfare Party had obtained power in municipalities,
Hüseyin Besli, the aide to the Officer of Cultural Affairs, said,

> Secularists would like to represent us as prejudiced with regard to cultural activ-
> ities. But in our opinion, only a monist cultural understanding has prevailed in
> institutions of the state up to this point. The historical culture that has seeped

into the genes of our people was not represented in the institutions of the republic. We are the first to introduce a multivoiced cultural understanding to municipalities. We will offer room in public halls to those whose voices have not previously been heard. And we will give priority to the culture of the people. Our administration will be the transparent representation of the plural culture of the people.

A central activity of his office had been the organization of a number of conferences to be held in the cultural centers Tarık Zafer Tunaya in Beyoğlu and the Ataturk Library in Taksim. There were few days of the week when one event or another was not being held in these cultural centers that were administered by the new Welfarist municipality. At each of these events, there would be thirty to sixty people. A group of regular attendees had formed from among Islamist intellectuals and students. Yet, in time, secular intellectuals, certain leftists, feminists, and non-Islamist students also began to attend the events, even if in smaller numbers. The subjects that the conferences addressed were highly intellectual, abstract, and theoretical. The speakers mostly came from a circle of Islamist intellectuals gathered around a number of Islamist magazines and newspapers. Among the topics discussed were critiques of modernity, Islam and aesthetics, and Islamic philosophy of science.[28]

In these particular cultural centers, far from reflecting "the plural culture of the people," Islamist intellectuals were formulating an alternative high culture to replace that of secular elites. The conferences at the cultural centers, where men and women were often asked to sit separately, were heralded as a form of urban entertainment to replace the high cultural life of Westernized elites who frequented the Istanbul Festival of Arts in summers, the Western classical music concerts in winters, or plays in Istanbul's public and private theaters on the weekend. The Welfare municipality was structuring another sort of (high) cultural domain for the city. Those who felt most comfortable and in place at these activities were highly educated Islamists of middle-class aspirations (if not of middle-class backgrounds). And Welfare Party officers insisted on representing the cultural activities that they organized and sponsored as a reflection of "the culture of the people" or as "the voice of civil society" unspoiled by loci of power, especially that of the state.

There was important difference between Welfarists' uses of the terms of modern statecraft and the use of the same terms by secular politicians: Welfarists promised the ideals of democracy in following the path of God. Integral to this vision was a critique of the secular-Turkish version of democracy. Because of their desire and need to express publicly their religiosity, Islamists felt like the outcasts within the republican state, founded as it was on the idea of a nation of secularists. Islamists identified with their religious predecessors in the formative years of the secular state, their predecessors who had received capital punishment for expressing their religiosity in public. Accounts of the lives of religious men, punished in "Courts of Liberation" (İstiklal Mahkemeleri) for maintaining religious garb, were popular reading material among Islamist youth. Young Islamist women, being banned from public service in hospitals, courts, and universities for veiling, believed that the story was not yet over. Feeling repressed and humiliated by secularists for looking religious and maintaining religious life practices, Islamists thought that their experience exposed a weakness in a system of government the rationale of which was an impartial notion of citizenship and egalitarianism. Despite the government's claims to the contrary, my Islamist informants felt that they were not, in their words, treated as "equal" under institutionalized "secular-democracy." "Isn't it paradoxical," their objections often began, "that in a country where 98 percent of the population is Muslim, the Muslim community is experiencing discrimination for practicing Islam?" It was with such a historical consciousness about what secular Turkish democracy meant that politically active Islamists in the Welfare Party sought a democracy truer to its universalist principles of impartial government. And they sought this in otherworldly inspiration. In their belief in an Islamic social order, Welfare Party activists found guidance for a modern state order that would deliver better social justice, one where "the Muslim society" would no longer be outcast economically, socially, or culturally. Accordingly, Welfarists never ceased speaking of themselves as "the victims of the state," as "members of society," or as "the community of Muslims" that had been deprived of power.

Many Welfarists were leftists in the 1970s. And it was in reading and interacting with leftist critics of the state, such as Murat Belge, in the 1980s, that many of these Islamist intellectuals picked up the vocabularies of civil society and democracy. Yet something interesting happened in this culturally specific appropriation. The terms of modern statecraft did not sit awkwardly in the language of the Welfarist officials who were my informants. A politically significant group of Welfare Party activists, that is, those who have climbed the ladder to state power with popular backing, developed a proper synthesis of their own in their calls for "better democracy." They introduced the Islamic tradition of the time of the Prophet Muhammad as a model of democracy more pluralistic than the modern version that exists in contemporary Turkey. They began to present şeriat (Islamic law) as "pluralist democracy." This they juxtaposed with the monist authoritarianism of the secular Turkish state, restrictive of religious lifestyles and of minority cultures, most importantly of that of Kurdish communities. Welfarists extolled Islam as a system of statecraft that was based on an understanding of the peaceful coexistence of a multiplicity of lifestyles, cultures, and beliefs under the protection of the Islamic state. Because of this worldview, the Welfare Party won many votes from Kurds in southeastern Turkey.

The prominent Islamist intellectual Ali Bulaç has been most active in influencing the Welfare Party's politics of multiculturalism. To Istanbul's public culture, fraught with conflicts in identity, Ali Bulaç proposed the Prophet's city, Medina, as a model for contemporary peace. In 1989, in his research into early Islamic history, he had come across descriptions of "the Medina Covenant." To Medina, tired of tribal wars between Jews and Arabs, the Prophet Muhammad had introduced a truce that would guarantee cultural and legal autonomy to each religious community. Jews would be subjects of Jewish law and Muslims of Islam. Medina, according to Ali Bulaç, was a society of a plurality of legalities. Istanbul could be so, too. Inspired by such presentist narratives of the Prophet's times, Islamists have been promising to bring a version of "a multiculturalist" understanding to Turkey's legal system, one where each will be judged under the law that she or he prefers, Muslim, Jewish, Greek-Orthodox, or atheist. As Ali Bulaç refashions "modern citizenship" with a Prophetic example, other Islamists have revived the Ottoman *millet* system as an example of government they argue to have been more just, humane, and superior to the monism of the secular nation-state. *Millet* was the name for religious communities in the Ottoman Empire, communities that had their autonomous legal systems. Welfare Party activists share in this revivalist vision of Islamist intellectuals. They believe that the pluralist example from the past can serve as an alternative model of citizenship to the faulty modern one.

There was an effort on the part of Welfarist officers to implement and practice their version of a democratic ideal as soon as the party won municipality elections throughout the country. Among the first acts of the new mayors was the institution of what were called "peoples' parliaments" (*halk meclisleri*) as an effort to move statecraft toward a version of what Welfarists had learned to call "direct democracy" (or, *doğrudan demokrasi*). The neighborhood of Kağıthane, a shantytown of Istanbul where I did an important part of my fieldwork, was the first to have a peoples' parliament. Here the Welfare Party had been in charge since 1992, even before the widespread victories in 1994.

One evening every week, the district mayor would appear in a public coffeehouse for men and would ask neighborhood residents to voice their wishes and complaints. The mayor of Kağıthane defined "direct democracy" as a right for human beings ordained by God. Before beginning the interchange, he always reminded neighborhood residents that these gatherings were in the model of Prophet Ömer's mode of governing in the early centuries of Islam. According to the mayor's narrative, Prophet Ömer used to greet the people under his sovereignty face-to-face and would allow them to challenge him. Those attending the weekly parliament, almost exclusively men and mostly Welfare Party supporters, voiced their concerns about problems in the neighborhood: broken pipelines, uncollected garbage, traffic accidents, unpaved roads, and lack of water, electricity, and so forth. The mayor and his officers were quite efficient in noting and following up on these complaints, and indeed more effective than former municipal governments in doing so.

The mayor knew that residents of Kağıthane had suffered much from corrupt bureaucracies. It seemed that the old municipalities had done more to line the pockets of their officers than to serve the needs of the district. The peoples' parliaments were presented first and foremost as a way for citizens to make officials publically accountable. The mayor advertised these gatherings as a demonstration of the Welfare Party's commitment to what he called "transparency" in government. "Not everyone has the courage to make an appearance in front of people every week in order to be accountable," he said. In his words, he would only be "a servant to the needs of society."

The mayor knew as well that residents of the shantytown that he administered felt much estranged from organs of the state. The state had never worked for the benefit of shanty inhabitants. People preferred to resolve their problems among themselves without resorting to any institution of state. In fact, the notion of the state represented danger to the poor residents of Kağıthane. The mayor initiated the peoples' parliaments to create, in his words, "a society of service in place of one of fear." The peoples' parliaments, he hoped, would encourage people to interact more with the state, to ask directly for their rights, and to participate in goverment. "Could a higher image of justice be conceived?" he often asked. In using the term "direct democracy" to characterize his municipal practice, he was trying to argue that he was no "representative of the state," but "a member of civil society." It was "society" that was "directly" shaping his municipal practice.

The mayor had coined the phrase "a peoples' government based on Right," for his project. There is an implicit pun in the mayor's use of the word "right." In Turkish, *hak* can be used to signify "rights." When capitalized in writing, it is one of the names for God. In this understanding, the concept of a just delivery of civic rights would be intertwined with a belief in divine justice. "I am not the one who is giving you this right to check up on those you have elected," the mayor told the people attending the coffeehouse parliament, "this right was granted to you by God. I am only preparing a suitable ground for you to use this right." In this use of "rights," the mayor understood something not too different from that defined within the context of the European Enlightenment. He argued, however, that civic rights were ordained not by the state but by God. A state office that approached the "right" of the people with "a fear of God," in his words, would be more just. Here, he was once again distinguishing himself from the state, in associating himself with God, and hence, in his understanding, with the people. There was "God and society" on the one side and "the corrupt secular state" on the other.

There were contradictions in what the Welfarist mayor called "direct democracy." The peoples' parliaments that I attended were more a reflection of patron-client relations than of the self-rule proposed by officials. Spatially, a division was always maintained between the public officers who were dressed in suits and ties and the people, the neighborhood residents, who attended the parliaments. The officers would sit in seats of honor behind desks and Welfare Party paraphernalia. The mayor would take the lead behind a podium and a microphone, arriving at the scene and leaving in a black limousine, applauded as he entered and left the neighborhood coffeehouse. The charismatic mayor tried to engender a cult of personality around himself. In his speeches, where he always maintained the upper hand, he primarily praised the activities of the Welfare Party. Most peoples' parliaments were arranged before elections, in other words, when the Welfare Party needed electoral support. The people who attended the parliament did get a slight chance to voice their concern about the practical workings of the neighborhood infrastructure, but their voice was restricted and cut short by Welfare's officials keeping track of the time. Moreover, people who opposed the Welfare Party rarely appeared in the parliaments, thinking that this was a Welfarist affair. And there were never any women in attendance, except myself as participant-observer, as the "parliaments" were organized in spaces traditionally attended by men—the men's coffeehouse was not a space used by shantytown women. Therefore, far from being an example of "society" governing itself, the peoples' parliaments were part of the Welfare Party's campaigning strategy; a kind of tool of propaganda; it was one way in which they hoped to obtain more votes in order to rise to state power. And that is what they were able to do skillfully in the national elections of 1995 and 1996.

Using the term "civil society" to characterize the activities of local governments under the Welfare Party might have the effect of overlooking the complex relations of power in operation and the discursive use of the term "civil society" by officers seeking power in the state. In this section, I attempted to demonstrate that the state-versus-society distinction, in the abstract, is a concept used by Welfare Party officials. Even after obtaining a majority of seats in parliament and the cabinet of ministers, Welfarists persisted in presenting themselves as "the separate realm of society," as the domain that lacks power. Here, I have attempted to compare this discourse with the actual workings of power on the ground. It rather seems that the Welfare Party is an alternative locus of power in Turkey, defining what is and what isn't civil society or the culture of the people, in opposition to other loci of power, some of which are secularist.

Welfarists expressed their populism through a discourse of society versus the state. They presented their municipal undertakings as well as their particular practices of everyday life as if they were an archetypal representation of the preferred cultural practices of Turkish society at large. They pitted this reified construction of the people (or Islam) against the state, *as if* there had been no historical relations between the two. Instead, I will argue that this was a particular discourse on society as well as a specific cultural practice that represented what was being invented as (rather than what was) Islam and presented as (rather than being a reflection of) the culture of the people by outspoken and powerful Islamist intellectuals.

"A Holiday of the People"

The distinction between state and society has also been employed by secularist officials and by members of Ataturkist pressure groups and organizations.[29] Since 1994, a number of new Ataturkist social organizations have been founded by groups of secularists worried about threats to their lifestyle from the Welfare Party's vast electoral victories. One important example of such organizations is The Society to Support Civilized Life (Çağdaş Yaşamı Destekleme Derneği). Construing politics of identity with Islamists as primarily a gender-based issue, this organization is composed of middle- to upper-class, secularist women professionals. Other organizations include The Society for Ataturkist Thought (Atatürkçü Düşünce Derneği), composed mostly of older secular elites, and the Beyoğlu Platform (Beyoğlu Platformu), founded by secular artists and intellectuals to preserve the cultural life of the Beyoğlu district of Istanbul after Welfare assumed power in this municipal area.

Early on in their activism, members of these groups expressed the lack of knowledge that they had of "the people" (*halk*). Some of those I interviewed spoke of their restricted perspective on the city of Istanbul. They said that they had never visited Fatih or Eyüp (largely inhabited by religious families) and that they didn't know the back districts of Beyoğlu (poor shantytowns), where Welfare had obtained its votes. Yet, these secularists also thought they knew that the Islamist lifestyle they feared was not practiced by all the people. They believed that there was a fundamental basis for Ataturkism, that Ataturkism was the ideal not only of the privileged and educated urbanites but also of a large majority of the people who had not voted for the Welfare Party. They wanted to think that Ataturkism was not the established ideology of the state, but a tradition of Turkish society.

Yet these Ataturkist activists found that they had to prove their conviction. Reprinting history books about "the original Anatolian woman," who was unafraid of orthodox religiosity, was not of much use.[30] More organic links had to be forged with the secular communities among the people. Indeed, in the first few months of their meetings, called in emergency to react constructively to Welfare's victory in the municipalities, "the people" was an abstract notion for many of these Ataturkist women, something they thought they knew through their encounters with domestic servants, porters, certain students in state universities, or their employees at business or in the workplace. As an effort to reach out and ground themselves in society, activists of The Society to Support Civilized Life started "houses of learning" in various shantytowns around Istanbul. In these centers, "women from the people" would be taught all sorts of skills, from sewing to embroidery, childcare to hygiene. They would also be educated in the principles of Ataturkism.[31] The Ataturkist women who paved the way for these local centers often admitted that they modeled their practice on that of Welfare Party activists who had walked from door to door in shantytowns in order to recruit people to their electorate and worldview. Central to the Welfare Party's campaigning strategy was the distribution of food and other resources (coal, burning wood, clothes, etc.) to the people they reached out to. Activists of "Civilized Life" started to follow a similar strategy. Whenever they introduced themselves to women in shantytowns, the activist women would first offer their gift or donation packaged in cloth bags with the emblem of their organization.

A turning point in middle-class secularists' activism was their discovery, in the mid-1990s, of the existence of the Alevi community in Turkey. Here was a community, which could properly be defined as part of the people, who held a worldview and lifestyle that was radically in contrast to that of Islamists, most of whom were Sunni. Middle-class secularist activists began to read and learn about Alevism, to visit Alevi houses of worship (*cemevis*), to participate in Alevi ritual ceremonies (*semah törenis*), and attend meetings in Alevi organizations. In the 1990s, a number of Alevi organizations had sprung up in an attempt to organize Alevis politically against prejudice and to preserve and revive Alevi cultures and traditions. There is such a wide variety of Alevi practices throughout Turkey that different Alevi organizations often disagreed with one another as to how to group different Alevisms under one roof. This was difficult, not only because of the internal diversity of Alevism, but also due to the membership of many Alevis in a whole array of leftist organizations to which they wanted to remain loyal. For the "Civilized Life" activists who were my informants, the internal dynamics of the Alevi movement was mostly left unrecognized. My middle-class secularist informants were often naively enthusiastic about "Alevis," another abstract notion for them, like "the people." They felt that they had found exactly what they were looking for: the primordial inhabitants of Anatolia, the real Turks, against the habits of Islamists which they constructed to have been imported from Arab countries. From this point of view, Alevis constituted the society of Ataturkism.[32]

Ataturkist state officials, of the same political leaning as the secularist activists of "Civilized Life," began to employ the notion of society for their own ends around this time. Since their victory in the local elections, Welfarist officials had been arguing that they were the voice of society. Ataturkist officials found themselves in a situation where they had to invent a counter-definition of "society." Coming forward as representatives of the state, and preaching the principles of Ataturk, would no longer do, when the arena was left to the Welfare Party to define "society," "the public," or "the people" in its own terms. Ataturkist officials found that they had to incorporate "society" into their discourse and practice. At least, they had to produce an effect or an image of being representative of society.

The organization and celebration of Republic Day on October 29, 1994 is an excellent example of such an effort on the part of Ataturkist officials. In the late 1980s and early 1990s, anniversaries of the foundation of the Turkish republic had not been too meaningfully symbolic for most people in Turkey. Republic Day was about a disciplined school ceremony, an annual ritual of the military, a boring old program on state TV, an obligatory ceremony organized by municipalities and attended by state employees. Republic Day was better spent as a vacation day, a day off from school and work, not a day to observe a ritual. Even the old Ataturkist population did not celebrate Republic Day in the late 1980s and early 1990s. The Republic was taken for granted; it was, to a certain extent, naturalized, normalized, or commonsense. No exaggerated ceremonies were required.

In 1994, the story changed. A state ritual that ordinarily took place outside the full attention of the public assumed a different shape when Welfarist mayors, who had only recently obtained municipal power, refused to organize ceremonies for the republic's anniversary, contrary to what was expected of them by bureaucratic rules of etiquette. (In Turkey, mayors acquire their positions through elections, while governors are appointed by the state.) In reaction to Welfarist mayors, governors (*valiler*) all over the country decided to organize Republic Day 1994 as a major extravaganza. Because they are appointed by the state, up until now, governors have usually held old-school Ataturkist convictions. Hayri Kozakçıoğlu, governor of Istanbul, who took charge of orchestrating the big event, was no different. Ataturkist officials such as him felt that something had to be done to counteract the power of the Welfare Party. In refusing to celebrate the day, Welfarist mayors had been rebelling against the established etiquette of statecraft. Ataturkist officials were shaken to realize that they had to defend the state that they took for granted. The future of the republic was bleak, from their anxious perspective, not only because of the rise of an Islamist party, but also because of the ongoing war of the PKK against the Turkish army. Indeed, days before October 29, 1994, the PKK had planted two bombs in Izmir, one in front of a courtroom and one in a supermarket, killing one person and wounding many. Kozakçıoğlu and other governors organized Republic Day 1994 as a show of force against the Welfare Party and the PKK—what entrenched state officials saw as the two significant threats to the ideal of the longevity, integrity, and unity of the Turkish republic.

However, it would not have sufficed simply to aggrandize old genres of state ritual for the holiday. Governors had learned that those sorts of rituals alienated people; they didn't interest them. On the other hand, ceremonies organized by the Welfare Party, such as the anniversary of the conquest of Istanbul by the Ottomans (on May 29), were generating vast public enthusiasm and support. Something had to be done to transform the image of Republic Day from "a holiday of the state" to "a holiday of society." With the financial support of a number of large corporations, the governor of Istanbul invited thirty of the most popular singers to perform before the public in Taksim Square. These included singers of pop Turkish music like Sezen Aksu, performers of Turkish classical music, such as Muazzez Abacı, and even stars of *arabesk* like İbrahim Tatlıses and Orhan Gencebay, who were usually regarded without favor by the state's organs of culture. Advertisements and articles were submitted to the press, introducing the day as "a holiday of the people." Almost all mainstream newspapers and television channels characterized the preparations in the following way: "The most meaningful aspect of this year's celebrations is that, aside from official state ceremonies, groups of civil society, or, in other words, the people, are participating in the organization."[33]

Taksim Square, one of Istanbul's central sites for public demonstrations, was chosen as the location for this orchestrated celebration of secularism (see figure 6). It wasn't only that Taksim was an easily accessible central square for thousands of Istanbulis, but also that Taksim symbolized the "modern" (post-Ottoman / post-Islamic) phase of the country's history in contrast to other parts of Istanbul that held remains of the old Ottoman dynasty, presently reified by Islamists. In the middle of the square was the Monument of the Republic (*Cumhuriyet anıtı*), with a statue of Ataturk at its center. The monument had been erected in the first decades of state formation to symbolize Istanbul's new historical trajectory, toward secularism and modernity.

On the eve before the ceremony, Taksim Square was cleaned by streetsweepers of the Istanbul governorship. The square was to be transformed from its everyday "lived-in" appearance to a state of disinfection and cleanliness, the proper look of modernity. Yet those who labored to create this

Figure 6. Taksim Square decorated with Turkish flags in preparation for the "public" celebration of Republic Day, October 29, 1994. The banner reads, "Today think about Mustafa Kemal and the Republic. The Great Celebration in Taksim at 16:00."

sterility were to disappear discreetly before the celebration was due to begin the next afternoon; that would be the end of their assignment, until the finale of the ceremony when they would be solicited back to clean the remains of Republic Day paraphernalia. Traffic was redirected away from the square to make the whole area accessible to pedestrians. The square, then, would be reserved for the attendance of the people as constructed by the Ataturkist governorship.

Compared to previous years, there was indeed remarkably more activity around the holiday. With a flag campaign announced by the governor through the press, days before October 29, the entire city became peppered with Turkish flags. Red and white hats, flags, balloons, and pins and posters of Ataturk were on sale everywhere in the city (see figure 7). On October 29, Taksim square was quite full of people. Men and women of all ages, along with children, walked on İstiklal street toward the square with flags in one hand, sandwiches, candies, and other tidbits in the other. There were almost no veiled women in sight; I noticed only a couple. And the event was not even well attended by women immigrants from Anatolia who loosely covered their hair. Almost all the women standing to wait for the event were "open" (açık) in the contemporary Turkish idiomatic sense, referring to women who do not use headscarves in any fashion, who wear "Westernized" clothes, and who do not abide by Islamic prescriptions to cover. Nor did it seem well attended by the people from the surrounding neighborhoods, which had cast a high percentage of votes to the Welfare Party. Indeed, when I crossed the main street that separated the square from the (now) shantytown of Tarlabaşı, I noticed that October 29 was no extraordinary day in this part of the city. For the poor Kurdish, gypsy, Syriac-Christian, and other families and the gay and transvestite community of Tarlabaşı, Republic Day had no significance, despite the major ordeal orchestrated by the governorship to attract the public through musical events. The inhabitants of this neighborhood, most of whom dressed in village attire, were nowhere to be seen on the square, in spite of the fact that their homes were closer to the site of the event than it must have been for all those Ataturkists who would have had to travel a long time to come for this special occasion. Only the flower-selling gypsy women from across the street had taken their usual seats on the side wall of Taksim Square permitted to them by the municipality, going on with their trade on that "special day." Some street sellers from Tarlabaşı or other shantytowns of the city had come to make a living with their meatball and tripe stands, chestnuts on charcoal, cotton candies, popcorn, Turkish flags, Ataturk pins, and red and white hats. But these vendors were not allowed in the square, which was guarded by armed police. They could stand only on the edges of the festival.

The program began with a speaker on a large stage proclaiming, "For

Figure 7. Boy selling Turkish flags on Republic Day.

the first time the people are taking possession of their holiday with their organizations of civil society!" And then, in a condescending tone, "From now on, let us take charge of all of our holidays, promise?" "Promise!" cried hundreds of people, in response. The speaker was of course not referring to religious holidays, but to national holidays. "For what? For the republic!" the speaker cried again, and "How happy is the one who declares himself a Turk!" he exclaimed, repeating a saying of Ataturk, in an attempt to thrill the audience. "We have gathered in this square, which holds symbolic meaning for residents of Istanbul, around the monument of Ataturk. Below me, men and women from every walk of life are waving flags!" The band of the Turkish Armed Forces trotted its way through İstiklal street, and then, in a circle around the Monument for the Republic where a place for the soldiers had been reserved. A helicopter flew over the square as many waved their Turkish flags up in the air. The band of the Kuleli military highschool marched in as well, to be met with hearty clapping. A moment of silence was observed for Ataturk and "for soldiers who have died for our state's indivisible unity." The national anthem was sung, as a crowd of voices was heard from one corner, chanting "Down with the PKK!" The master of ceremonies screamed into the microphone as he announced the upcoming exciting events. "All these artists are here to celebrate Republic Day with you," he said. "They are here for our soldiers who are defending the Turkish state's indivisible unity!" The rest of the program was a concert, featuring all the best of Turkish music. The mass culture produced by the culture industry was here in Taksim Square posing in the garb of civil society: the image of popular support for Ataturkism desired by the governors.

But "the people's holiday" had to be organized with much security. Police and soldiers lined the square, perhaps outnumbering the people in attendance. At every corner, check-points had been installed to inspect the bags and clothes of all passersby. The governorship of Istanbul was worried that the Islamist terrorist group İBDA-C, the PKK, or a leftist organization would sabotage the event. Much police control was required for the national holiday to be staged.

On the evening of the celebration, secular mainstream TV channels, public and private, made a big deal of the event. "Today, citizens gathered in Taksim only for one thing: to protect the life of the republic," was the headline of the popularly watched ATV channel. And the report went on: "Taksim is living the cheerfulness of a major love for the republic. The only difference this year was the heightened interest of the people. From the ages of seven to seventy, the people were there. This gave a different meaning to the holiday this year." The state-supported TRT's news was not much different. "Every year the demand for national celebrations is increasing," according to the TRT report. "The people gathered in Taksim

Square voluntarily. For the first time the holiday was celebrated without a formal military ceremony." The news was followed with a program presenting statistics on the modernization of Turkey from the foundation of the secular republic to the present day: advancements in education, business, tourism, and industry; more railways, factories, roads, oil refineries, ballet performances, planes, women parliamentarians, and other indices of "progress." "It is due to Ataturk that our country was able to arrive at this stage," was the summary of the television report. The state of affairs was under threat, especially in 1994, after seventy-one years of the republic. Mainstream media was there, at least on that day, to protect it, preaching Ataturkism, with an implicit message both for the Welfare Party and for the PKK, the two social movements that were perceived to threaten the survival of the Turkish state.[34]

Even though Ataturkist officials and the mainstream secular press presented Republic Day 1994 as "a day orchestrated by civil society," as my ethnographic account illustrates, it is not easy to distinguish empirically between the state and society on the site of this event, any more than it is difficult and unwise, I argue, in many other cases. I will suggest that this was neither the state nor society, problematizing the analytical distinction state and society. What was, however, possible to illustrate empirically, is that Ataturkist officials, like the governor of Istanbul, were attempting to manipulate the term "civil society" for their own ends. There was, then, a discourse of society, and many people did attend the celebrations. Yet those among the audience who had not come merely to attend a free concert were there to stand for one (Ataturkist) as opposed to another (Welfarist or Kurdist) face of the state. One should perhaps be cautious in identifying this scene as an illustration of a reified notion of a public sphere or the organization of civil society in Turkey. Here, as in other ethnographic sites, it is unclear where the state ends and society begins, and vice versa.[35]

The Agency of "Society"

This chapter has been an attempt to critique analyses that have reified the category of "civil society" in descriptions of Turkey following the military coup of 1980. Rather than readily employing the state-versus-society dichotomy in an effort to understand social phenomena, I have used as my object of study the distinction between its public use and social scientific discourse. In this reversal of the question (and of perspective), civil society, the public, or the people did not appear as phenomena sui generis on the social ground. In the 1980s and 1990s, the concept of "civil society" was employed, incorporated, and implicated in competing discourses of power in a politics of culture. The notions of civil society, the people, society, and the public were appropriated and used in different fashions and contexts. Competing claims and meanings were projected onto society by Islamists and secularists involved in social movements aspiring to state power. The ethnographic material of this chapter illustrates that "society," "the public," or "the people" do not have singular or essential references. Rather, these terms are context-bound and contingent. The political is generated in their construction.

Given these observations, one may no longer find it helpful to search for separate domains for state and society, power and resistance. Perhaps the peculiarity that ought to be observed regarding the 1980s and 1990s in Turkey is the incorporation of the terms of civil society in discourses of power and not the linear development of civil society. Civil society was transformed into a symbolic ground on which legitimate state power was going to be based. Enforcing means of statecraft proved no longer to work without simultaneous efforts to generate statisms of sorts from society. State and society became enmeshed to the point where in most cases it was no longer possible ethnographically to distinguish spontaneous expressions of civil society from discourses of state power, and vice versa. New analytical terms and concepts are needed for the study of these complex relations of power in which the terms of "society" are implicated in discourses of "state."

Taking the references of the state for granted, social scientists have predominantly searched for it in the realms of formal government, public institutions, or official personalities. The material presented here directs us to new directions of inquiry for an anthropology of the state. In the first instance, we have encountered people from society organizing, through their own agency, shows of support for the state. Here I observed a particular enmeshed relation of sorts between people and state. The initiative for these rituals of statist thralldom did not appear to lie completely in the agency of statespeople. It is crucial to point out that a certain level of agency was in the hands and initiative of the young men who were walking in the streets holding flags of Turkey. I have indicated that young men benefited in various ways from this engagement with statist culture. Scholars of society have given little study to this kind of agency, which is, to a certain extent, spontaneously generated to reproduce the state. Here we see that the realm of society, if such a domain can ever be defined, cannot be mapped directly onto concepts of resistance to the state. Public agency is oftentimes deployed for conservative purposes, as in the context of fascisms. A reification of civil society keeps us from studying this sort of personal and collective, popular involvement with the state.

On the other hand, statism does not exist only spontaneously. In fact, there can be no absolute spontaneity in histories of power. Statism also persists because it is enforced. My ethnographic material also draws attention to this flipside. Consider, once again, the celebration of Republic Day 1994. Here I described a historical contingency when statespeople and Ataturkist activists deployed the terms of "society" and "the people" to produce a statist culture of the sort they desired. Republic Day was orchestrated, to an important extent, by statespeople in need of democratic legitimation. It is no wonder that, in the end, Republic Day appeared to be organized and attended by the people. This apparent public participation in the celebration for the republic was the truth effect of a statist discourse. Public support for the state, in this instance, was constructed and manufactured by statespeople.

Statism, then, persists through both repressive and productive mechanisms of power, not only one or the other as temporally privileged by Michel Foucault. There is a level of agency and spontaneity among the so-called people, a willing initiative to stand for the state. But, there is also an enforcement of support for the state. The difference between the two, spontaneity and enforcement, is blurred. It is perhaps within this blurred zone that power so effectively operates (and where it is regenerated) in contemporary Turkey and the statist world we live in today.

5

Fantasies for the State: Hype, Cynicism, and the Everyday Life of Statecraft

> A Mercedes automobile drove into the bottom of
> a truck, but perhaps it was the state that found
> itself under the truck.
> —Sabah *newspaper, November 16, 1996*

> Ideals of freedom ordinarily emerge to vanquish
> their imagined immediate enemies, but in this
> move they frequently recycle and reinstate rather
> than transform the terms of domination that
> generated them.
> —*Wendy Brown, 1995*

Does the "State" Exist?

In an article reviewing sociological work on "the state," Philip Abrams has suggested, "Since the 17th century the idea of the state has been a cardinal feature of the process of subjection" (1988, 75). Sociologists had been studying the state as if it were a real and unambiguous entity, coherent and unified enough to be empirically identified. Little did they realize, Abrams notes, that in assuming the existence of state as a tangible and decipherable object, they were reproducing what was the greatest device of modern power. The notion that there is such a thing as the state—real, neutral, and stable above governments, the army, political parties, bureaucrats, schools, or the police—is the greatest ideological myth of modern times (68). Power, or what Abrams calls "politically organized subjection," is about the careful maintenance of the illusion of state as reality (63). Were we not appeased by the mystical idea of state, Abrams proposes, the greatest means of modern power would collapse. So, he writes,

> The state is not the reality which stands behind the mask of political practice. It is itself the mask which prevents our seeing political practice as it is. It is, one could almost say, the mind of a mindless world, the purpose of purposeless conditions, the opium of the citizen. . . . The state comes into being as a structuration in political practice; it starts its life as an implicit construct; it is then reified—as the res publica, the public reification, no less—and acquires an overt

symbolic identity progressively divorced from practice as an illusory account of practice. The ideological function is extended to a point where conservatives and radicals alike believe that their practice is not directed at each other but at the state; the world of illusion prevails. The task of the sociologist is to demystify; and in this context that means attending to the senses in which the state does not exist rather than to those in which it does (82).

Abrams is arguing that the state, as such, doesn't exist. Social scientists and political activists have built their discourses and practices on a basic unquestioned premise of the existence of state as entity and unity. As Marx had unwrapped "commodities" in illustrating the social relations of inequality that went into their making, Abrams addresses what he conceives to be a prevailing false consciousness about the state. Employing the Marxist notion of ideology to unwrap, this time, the state, Abrams suggests that an overturning of this ideology lies in a massive realization of its fakeness, of the truth behind the pretension, the abhorrent secret behind the everyday order of things. In Marx, labor value was the kernel of reality that became glossed by commodity fetishism under capitalist relations of power. Extending the critical tradition from the domain of the economic to that of the political, Abrams would like to illustrate that unequal relations of power underlie what is imagined to be a real and stable state. Like the commodity, the state is not a thing with inherent value, but, in Abrams' words, "an idea." Writing within conditions of statist possibility, Abrams argues that the state looms above other ideas (ideologies) as a central artifact of modern power. If we were to realize that there is, in fact, no state (as such), the greatest means of contemporary political subjection, Abrams wishfully thinks, will topple over itself.

Two important contemporary thinkers, Benedict Anderson and Michael Taussig, have structured their critical projects on versions of a Marxist frame of lifting false consciousness. In writing the history of the nation as the result of print capitalism and the wide distribution of newspapers in one dominant language, Anderson (1991) would like to enlighten his readers as to "the imagined" (as opposed to the primordial, real, or autochthonous) quality of nations. Nationalist ideology pretends to the ever-present existence of the nation as if there were such an extra-historical or originally distinct entity or community. Anderson's work is aimed at what he has termed the "imagination" of nations. Implicitly, emancipation from nationalism may perhaps be achieved with an awareness of the lack of foundation under the notion of the nation. Michael Taussig undertakes a comparable exercise with the state. His guiding concept is not "imagination" (as is Anderson's), but "fetishism."[1] In this project, too, what initially seems to be a deconstructive approach to a modern discourse of power (in the Foucauldian or Derridean sense),[2] evolves, like Anderson's project, into a task of exposing ideology (in the Marxist sense), of illustrating the truth (the history of social relations) behind the construction (in this case "the fetish").

Bringing the notion of "fetishism" back home to the (Western) place where it was invented as a category to describe practices of the (colonized) "other," Taussig has advanced the study of the state. He draws attention to what he calls "the place of the sacred in the modern State" (1992, 117). Like the totem, which had been theorized by Durkheim to be worshipped for representing not a loved animal or object but the greater idea of society, the "State" too, according to Taussig, is revered (125).[3] The state is the greatest fetish of contemporary society. Answering an age-old sociological question, Taussig suggests that with the historical dwindling of religious power, the idea of the state replaced that of God (130, 114). "It is to the peculiar sacred and erotic attraction, even thralldom, combined with disgust, which the State holds for its subjects, that I wish to draw attention in my drawing the figure of State fetishism," Taussig writes (111). The work of colonial officers, public administrators, governors, the army, or police is about upkeeping a god-like notion of the existence of a state. Yet, what is more worrisome, from Taussig's point of view, is the complicity of those in the margins of stately power in the activity of reifying the state (132).

In following Abrams's sociology, Taussig's ethnography is a critique of reification in the Marxist sense. His work on medicine, titled "Reification and the Consciousness of the Patient," is an even better illustration of the ethnographic task he has mapped out for himself. Disease, too (like commodities and the state), is a site of power in contemporary conditions of capitalist possibility where power conceals itself in the form of a fetish. If "disease" is not disease, then what is it? (The same question could be posed for the state from this particular critical perspective, which ponders what lies behind the representation). "I am going to argue," Taussig writes, "that things such as the signs and symptoms of disease, as much as the technology of healing, are not 'things-in-themselves,' are *not only* biological and physical, but *are also* signs of social relations disguised as natural things, concealing their roots in human reciprocity" (83, his emphasis). For example, when a doctor announces that "this patient is a hysteric!" he denies the agency that he employed in reading the pieces of available information and gathering them in the consulting room. The doctor has pulled the fragmented bits of medical results together to create an account of hysteria (a category of disease). Yet, in the final instance of declaring his diagnosis, he conceals the social relations that went into manufacturing it (88). Taussig's ethnographic reading is a political critique of the "thingification" of historically situated relations of unequal power between social individuals. Beyond reification, he would like to generate consciousness in the patient. In the following statement, he outlines what he would like ethnography, like therapy, to be: "The real task of therapy calls for an archeology of the implicit in such a way that the processes by which social relations are mapped into diseases are brought to light, de-reified, and in doing so liberate the potential for dealing with antagonistic contradictions and breaking the chains of oppression" (93). In overcoming false consciousness, the patient will be cured, the colonized will overcome the imprint of colonialism, the citizen will emancipate herself from subjection under the state. In exposing "fetishism" (in coming to realization), the social relations that operate under the aura of a constructed signifier will collapse.

Taussig is a secularist. He does not appear to believe in the sacred.[4] One could perhaps even argue that he is heir of an Enlightenment tradition of secularism, where religion (belief, deification, reification) is understood to be at the heart of evil. Taussig's work on the state is meant to demonstrate the religious qualities of a system that soberly poses to be secular. One could read Taussig's work, as represented in *The Nervous System*, through Marx's famous aphorism that religion is "the opium of the people." In his critiques of power in this book, Taussig attempts to illustrate that this is, in his words, "a man-made world," socially, politically, historically (89). Illusions to the contrary only serve regimes of subservience.

This ethnography follows on Michael Taussig's work on the state. Soldiers' farewells, rallies for national sports teams, and flag campaigns (among other everyday practices of ritualistic exaltation of the Turkish state) can be read as Turkish examples for what Taussig calls "state fetishism." Taussig's work is valuable in pointing at the statist culture that persists, at times, in the domains of society.

Yet, there is further ethnographic material that a Taussigian approach to relations between society and the state (at least in Turkey) would fail to bring to attention. There is, indeed, that realm of "state fetishism" of the sort I have exemplified, among pan-Turkists, secularists, Islamists, as well as leftists. However, what is also the order of the day in contemporary Turkey, along with public demonstrations of thralldom for the state, is mundane everyday criticism of statespeople and ridicule of the state. If we were to approach the subjects of the Turkish state as "falsely conscious" (as an ethnography of state fetishism would have it), we would overlook the widespread everyday habit of narrating stories of disgust and abhorrence vis-à-vis the state. Taussig's approach to the state is limited in addressing this ambiguity, or the inbetween of thralldom and critique (ideology and resistance) where the political in public life may be positioned. In this chapter, I study ordinary everyday practices of producing stories and critical commentary about the state. My informants did not appear to be "falsely conscious" as Abrams, Taussig, or Anderson would present them by implication. But, and this is a crucial point, I am not proposing a critique of false consciousness, here, of the sort developed by James Scott (1985) in his famous work on resistance. As I have argued in the last chapter, studies of resistance (as well as of civil society) in anthropology have risked overlooking the more remarkable phenomenon of public participation in reproducing systems of power. On this point, I follow Taussig. What I am suggesting, then, is not another move to study resistance: resistance studies have, we could argue, missed studying how power is regenerated in the very domain of so-called resistance. But we do not have to choose only between power or resistance, state or civil society, state fetishism or the lifting of false consciousness. Approaches that would tilt either side of these binary oppositions wishfully promise liberation on the horizon, after the disentanglement of ideological constructions. In the ethnographic context I have studied, it was not possible to analyze such an overturning in consciousness.

In following Peter Sloterdijk and Slavoj Žižek, I will propose that "cynicism" was the common structure of feeling in the historically specific context that I studied. "Cynicism" describes the public experience of the political in contemporary Turkey. I argue that cynicism encapsulates both state fetishism and everyday public critiques of the state. Like a self-fulfilling prophecy, cynicism as a habitus (Bourdieu 1991) of public and everyday life in Turkey during the 1990s reinstates the state over and again, even when it is obvious to everyone who doesn't have their head in the ground that the state is not a unity. I agree with Žižek in arguing that contemporary state power needs cynical subjects to maintain itself, and with Sloterdijk, who suggests that cynicism is the necessary condition of contemporary fascisms. In other words, cynicism does not help us to achieve emancipation from the chains of statism, but to remain forever (foreseeably) locked into it.

What is cynicism? In a section of his work entitled "Cynicism as a Form of Ideology," Žižek differentiates his analysis of the political from that of Marx and certain Marxists.[5] In Marx, the subject was understood necessarily (or originally) to relate to the world with a certain lack of consciousness, with "a misrecognition" (Žižek 1995, 2). "They do not know it, but they are doing it" is the phrase that summarizes Marxist approach to ideology (28). In following Lacan, Žižek grants more agency to historical subjects (which makes him not more, but less optimistic than Marxists about possibilities for social change). He counterbalances the classic Marxist phrase about false consciousness, with "they know very well what they are doing, but still, they are doing it" (29). Žižek perceptively argues that in contemporary societies, people are aware of the falsity of ideology. They see through ideological pretension and consciously verbalize critique. Even more, contemporary subjects are conscious of the reality of social relations that underlie icons of reification. And yet (and this is the point), the same people take actions upon the world as if they did not know, as if they were deluded by ideology, as if ideology were reality. This is cynicism. And it is what more accurately characterizes contemporary experiences of the political in Turkey. In Žižek's words, "the prevailing ideology is that of cynicism" (33). He writes,

> [I]n contemporary societies, democratic or totalitarian, that cynical distance, laughter, irony, are, so to speak, part of the game. The ruling ideology is not meant to be taken seriously or literally. . . . The cynical subject is quite aware of the distance between the ideological mask and the social reality, but he nonetheless still insists upon the mask. . . . Cynical reason is no longer naive, but is a paradox of an enlightened false consciousness: one knows the falsehood very well, one is well aware of a particular interest hidden behind an ideological universality, but still one does not renounce it (28–29).[6]

Žižek puts Lacan in dialogue, or argument, with Marx. He borrows his understanding of "doing in spite of knowing" from Lacan's definition of the psychoanalytic "symptom." The traditional psychoanalytic procedure was based on the process of interpretation. It was assumed that if the subject were made aware of his symptom (the childhood events that held a determination over him), the symptom would disappear, the subject would be psychologically cured.[7] But for Lacan, the problem was located elsewhere. The procedure of interpretation does not usually deliver the results that it promises. Analysis is often stuck, even (or especially) at the moment when the subject appears to be crisply conscious of his symptom. The question, then, for Lacan is "why, in spite of its interpretation, does the symptom not dissolve itself; why does it persist?" (Žižek 1995, 74). Lacan analyzes this psychoanalytic roadblock through the concept of "enjoyment" (*jouis-sense*). The subject enjoys his symptom; his symptom has become his reality; it is his character; it is what distinguishes him from others, what gives him meaning and consistency in life; he does not know how he would manage without it (74–75).

The term in Lacanian psychoanalysis for a symptom that persists in spite of interpretation is "fantasy." The *jouisseur* maintains the symptom even though he has come to understand its cause. A pathological situation which remains even beyond "fantasy" is, in turn, termed "sinthome" (Žižek 1995, 74–75). And so, even though he knows, now full well, that this symptom is gradually eating him up, the subject persists in repeating it. He chooses to live with it, rather than without it. The imagined consequences of overcoming the symptom (what looms in the subject's mind as a possible future of liberation) produce more anxiety (even fear) in the subject than the state of surrendering to it. The subject signs his own death statement. He'd rather do that than risk the unknown.[8]

What Lacan analyzes in the (psychoanalytically) "fantastic," Žižek studies in the political.[9] I will use his insights in dialogue with Taussig's as they prove extremely helpful in studying the political in contemporary public life in Turkey. In a Taussigian narrative of history, the Turkish state (with the violence and deceit that underlies its ideology of secular democracy) could be overcome (dissolved) if its fetishists were made aware of their complicity in upkeeping it. As I illustrated in the last chapter, such fetishism of the state exists in contemporary Turkey. However, the situation shows itself to be more serious (or, in Lacanian terms, "fantastic") than Taussig's implicit faith in a future overcoming. Fetishists of the state are not duped by ideology. If that were so, it would be easy to make them realize (on the part of organic intellectuals or shamans in yagé nights)[10] that they were mistaken. There is more agency in public fetishism than Taussig's reading will allow (or, for that matter, than will a Foucauldian approach, which sees such fetishism as immersion in a statist "discourse"). As they perform everyday rituals of reification of the state, fetishists know that the state does not exist as an entity, as such. Yet, as Žižek's insights would have it, they persist in carrying on with their everyday practices *as if* the state were a unity, actively and with agency reinstating the fetish.

Since the mid-1990s (a time of stately dissolution with a public awareness of circles of violence and corruption), people of various political affiliations in Turkey have become conscious of the contradictions and complexity of the notion of the Turkish state. The social reality behind the ideological façade is evident probably to most people in today's Turkey. "People," to use tentatively this problematic category, do not have to be rendered formally conscious; they have more consciousness and agency in their everyday actions upon the world than a Marxist reading (i.e., in its Taussigian version) would have it. The question to ask is, Why do those who have critical consciousness available to them persist in "doing," in Žižek's terms, *as if* the notion of the Turkish state were straightforward?

The problem resides not in the knowing, but in the doing, according to Žižek. And this is why I would propose that Žižek's (Lacan's) notion of "fantasy" is more useful for ethnography than Anderson's concept of "imagination," Taussig's interpretation of "the fetish," and certain uses of Foucault's notion of "discourse." This is because Žižek's interest deliberately lies in the practice of everyday life, the domain studied by anthropologists. Consider the following passage:

> The lesson to be drawn from this concerning the social field is above all that belief, far from being an "intimate," purely mental state, is always materialized in our effective social activity: belief supports the fantasy which regulates social reality. . . . [What needs to be illustrated is] the mise-en-scène of the fantasy which is at work in the midst of social reality itself: we all know very well that bureaucracy is not all-powerful, but our "effective" conduct in the presence of

bureaucratic machinery is already regulated by a belief in its almightiness. . . . What we call "social reality" is in the last resort an ethical construction; it is supported by a certain *as if* (we act as if we believe in the almightiness of bureaucracy, as if the President incarnates the Will of the People, as if the Party expresses the objective interest of the working class . . .). (Žižek 1995, 36).

Žižek draws our attention to the habitual performance of everyday life practices that is done in full consciousness of their counterproductive (or self-destructive) quality.[11] This is the cynical contemporary agent. This is what more characteristically describes political subjectivity today. We are automatons and we know it.

However, somewhere along the line, Žižek confuses the knowing with the believing. He writes on behalf of an all-encompassing "we." In his reading, "we" (all of us in the contemporary world?) recognize ideology. "We" are conscious of it as farce. And yet, "we" pretend as though we were unaware. On the sites for such pretension (in our material actions upon the world, in our activity), Žižek analyzes a "belief." According to him, in doing as if we didn't know, we ultimately start to "believe" in what we do. In ethnographic sections below, I attempt to situate Žižek's "we" more historically, to move beyond it in analyzing my informants' lives in the context of their particular social experiences. Žižek's "we" contradicts anthropological attention to specificity and historical contingency. As Žižek would have it, certain social groups in Turkey indeed begin to "believe" in what they do. The participants in the ritual for the departing soldier, especially the pan-Turkist nationalists among them, and certain of the ralliers for Turkish soccer teams, for example, may have become believers in Žižek's terms. And yet others were conscious of ideology, even as they reinstated it by default. They took action upon the world as if they weren't aware, but they did not turn into believers. They pragmatically held onto their "symptom" (their alienation) in order to survive within the limits of the constraints upon them. They recognized, but could not discard their symptom. Knowledge of ideology may, at times, mesh with belief, but not at others. There isn't a "we" that universally approaches ideology in an identical manner. We need to study situational and relative, positional relations with the state. This is where an anthropological approach is needed.

Žižek argues that the condition of conscious submission to the state is more a necessity than an unexpected default of contemporary regimes of power. Power would not be power if it were to expect rational submission from its subjects, if subjects were to submit only after having reasoned that "this is justice." Likewise, one would not be a believer if one had to rationalize the existence of God; if religious ideology were dependent on such positivism, then it would not be stable, for the day would come when one or another person could prove the opposite. On the contrary, Žižek argues, power requires a form of irrational submission whereby the subject is conscious of the fact that there is ideology, but prefers to pretend that there isn't. Žižek writes, "It follows, from this constitutively senseless character of the Law, that we must obey it not because it is just, good or even beneficial, but simply because it is the law" (1995, 37). Žižek once again argues that the site for such submission is everyday practice. As one is already aware of ideology and would not submit to it consciously, one acts upon the world as if she or he didn't know. And in the process of pretending, one ultimately (consciously yet irrationally) ends up actually believing in the ideology. Žižek cites Pascal in his analysis of this experience of the political: "Leave rational argumentation and submit yourself simply to ideological ritual, stupify yourself by repeating the meaningless gestures, act as if you already believe, and the belief will come by itself" (39). I will agree with Žižek that in cases of extreme disenchantment (when the doing as a disciplinary activity may overtake the knowing), belief may ensue. Up to here his argument is deeply insightful in deciphering experience under certain forms of totalitarianism. And yet I will illustrate that there are other ways of doing and relating to ideology, ones that do not transform into belief in nationalism.

The context for Žižek's theory and history-writing is Eastern Europe, which he interprets as neither "totalitarian" nor "democratic" in its regimes of state.[12] The case of the Turkish state is complex, but perhaps it could be characterized (at present) as a "totalitarian democracy."[13] The context is different from that described by Žižek for Eastern Europe. As my ethnographic examples of Islamists' and Ataturkist officials' organizations suggest, there has recently been an effort on the part of statespeople in Turkey to render their executions and ideologies "rational" from the point of view of "the people." There has been a procedural democratic process of legitimation at work, which asks politicians for proof that they are more just than their competitors from other parties. The point of the matter is, however, that few politicians are successful in convincing their subjects that they are just. And behind them stands the coercive force of the army and the police (the precipitation of the last military coup), which reminds citizens that if they were to refuse to act as though they believed in the ideology of the state, their freedoms would be at stake. The state of affairs in Turkey during the 1990s was complex enough not to be decipherable by only one or another (Weberian) ideal type of power.[14] Yet in its historically contingent complexity and situational variability, a certain form of cynicism, comparable to that described by Žižek, exists. Cynicism, or doing as if one doesn't know, is a technique of contemporary Turkish state power. Arguably, cynicism is the condition on which the Turkish state still maintains an existence despite having repeatedly reached the verge of a breakdown.

In his *Critique of Cynical Reason*, Peter Sloterdijk, on whose insightful work Žižek's comments on "cynicism" are based, draws an interesting picture of the cynical social agent. Sloterdijk's critique is written from the context of Germany in the late 1970s and early 1980s, time of the demise of the 1960s student movement and of the incorporation of former radicals into the lifestyle (if not the consciousness) of the system. So he writes, in particular, about those who were enlightened by the tradition of critical theory, who were politically active, yet who, in the interest of self-preservation in "the new world," ended up "being realistic" (or "grown up," as he ironically puts it) and adapted (at least only their actions) to contemporary expectations. Such is his description of former leftists who turned into businesspeople, bankers, lawyers, parliamentarians, and advertising agents. What is interesting about this social group is that, in spite of being successfully integrated, they have not shelved their political awareness, because, as Sloterdijk claims, "consciousness-raising is irreversible" (1988, 5).[15] They can see the fraud and the violence behind the everyday order of things, yet they prefer to do as if they didn't, in order to carry on. And they have transformed enlightenment into a "chic bitterness" about the activities in which they are involved (5).

Sloterdijk's description of the afterlife of the 1960s generation in Germany is interesting for someone reflecting upon the equivalent of this social group in Turkey. Indeed, in the 1980s and 1990s, intellectuals and activists from a variety of lower- to middle-class backgrounds who used to be active in 1970s socialist groups in Turkey became the forerunners of the culture industry, the organizers of a consumer capitalist culture in favor of economic liberalization. Although significant numbers among them pursue politics through a conviction in democracy, liberalism, and civil society, Sloterdijk's characterization would be welcome here as well in describing the actual everyday practice in which such people are cynically involved (in Turkey, especially journalism and advertising). What I have observed in this social group in Turkey is an attitude of cool resignation, affectation, and put-on apathy that permits the upkeeping of everyday practices. Along with this, is a crisp knowledge and consciousness of the terrifying state of things expressed in a language of ridicule. The idea is that things are "just bad" and there is not much hope in trying to change them. Better to try to save one's self and one's immediate family within the wreckage created by the state. "We have accepted the situation as it is; we have become indifferent," was the most common expression I encountered among intellectuals in Istanbul in the summer of 1997. Cynicism. There is consciousness about the terrifying state of affairs, there is also consciousness about one's own indifference to it. This is not a bowing-down form of submission. This submission to power involves a high degree of agency.

I do not, in this ethnography, give detailed attention to those from the generation of the 1960s, a good number of whom constitute today's professional middle class in Turkey. Sloterdijk writes the history of the incorporation of this generation into capitalist disciplines of power and finds hope in another group, whom he presents as the "kynics" in juxtaposition to the "cynics": those who do not adapt, but who resist the system through irony and laughter.[16] Through the characterization "kynic," Sloterdijk would like to refer to groups from lower social classes who do not have the means to adapt to the capitalist system and who turn it topsy-turvy through humor. Against his "cynics," the generation of the 1960s, Sloterdijk upholds his "kynics" as a subaltern group among whom the kernels of resistance may be located. In turn, in the context that I study, I have not come across such a subaltern group or practice to idealize (or to reify). In the interest of furthering the critique of cynicism, I will take Sloterdijk's argument one step further and suggest that the "enlightened false consciousness" he writes about (1988, 5) is the prerogative not only of the formerly organic intellectuals but also, albeit in a different way, of those who are idealistically referred to as "the people." As Akhil Gupta suggests, every sort of relation to the state is situational (1995, 390). I encountered forms of enlightened false consciousness in relation to the state among members of lower and working classes who have never gone through "consciousness-raising." Here, there is consciousness about the state as farce, a recognition or awareness of alienation. And yet, simultaneously, there is a pragmatic recycling of statism in everyday life. To put it in Lacanian terms, the so-called people have discovered their symptom, but they cling to it out of worldly necessity. For these cynics, the line between carrying or deconstructing the symptom is thin: it is the mark between livelihood and death; the symptom is a tool of survival. In most cases, the symptom is about an income, about bread and butter. Alienation is self-evident, but what else could be done? The material effects of the idea of state as a construction are sharply felt and they have to be accommodated. But in the process of this accommodation, the state is regenerated. It is in the activities of such individuals (coined "the people") in which the idea of the state is maintained in the manner in which it prevails. It is in these margins of statecraft (Taussig 1992) that the state is located. In the realm of this mundane cynicism, some, at particular times, turn to be more statist than the state, even favoring a military intervention.[17] Technically, there is a very thin line between this cynicism, which is about survival, and a statist culture. Public statism, as reproduced in the margins, may keep a politician from endeavoring or achieving favorable change; it may prevent a general from suggesting that the Turkish army withdraw from Cyprus or scare a politician from suggesting that Kurdish be recognized as a legitimate language. It is on this kind of situated cynicism that I focus my attention in this chapter. Ignoring this, in a wishful search for a subaltern group that resists, would be to overlook sites, in the margins, where the state is reproduced through mundane everyday life practices. In the case of certain situated actors, an awareness of the fraud of state is an ordinary as well as a cynical approach to organizing everyday life in order to be able to survive in this world. It is to the life of one such person that I now attend.

Mundane Cynicism

Saniye worked as janitor in a municipal office building in Istanbul. She had worked doing odd jobs—housekeeping, cooking, and cleaning—for as long as she could remember, like most immigrants from her village in the Black Sea region of Turkey. Saniye had arrived in Istanbul as a teenager with her husband, Cemil, and they now lived with their three children in a shantytown that bordered one of the wealthiest districts of Istanbul. A busy highway separated her neighborhood from that of duplex cottages inhabited by upper-class families. For many years she had commuted on a daily basis to work as a servant in a large four-bedroom apartment in that posh part of the city. Now she worked all day doing similar things for the state: wiping the floors, cleaning the windows, cooking, and washing dishes in a municipal building. In the evenings, she would return home on a minibus shared with coworkers from her neighborhood. Saniye's husband had been unemployed for a long period. Therefore the survival of the family was largely in Saniye's hands, with assistance from her elder daughter who had recently started to work as a sales clerk in a clothing shop. In the evenings, Saniye would quickly prepare a meal and spend the rest of her night ironing or sewing and chatting, while watching TV.

The seven or eight o'clock news on one of the private TV channels was not to be missed in Saniye's home. Keeping up to date with the news was a matter of survival, especially in big cities like Istanbul. Saniye could not read; she had never been sent to school. Through TV, she tried to get the information about politics that she needed in order to know what to expect in her environment. Having lived in Istanbul for all of their adult lives, Saniye and Cemil had developed a habit of watching the news, as if they had decided that the condition of the state had direct implications on their livelihood. Survival was about maintaining a source of income, and as such it was also about managing one's way within an unpredictable domain of state politics. It was as though Saniye knew, if she didn't articulate it as such, that the state was everywhere and that life was about walking through cracks and interstices that eluded the mechanisms of state. Saniye worked for a state office; she frequented the state hospital when one of her family members was unwell; her husband received a small amount of pension from the state every month; her younger daughter attended a state school; she often stood in line in the municipality's subsidized bread shops; she made sure she voted at election time—she had these sorts of relationships with the state. Yet she tried to keep a distance from the police, the court, and other more coercive organs of the state as much as she could.

Saniye had led a number of protests to demand better municipal services for her shantytown. On one occasion, she had called her friends and neighbors to walk to the district mayor's office when her neighborhood had been deprived of water for more than a couple of months. She had sat in the waiting room and refused to leave, until officers would allow her to speak to the mayor face-to-face. This was a conscious act of resistance in cooperation with other women from the shantytown. It was an act of resistance that took the state for granted. Saniye approached the mayor as if he were the state personified. She had gone to the state to complain about the state. Her act of resistance was by default a reinstatement of the state; in order to demand water for her neighborhood she had to behave, in her everyday life, as if the state were real. There was no other way of reestablishing the water. In order to survive, the habitus of an established statecraft had to be reproduced on a daily basis. Going to the mayorship to register a complaint was an everyday practice within (and not outside) the expectations of statecraft. One had to work within the parameters of the state in order to manage. In our conversations, Saniye would often remark, "The state has never worked for our good."

Saniye did not participate in any of the groups, gatherings, or demonstrations of Sufi orders active in her district, nor in any Islamist groups, which she explicitly abhorred. And as she felt distant from Islamists, neither did she feel a shared sense of purpose with the socialists who lived in her neighborhood or those she learned about through TV. There was an element of fetishist respect for certain representations of the state in Saniye's thoughts and consciousness. She spoke of the instigator of the military coup of 1980, General Kenan Evren, as "a man like Ataturk." Like many others who had rationalized the coup, Saniye would say, as if she were speaking common sense, that "if it weren't for him [the general], we would be gone." (She was referring to what was officially called "the state of anarchy" in the 1970s, with factionalism between right- and left-wing groups.) The generals had justified their intervention by arguing that they had come to rescue the state from dissolution. "After 12 September," Saniye said, referring to the date of the military intervention, "I was able to send my daughter to school with peace of mind." (Before the coup, she had been fearful of violent clashes between political groups in the high schools.) Indeed, Saniye revered the army and generals who had organized the coup. If she had been a member of any socialist group in the 1970s or 1980s, a critique of the army would have been part of her discourse. Saniye was fearful of leftist groups, including the PKK, and referred to them as "terrorists." In 1996, when the corrupt affairs of statespeople were revealed, Saniye said that she just wished the military would intervene.

When she watched TV in the evenings, Saniye listened to the voice of reporters with one ear turned off. She would carry on conversations with her children or neighbors as she simultaneously noticed important events depicted on the screen. However, in times of political crisis, she would deliberately stay up, sometimes until four in the morning to listen carefully to political discussion programs on TV and follow the news. She would absorb the statements made by representatives of different political groups; she would argue aloud with those with whom she disagreed (especially with Welfarists at the time); she would make fun of them, make faces at them, and curse at them as she watched. During such evening gatherings, sitting together to watch the news, people in Saniye's household talked about "the fraudulent nature of statespeople" and about "the wretched quality of the state." Making clever, funny, and cynical remarks about statespeople and about the state was a favorite pastime and preoccupation for Saniye and the people in her life. She liked especially to catch politicians tripping over their words or contradicting themselves when they wanted to deliver morally wholesome self-portraits.

In each of our daily meetings, Saniye would reflect on the TV news from the previous day. TV was a central medium through which she related to the state, a role TV has occupied more generally in Turkish public life over the last couple of decades. Saniye was extremely interested in what happened in the state and she followed the episodes through the media. She remembered minute details about the underhanded activities of particular statespeople. She talked at length about corruption scandals. She repeated criticisms of ministers, parliamentarians, mayors, and the police to her friends at work, on the minibus on her way to the municipality, and to her family at home. At work as a state employee, she would recount funny stories about the state to the municipal officers, the secretaries, and to others who ate her food and used the offices that she cleaned.

When news came of the secret dealings of a Welfare official called Mercümek, for example, Saniye was shocked. Journalists had revealed that funds which the Welfare Party had collected in Turkey to support Bosnian refugees had gone to the party's private bank accounts in Germany. The event was on the agenda of TV stations for a whole month and so it came up in Saniye's everyday conversations. Saniye was very upset to learn that money for charity had found its way into the pockets of the Islamist politicians she especially disliked. Later, when she learned about the excessive private property of the then Prime Minister Tansu Çiller, she said "I am not surprised," and counted each and every holding of the prime minister: her supermarket and house in the United States, her land in Istanbul, her extensive savings and numerous properties and companies. Saniye had no doubt that the prime minister had accumulated this much wealth by embezzlement. She was appalled but not surprised. The persona of the prime minister coincided with Saniye's characterization of statespeople at large (except for Ataturk and General Kenan Evren whom she placed on a pedestal). "When Tansu Çiller came to power, we were happy that we would have a woman statesman for a change," Saniye said. "But she turned out to be a disgrace to women. That is what I call her."

In elections during the 1980s and 1990s, Saniye had mostly voted for ANAP, one of the right-of-center political parties, reasoning that it was the least of the evils. Before the national elections of December 1995, when the Welfare Party was being reported to have the highest chances of winning, Saniye said:

> We are voting against the Welfare Party. Everyone is doing that in our neighborhood. Anyway, no one is doing anything for the people (*halk*); they all come, fill their own pockets, and leave. At least, we are thinking, let it not be worse, let us prevent someone worse [the leader of the Islamist Welfare Party] from coming to power. We were going to vote for the CHP [the secularist social democratic party]. Me, Cemil, and my elder daughter, three votes. But now, so that our votes are not wasted, we will perhaps vote for ANAP.

Saniye maintained that statespeople practiced the most immoral of trades. She thought that those involved with the state could only possibly be motivated by a self-interested drive for more money from funds received and reserved for the public. And more money meant more comfort and further power. Yet, there was something that worried her more than plunder and pillage by politicians. She worried that, if the Islamists came to power, they would enforce all sorts of rules on everyday public behavior. She imagined that Welfarists would impose the veil and seclusion on women. That is how she expressed one of her greatest anxieties. If she wore the veil, she would be able neither to work nor to make a living for her family. Islamists would threaten her very mode of survival.

Even as she worked for the state on a daily basis (cleaning office floors and windows), Saniye made fun of the state for its corruption, its fakeness, its inefficiency, and injustice. These two everyday practices—working for and in relation to the state, on the one hand, and ridiculing it in everyday conversation, on the other—were coeval in Saniye's life. I will suggest that Saniye had a consciousness of what was behind state ideology. Yet, she had to keep working for statespeople *as if* she were unaware. The state was her bread and butter. Saniye clung to the state for pragmatic reasons. She did not believe in what she did, not in the state. She only had to continue working for the state to remain alive and intact as a poor person with a family to take care of.

Saniye was highly respected by her coworkers as well as by the officers of the municipality. She amazed almost everyone with her spirit and intelligence. It had become common for her colleagues to remark to her that if she had had the opportunity for schooling, she would have become mayor of her district. Saniye knew that they were sincere. Yet, she would always snap back at such remarks saying, "Being a statesman is for the liars, for the tricksters, for those who are out for self-interest, for money, for fame. That's not for me!" And once again, she would recount a story about one of the last ordeals of the prime minister, who had been reported to have channeled state resources to her own account. In Saniye's perception, the ambition of (especially higher-echelon) statespeople could be guided by nothing but self-interest. That was what being a statesman was about. Power was about looting resources that were meant for the people or about striking it rich after occupying a seat for some time in a state office. She was furious to learn that everyone who worked as a parliamentarian, even for a short period, had the official right to an expensive pension.

The mundane cynicism in Saniye's everyday practice of life is the most common sort of relationship with the state in contemporary Turkey. There are numerous civil groups that have organized themselves in a critique of the state: mothers of the disappeared who have gathered in the Galatasaray neighborhood in Istanbul every Saturday, feminists who formed coalitions to help defend the court case of a young woman who was raped and tortured by her former lover, members of a diversity of socialist groups marching in protest at the funeral of a journalist murdered by police, activists of the newly formed Freedom and Democracy Party (ÖDP) who have been organizing themselves against state corruption, and so forth. There were many such acts of protest, organization, and civil disobedience in Turkey of the 1990s. Yet, cynicism is still, I argue, the predominant sort of relationship with the state in contemporary Turkey.

What do I mean by cynicism in this ethnographic context? Saniye is not a brooding type of person, setting up a dark narrative for herself in the world. She is, in fact, an extremely hopeful person, especially regarding the prospects of her own family. She believes in the future of her children, for example, even at times when all odds and chances are against her; she wants them to have comfortable lives so much that she really thinks it will happen. So her cynicism is not of the sort that harbors no personal wishes for the future. She *does* imagine favorable change, even though she has mainly seen change for the worse in her personal circumstances. Specifically, Saniye is cynical about the Turkish state. She believes that statespeople's motives are bad and selfish and she shows this in her verbalized contempt for them. Her everyday discourse is imbued with sneering remarks about the state. From Saniye's perspective, the Turkish state, at least as it currently stands, is a joke. She mocks state officials and produces comedy about the state all the time in her everyday life. She does not (completely) fetishize the state, as a Taussigian narrative would have her do, even though she holds Ataturk, General Kenan Evren, and the army on a pedestal. She conceives of statecraft as a game of deceit in pursuit of self-interest, as the social relations of power that it is. Falsely conscious? Not at all. Consciousness about the farce of state is the everyday matter of Saniye's life. Yet she keeps on "doing," in Žižek's terms, as though she were unaware of this. And how else could she behave? She organizes her everyday activities *as if* the state were there to deliver justice, *as if* it were an institution, a person, something tangible, *as if* it were a wholesome entity. She reproduces and reinstates statecraft as it is through her everyday actions upon the world: she works for the state, negotiates with municipal officers and doctors, solicits social benefits, and so forth. In her daily life, she goes through the motions of state practice. The Turkish state endures in the domain of these sorts of habitual everyday practices for the state, as if nothing happened, as if all were normal, or as though one were unaware.

I will argue that the signifier "state" can remain intact, in spite of public consciousness against it, because a material and tangible world has been organized around it. The state has to be dealt with, in everyday life, as an object because it functions as though it were. A whole economy has been mobilized around this symbol. Even when we have come intellectually to disentangle the state, we need to keep on treating it as a reality, because there exists a reality that has been activated through this symbol.

The Truck That Crashed into the "State"

On November 4, 1996, Turkey woke up to a scandalous news report. An unbelievable event had taken place the night before. A truck had crashed into a car on a highway that went through a town called Susurluk. The bodies of four people were found in the car: a parliamentarian, Istanbul's former vice-head of police, a pan-Turkist mafia dealer, and a prostitute with a false identity card. All had died but the parliamentarian, who was seriously injured. The story on the news sounded like the scenario of a gangster movie. That politicians and the police had relations with the mafia was now official. Yet the event did not awaken a Turkish public that false consciously imagined otherwise. The incident had taken place at the right historical moment when conditions of possibility were ripe for its public reception and interpretation. Most people in Turkey had received confirmation of their suspicions. During the two months following the accident, "Susurluk" (as the event was called) became the preoccupation and subject of everyday public conversation in Turkey.

What were these four people doing together? What were they after? Where were they traveling? What was their relationship with one another?

Which politicians had been aware of this meeting? Who had organized this? Public discourse became saturated with question marks. Mainstream TV and the press presented themselves as "the saviours of the nation": journalists would go after the questions and reveal the true face of the state. Reporters directed all their energy to understanding and deciphering the event, and they ended up producing still more questions. The maze of confusing details about the connections and undercover dealings of one obscure character after another served to inflate rather than eradicate that great question mark of the state. Everyone knew that the Turkish state was somewhere underneath the series of queries and conspiracy theories, yet it seemed that the questions and theories were also serving to maintain the aura of that farce intact. It was becoming harder, by default, rather than easier to understand or grasp what was going on. The media was ultimately confusing rather than informing people. The state remained the privileged and big unknown.

A small amount of information on the biographies of the accident victims was publicly available. The mafia dealer in the car was Abdullah Çatlı, a pan-Turkist who was responsible for the massacre of seven members of the Turkish Workers' Party (TİP) in the 1970s. There were still charges against him on this case as well as on a number of other murderous political acts, primarily against leftists. He had also been caught smuggling astronomical amounts of drugs to and from Turkey. Apparently, Çatlı had changed his identification papers several times. Somewhere along the line, he had been hired to perform undercover operations and assassinations for the state of the sort that politicians could not organize through "legal" organs like the police or the army. It seemed that Çatlı had led an easy life in the 1980s under the military regime. He had an established life, a home and a family, and he owned a number of companies. Not only had he been spared from a prison term under the strictest of martial laws, he had, on top of that, been granted a special green passport, of the sort held by senior state employees, to travel abroad without visas, and he was given official permission to carry guns. It appeared that Çatlı was the state's hired gunman. Before his death in the car crash, the public learned that he had been involved in the orchestration of a pro-Turkey coup in Azerbaijan. The coup fell through, yet it turned out that this exercise was authorized by heads of the Turkish state. Knowledge about the Susurluk incident created a major uproar in public life. The idioms of "agitation," "tumult," "sensationalism," and "panic" abounded in expressions of the experience of the political at the time.[18]

"There clearly are relations between the Turkish secret service and the pan-Turkist mafia," journalists wrote. And this was a relationship of give and take, where, in return for accomplishing prostate activities (assassinations, coups, and other undercover operations), mafia dealers received cash returns and were spared from control over their smuggling rings. News-papers carried large headlines declaring "Illegal Organization Within the State." Forums on TV were programmed to discuss "the Police-Mafia-State triangle."[19] Everyone who read or watched the news constructed stories about the connections. The names of the suspect mafia dealers—Çatlı and Çakıcı—their stories and personas, grabbed the public imagination. Suspicions of conspiracy abounded. The idea of "the plot" became the central metaphor of power. The public became detectives of the state. Public representations of the state were crowded with numerous open-ended schemes about the involvement of politicians in "dirty work." The state was now the greatest social suspect. The public was now alert to the covert side of state officials' practices, their engagements with the mafia, and corruption.

The luggage of the crashed car contained a load of weapons. The parliamentarian injured in the crash, a formal representative of the state, was Sedat Bucak, who belonged to the True Path Party (DYP), under the prime minister. This party was leading the governing coalition along with the Welfare Party at that time. He was also the lord of a right-wing and pro-Turkey Kurdish tribe in the southeast. His tribe was known for its anti-PKK sentiments and had been collaborating with the Turkish army in its war with the PKK. One newspaper suspected that the mafia dealer Çatlı had recently been employed as bodyguard to this parliamentarian, after having worked in the same capacity for the owner of a major gambling ring. The parliamentarian was the only one saved from the accident on the Susurluk highway. In intensive care in hospital, he was surrounded by hundreds of relatives from his tribe. His brother, interviewed, did not seem alarmed or ashamed by the event, nor did he make an effort to conceal his tribe's commitments. "We are a nationalist, right-wing family," he said. He recounted working against the PKK and not being honored sufficiently by the state. He took pride in his tribe doing what the state should have done in the first place (Bakiler 1996). He spoke as if he were the personification of what the Turkish state should be. For two months, journalists waited at the doors of the hospital for the parliamentarian to regain consciousness. "His condition is unstable" was the answer of his relatives and of the Minister of Internal Affairs who visited him. Somehow, in that atmosphere of hype and confusion, journalists were not allowed to see for themselves whether this was really the case. The state's technique of power was at work. The big unknown had to be maintained, as it usually and successfully had been after political assassinations. Most of such events in Turkey of the 1980s and 1990s—disappearances of those arrested, murders, and torture—were somehow left unresolved. The perpetrators of such crimes were never identified. Those who knew too much, such as the journalists Uğur Mumcu and Kutlu Adalı, were "somehow" murdered.[20] And so the questions and secrets grew and grew. In this case, too, the parliamentarian had to be kept from accidentally speaking. It might have been better for the state if he had not survived the accident.

When Sedat Bucak finally recovered (when it was no longer possible to say that he was repeatedly losing and regaining consciousness), he was interviewed once again about the event. The parliamentarian's words did not match one another as his answers expressed only a general ambiguity. When shown video clips of his first statements in momentary consciousness while still in the hospital, Bucak put on an air of amazement. "What was I saying?!" he said, and denied his former testimony, claiming that he must have lost his mind as an effect of the accident. He said, this time, that Abdullah Çatlı had presented himself as "an official of the state" and "an expert on terrorism." He said he learned of Çatlı's real identity only the previous summer, without clarifying what he meant by "real identity." The only thing the parliamentarian was uncompromising about was his statism. When asked whether he and the other three in the crashed car were preparing an undercover operation against Abdullah Öcalan (the leader of the PKK), Bucak said, "It has nothing to do with it. I wish it had. That is my ideal. It is the ideal also of the former minister of interior affairs, it was the ideal of Çatlı, as it should be of anyone who loves his motherland (*vatan*)."[21]

In the middle of absurd stories and questions, the reception of this news on the part of a significant proportion of the public was not unprecedented. People had found a confirmation for something they already knew.[22] This was no dark cloud suddenly appearing on Turkey's horizon. It was not a bang on the head for the naive citizen. It was the normal condition of the state only more obviously revealed through an abnormal accident. Those who were already cynical about the state only sharpened the note of disgust in their voice. Among the representations of the state in popular use in those two months that followed the Susurluk incident were "swamp," "rottenness," "filthiness," "putrefaction," "vulgarity," "crookedness," "disease," and "degeneration." Adjectives were, in turn, derived from these nouns to develop ever more grotesque narratives about the state. In public representations, the state was described through images of abjection, of excesses of filth, immorality, and violence. An imaginary of offal or refuse colored public discourses about the state, in which expressions like "This country is a pile of shit" or "This is a state to be vomited over" were common.[23]

Now, in this context of sensationalism and its Janus-face of "normality," the state was experientially perceived as something that could not be pinned down. In the disjointed stories available for public consumption, the construct of state appeared in many guises and faces: the reporter on television, the mafia dealer, the police officer, the parliamentarian, the soldier, the spy, the figure of Ataturk, and so on. No sooner did the state appear in the garb of military officer than it disappeared and reappeared in the cloak of mafia. The state went through several metamorphoses in public consciousness. It wasn't stable. If people wanted to hold on to a notion of the state as thing, through processes of reification, the state soon transmogrified and appeared through surreal stories that belied belief. Through the metaphors of plots and counterplots, the state emerged as an apparition—now you see it, now you don't—an intangible nonentity that appeared constantly to change hands.

Here, the spectral quality of the state (see Aretxaga 2000), or the hide-and-seek factor, is experienced as an existential problem, by those who would like to have believed in the state as an item. The metamorphosis effected by the change of hands in under-and-overground networks is precisely and ironically how the reified notion of "the state as unity" is able to survive. The production of confusion can be studied as a tactic of power. When experientially and existentially unsitable, the notion of the state remains abstract in public discourses, as though it were indeed an item. Consciousness of the multiple skins of the state is coeval with the reification of the state in public life.

There was acute public consciousness about what was often called "the horror," but many also reflected on their complicity in maintaining the status quo by not "doing something." "And we are not doing anything! We are waiting just like that!" was a common comment of those perplexed by their own cynicism. "We have become used to dirtiness," one person said, "we don't react to it anymore, as if we were vaccinated and got used to having the microbe around." "We have been immunized against such infections," was another comment. "We don't react any more." At this time, it appeared that there was public awareness of the ordinary cynicism that was prevalent. Beyond the sort of consciousness that Žižek allows the subject, I will argue that there was even consciousness about one's own cynical acts in this case. Not only an enlightened reflection on ideology, as argued by Žižek, but also a self-critique of the cynical state of submission and lack of reaction.

Three months after the Susurluk incident, many were already saying, "There is nothing going on, everything is as usual." Many used the phrase "We have accepted the situation as it is; we have become indifferent" in self-critique. Very soon after the scandal, the hype, the uproar, and the public critique of the state, the Susurluk event was on its way to being normalized, dropped from journalistic agendas, pushed to the back of public consciousness, at least temporarily forgotten. This normalization became a vehicle, I will argue, in the further entrenchment, or reproduction by default, of the state. The extraordinary force of the signifier "state" had recovered from another major blow. The idea and abstraction of state could remain and persist. Cynicism reemerged as the ordinary habitus of a state culture in operation.

Consciousness and amnesia were informed by the same contingency in public life. Apparently consecutive, they in fact formed the flipside of a dialectic. As public representations of the state were informed and filtered through a culture of news, the same organs of the press that had constructed the "event" also manifested its dissolution from public discourse through the circulation of further news. In the culture of hype, alarm, and agitation encouraged by the media's bombastic style, panic and its normalization were almost coeval.

Popular publications in Turkey have generally followed journalistic constructions of public events in the 1980s and 1990s. Soon after the Susurluk event, the earthquake, and the more recent incidents involving Hizbullah, numbers of books have appeared on the market depicting and renarrating the events. As significant as such publications may be in inscribing incident in public memory, they are also emblematic of the commodification of event, disaster, or scandal. For very soon after they have been consumed, these best-sellers are replaced by others, depicting the newly framed "news." The production of consciousness of event and the subsequent replacement of one event by another is almost consequential. In other words, the appearance of every new piece of news on the agenda as consumer item triggers the erasure of the former from public consciousness and active memory. Every new event produces amnesia or apparent oblivion about the former. Or rather, former events are submerged in public consciousness, pushed to the back or to the political unconscious, as new events dominate the center stage of public discourse.

Even though cynicism quickly became the most common reaction to "Susurluk," there were those who were not cynical. Some, for example, embraced the image of the dead mafia dealer in declaring him "a saviour of the country." His coffin was covered with a Turkish flag as it was carried by a cortege of pan-Turkists in his funeral.[24] Likewise, columnists in right-wing and conservative newspapers such as *Türkiye*, praised the victims of the car crash for their "dedication to the state and the nation." One of these writers even justified the politician-police-mafia relationship, arguing that such deals were necessary to maintain states. This writer wondered whether the United States, Israel, Russia, and other states did not organize such undercover operations to annihilate their enemies (Bakiler 1996). All was positive when done for the state, according to these unabashed state fetishists. Soon after the Susurluk scandal, a book was published by pan-Turkists in praise of Abdullah Çatlı, the state's hired gunman. The book was entitled "Our Çatlı" (Yıldız 1997) and was written with compliments to the statist mafia dealer for using all means to defend the Turkish state and nation against its "external and internal enemies."

What was worse was that certain official representatives of state were taking comparable positions and making similar remarks. The then president, Süleyman Demirel, urged all politicians, journalists, and judges to "go after the Susurluk event wherever it may take you." But he refused to volunteer any information himself, to give any help, or to offer any clues toward a clarification of the issue. The head of state was playing a double strategy, wanting to appear morally wholesome in front of the public, on the one hand, yet attempting to maintain what he called "the integrity of the state," on the other. When he refused to comment, he justified himself, as if he were protecting the law of God, in saying that he was doing so out of a "state custom." His primary commitment as president was upholding and perpetuating the Turkish state. He would allow research into the Susurluk affair only as far as it was studied as an anomaly, as an event that implicated *certain* dubious politicians and police, but *not* the state. This had nothing to do with the state, according to the president. A similar sentiment was expressed by the Minister of Justice, who belonged to the Welfare Party. Şevket Kazan said, "While some people in the state might have relations with the mafia, the idea of the state is not that cheap." He was willing to concede the fact of corruption as long as it did not stain the Welfare Party, which was sharing the coalition in government. Islamist politicians like him had ambitions to obtain power over the state on their own. Yet the politician that made the most outrageous statement was Vice-Prime Minister and Minister of Foreign Affairs Tansu Çiller. It was her party's parliamentarian who had been caught in the car with the mafia dealer. Çiller declared that "Sedat Bucak is a national hero." When he gained consciousness, Sedat Bucak defined the pan-Turkist mafia dealer Çatlı as "a great patriot." That was the last straw for most people in the peripheries of the state. Yet most only kept producing more cynical remarks and criticisms.

According to simplistic observation of the state of alarm in those two months that followed the Susurluk event, the Turkish state was on the point of collapse. With heightened cynicism about the state among citizens and publicized disfavor in the media, it could indeed have seemed like the notion of the state was in danger. Yet, the notion of the state survived public criticism. My question is how? The thoughts of a columnist in the *Sabah* newspaper are, I think, helpful in probing for answers. Cengiz Çandar writes, "When looked at from one angle, the state is very much rotten; yet when looked at from another angle, the state is extremely strong in its ability to gloss over these sorts of events" (1996). Indeed, this is where contemporary Turkish governmentality is located. The notion of the state has somehow (always) survived scandals about its terror. It could not afford to lose one game of imagery or signification. This is power. This is command. It is not so easy, with raised consciousness, to deconstruct such a loaded signifier. A fantasy for the state, as I analyze it, allows this signifier to be reerected after every public effort to challenge it.

What has been significant in the public life of contemporary Turkey is the quick shuffling of squares on a hopscotch of remembering and forgetting. What is cynically remembered for a couple of months is in no time (in some way) forgotten. That media that prides itself in exposing the problems of the state has, in the interest of presenting fresh news for better ratings, dropped items down from its agenda and created newer topics for public consumption in little time. So, a few months after the Susurluk event, mainstream media began to define Turkey's issue as the conflict between secularists and Islamists. Just at the time when people were uniting and organizing themselves to protest against state corruption and violence, the press targeted the Welfare Party as an object for critique. A public critique of the state was transformed, in a short time, into a critique of the Welfare Party, as though Ataturkism represented stately "cleanliness," and Islamism was responsible for the "disease."[25] A secularist discourse about "the Islamic threat" was hyped up, at this strategic time, to reclaim conventional legitimacy for the state.

Public uproar quickly became public oblivion with the help of privately owned media channels. It was not clear, in this process, whether the media was a representation of civil society or an institution caught in contemporary techniques of state' maintenance. Cynical relations with the state had become the condition of the state's survival.

In the weeks that followed the Susurluk incident, there were significant public demonstrations against the state. Supporters of the recently founded Freedom and Solidarity Party (ÖDP)[26] organized a "Cleansing Demonstration" where people took to the streets of Ankara with brooms in hand symbolically to clean the capital city of what was referred to as "political dirt." Members of one of Turkey's biggest labor unions (Türk-İş) organized a protest in Ankara attended by 150,000 people, calling "Workers out, Gangs into prison!" Everyone knew that the state was run at least partially through the social relations of interest between mafia gangs and politicians.[27] Numerous other such public demonstrations took place, warning about "the mafia behind the state." All who had access to pen, paper, and press angrily wrote their critiques. Publicly circulated writing was full of comments on Susurluk. Thus there was also some organized political resistance, even though an everyday practice of cynicism was more commonplace. Yet, as journalist Cengiz Çandar suggested at the time, "For the time being society does not have the organization and preparation to combat the command and authority of the state" (1996).

The state endures as idea and reality (1) because significant numbers of ordinary people normalize the idea of the state through their habits of everyday life, (2) because statesmen, generals, mafia dealers, journalists, and other people with power[28] are successfully able to produce truth about the existence of state through their bureaucratic practices, their under-cover operations, and their influence over culture industries, and (3) be-cause the materiality—force, economy, bureaucracy, technology, and so forth—that has been functioning in the name of the symbol of state is still intact. Through a number of different practices in a variety of sites (some of which I have studied), an effect of an idea of a state is generated by those who find such an effect useful for their social relations. In fact, there is no such unified entity as the state. The state remains because actions upon the world are taken as if there were such a thing *sui generis*. Rituals for the state of the sort I studied in this and the previous chapter (fare-wells to soldiers, rallies for national sports, flag campaigns, the organization of cultural activities in municipalities, celebrations of national holidays, routine applications to the state for jobs, education, health, and pensions) are done on the assumption that the state, as a whole, exists. And, in terms of the effects that it engenders, it really does. The state remains as long as ordinary people are able to pretend that it exists in their everyday practices of life. Likewise, statespeople collect gains if they act *as if* there were some thing like the state, if they employ this symbol, even at times of bureaucratic dissolution. Contemporary governmentality requires (is based on upholding) this *"as if"* quality. As long as what I will call *the everyday life of statecraft* is maintained, the state is reproduced. A *pretense to nor-mality* is coeval with a critical consciousness about state. As Žižek suggests, we continue to *do* as though we did not *know*. Normalization takes over through ordinary habiti, in Bourdieu's terms, of cynicism, where the con-sciousness of state violence and corruption dissipates. The state endures. It is regenerated again after every public effort to deconstruct it. Fantasies for the state keep it up.

"Turkey" is a signifier that was constructed not only in the sphere of signification. Construction was also, and crucially, about a foundation of a materiality of tangible objects, networks, and processes. Real things—institutions, a national economy, a market, borders, motorways, schools, police, an army, factories—were composed out of the signifier "state." A whole set of life processes now run through the materiality of networks that function under the emblem of state: one has to deal with bureaucracy to be granted healthcare, to receive an income, to apply for a passport, to conscript in the army, to get working permits. One's freedom of habitation, of speech, and thought are at the mercy of people who represent the state. The state is a construction, and an effective one at that. One feels and has to maneuver through its real effects for actual and everyday survival.

It is easier to deconstruct a signifier ("the state" as text) than it is to dismantle its effects of truth. In fact, my ethnography illustrates that truth effects, or the-state-as-materiality, persist even if and even after "the state" as signifier has been intellectually (and publically) deconstructed. We know and yet we persist in doing as if we didn't because we have to: the materiality of state remains and we are dependent on it. Our life depends on a pretense to normality, in spite of the pervasive availability of crisp critical consciousness. In our recycling of statecraft on the ground of everyday activity, "the state" as forceful and ultimate contemporary signifier of power survives even deconstruction.

The Magnetism of State Crime

In his recently published novel *Bin Hüzünlü Haz*, or *Pleasure of a Thousand Sadnesses* (1999), Hasan Ali Toptaş writes:

> What worries me the most is my purification from crime. For a long time, I have been feeling this intensely in the depths of my spirit. Sometimes, so I can plunge myself in filthiness and well understand who I am, I fearlessly throw myself into this city's alcohol-smelling darkness and get involved with whatever trickster I find in a corner or whichever tramp or drunkard I meet on the street. I venture with them to those unexplored points of life and dive into puddles of mud decorated with the flickering lights of the night. I make a home out of the main dirthouse and stay there for years. As all of this is happening, I feel like attracting all the crimes possible for homo sapiens to commit, like a magnet, in my being. But I am just not able to achieve that. . . . (9)

I read what may appear to be the phantasmatic imagination of an author, here, as an entry into the structure of feeling, in Raymond Williams's terms, generated by an entanglement of state, contrastate, and mafia practices in the present contingency of Turkey. The dialectic between desire for crime (see "pleasure" in the title of the novel) and the fear or repellence from it ("a thousand sadnesses") can be read as an ethnographic depiction of the political in Turkey of the 1990s. The magnetic pull and push of crime is depicted by the author in what can be read as an ethnography of the excesses of the political in contemporary Turkey. The surreal element in the protagonist's life in Istanbul, the floating through tides of criminality and involvement in layers of dirty relations, is not only a situated representation of the political culture, as constructionist anthropologists may want to study it, but also a sensitive presentation of experiences of the real. The surreal element, here, is generated by and generates the real.

In the aftermath of the exposure of relations between mafia gang leaders, police, and representatives of the state connected with the Susurluk event of 1996, when consciousness about underground politics was available in public life, a story was told to me of a man who walked onto the Bosphorus bridge and began to scream "I want to be mafia, I want to be mafia," threatening to commit suicide, until he was saved by police. The allure and the danger of criminality were integral in that instance on the side of the bridge. The protagonist articulated a desire for life (and upward mobility) through a fascination for mafia, with a recognition of the flipside of his desire, the brink of suicide. His scream can be read as a commentary on Turkish society, as well, at a time when the prevalence of mafia was available to the consciousness of the public. Here, notice the dialectic between motivations that may appear contradictory. The mafia, now, has a grip on public consciousness as fantasy. But there is curiosity for the very symptom of one's destruction. What I want to draw attention to is this complexity of relations with crimes involving the state.

It is not mafia as thing or as object of study that motivates my interests here. A number of anthropologists have successfully studied mafia circles and circuits (e.g., Blok 1987) and this is not an attempt to replicate an ethnography of the mafia-state-police triangle in a new context. I am interested neither in describing the actuality of undercover political and economic relations involving pan-Turkist mafia dealers and representatives of the state, nor in only citing the resulting constructions of the state (for example as "gang leaders" or *çeteciler*) in public life. Rather, I would like to draw attention, beyond the study of the state and mafia as items or constructs, to the effect of underground politics on the sensing of political existence and on political life.

Much more than a study of institutions and social relations, an anthropology of the state can also address the political culture generated by specific political practices. This is not to culturalize or essentialize what emerges from a specific historical contingency. Rather, it is to draw attention to a little studied arena for the efficacy of state power. I would like to argue that a proper ethnography of the state must study the state beyond its tangible manifestations in the garb of institution and its production of discourses and representations. In what I would like to call its visceral (habitual, psychic, phantasmatic) effects on subjects of a political culture, is located an important and intangible site for ethnography. It is in the physicality of the political that the state attains an effect. A political culture of fear and unknowing is embodied, to the point when the state is carried in the bodies, habits, and internalized reactions of its subjects, whether they be within the borders of Turkey or abroad. Indeed, once visceral, or physically and psychically internalized, the panic that the entanglement of crime with the political generates can be carried within one's self anywhere. A political culture of uncertainty and fear marks the bodies of its subjects to the point of haunting them.

In their article "Bad Endings: American Apocalypsis," Kathleen Stewart and Susan Harding write on the proliferation of discourses of conspiracy in contemporary America. In a Foucauldian framework, they study conspiracy in American narratives as belonging to a discursive field (1999, 290). So they write, "Conspiracy theories can identify absolute truths about the world while dismissing holders of power as sinister, corrupt, and deceptive" (294). But studies like this that would focus on conspiracy as representation, face by default the danger of trivializing and normalizing a state's discourse of unity and transparency that would represent power otherwise. In the context I am describing in Turkey, the plotting in public narratives about politicians has to be studied not only as representation but as a sense generated from actual experience. There are, indeed, what could be called certain conspiratorial relations between representatives of the state and leaders of the underground who are ready to commit Machiavellian acts for the interest of the Turkish state. In the event of these sorts of social relations, the self-interest of these particular politicians and mafia dealers is rendered indistinguishable from that of the state. It is not possible, in contexts like this, to dismiss conspiracy theory so easily or to evade it by studying it as a discourse or a representation.

The anthropology of the state in Turkey, if not defined as such, has been dominated by two approaches. The first, the more conventional, assumes state and society to be "things," as it were, and studies their relations. This approach, represented in the ethnographic works of Stirling (1965) and others studying the state's influence on village societies, is no longer predominant. The second approach, informed by the constructionist turn in the social sciences, focuses not on materiality or social relations but on their representations. In works such as the volume edited by Reşat Kasaba and Sibel Bozdoğan (1997), the site for ethnography is the social institution and its production of national discourse or ideology. I argue that not only is the social institution taken for granted as "site" in such a framing of the question, it is fetishized as the arena for the production of political culture. In studies that would focus on institutions and their discourses as the sites par excellence for the political (in following Benedict Anderson's work on the printing press as site for the production of the national imagination), a rationalized portraiture of the political remains. Pick an institution and study the production of national discourse on site. When the project for the ethnography of the state is framed as such, rationalized or disciplinary mechanisms, in Michel Foucault's terms, take center stage, as the sites for the manifestation of political discourse. Begona Aretxaga (1997, 2000) has argued and illustrated the pitfalls of privileging the study of rationalized institutional practices against the effects that the political engenders.

I would like to argue that the political eludes attempts by social scientists to pin it down in either state or mafia as objects of study (fetishized as such) or in the topsy turvy focus on representations of state and mafia in political culture. The fear, uncertainty, and panic that is generated by the entanglement of crime and politics in public life bears a mark. Through the rising and receding tides of consciousness and amnesia, at least partially generated within a culture of news, the panic caused by the Susurluk story remains submerged in the bodies, psyches, habits, and unconsciousness of subjects of the Turkish state only to be recalled with the emergence of fresh anxieties. It is in this visceral domain where the political is shown to have ultimate power for reproduction and effect that I situate my work on the state in Turkey. It is in those intangible reactions—unarticulable, internalized, unconscious—that the political perhaps becomes available for analysis.

The Afterlife of the "State"

The theoretically attuned reader will be quick to realize the affinity of my analysis of "the state" with historical materialism. Throughout this and previous chapters, I have given ethnographic examples of the everyday practice and the social relations of power that go into the making of the state and I have argued, like certain Marxist theorists, that the notion of the state is an abstraction. In a brilliant review of Karl Marx's work, Derek Sayer (1987) maintains that Marx studied the state as an ideologically produced abstraction that positions itself at a distance from relations of production in order better to manage them. Marx, according to Sayer, interpreted the category of the state to be intrinsic to a capitalist mode of production. The state was the most convenient ideological superstructure for a base of capitalism. I would argue that those post-structuralists who pit their analyses in critique of historical materialism have not gone much further than Marx in noticing the constructedness of the category of state. In an invaluable analysis, Timothy Mitchell (1990), for example, makes reference to Foucault in demonstrating the embeddedness of the categories of "state and society," "power and resistance" in relations of power. He and Foucault differ from Marx in their interpretation of the content of those relations, that is, a capitalist mode of production would not solely describe it, nor would the bourgeoisie and workers be defined as social actors. Foucault has written the history of strategies of power that cannot be contained in the bodies of social individuals; in fact, he has endeavored to write a nonsubjective or trans-subjective history of relations of power. Yet, as Derrida has objected, there is still a content (a metaphysics of presence) in Foucault's deliberations on "discourse."[29] If it is not the historical materialist content (the material mode of production), then it is disciplinary mechanisms of power. There is, I would agree with Derrida, more of an affinity than a contrast between historical materialism and Foucauldian post-structuralism. (Unlike Derrida, I would suggest that this is for the better.) See for example, Timothy Mitchell's interpretation of what is behind the state as a modern discourse of power:

> The binary world constructed by the new forms of power includes a series of novel practices that appear to create outside the world itself a separate realm of intentions, ideology, or meaning. The effects of externality, fixity, and permanence achieved by the new modes of domination coincide, therefore, with the more general effect of the existence of meaning as a distinct order of being, opposed to what it will now be possible to call mere reality, a merely "material" world (1990, 573)

In another passage, Mitchell writes,

> The distinctive nature of the modern "world-as-exhibition" in which we live is that more and more of social life has been so arranged that we mistake these effects of certain coordinated practices for the existence of a distinct metaphysical realm of structure or meaning that stands apart from what we call material reality (561).

Then, it is the world, history, and relations of power in material reality that have constructed "the world-as-exhibition" as a more effective mode of power. There is a historical materialism that underlies Mitchell's post-structuralism. He writes the history of social relations that are the corollaries of historically situated abstractions (such as "the state"). Mitchell is writing about the world that imagines itself "as-exhibition." Yet it is the world that he is talking about. If we were to take Derek Sayer's reading of Marx seriously, the task of post-structuralism is not so remote from the project of historical materialism.[30] Some functionalist and determinist Marxists might have rendered Marx's work foreign to the interests of post-structuralism. Marx, Sayer argues, did not conceive of "superstructure" as an epiphenomenon or as a derivative or result of material relations of production. Rather, according to Marx, specific social relations have historically arisen with specific abstractions that serve to reproduce those particular sorts of relations (in this case of production) in the world. According to Sayer's reading of Marx, contemporary social relations could not exist were it not for the simultaneous invention of abstractions. The latter are only apparently independent of social relations. In fact, they are the correlates of these particular (capitalist in Marx's sense) sorts of social relations. This particular historical contingency (in Marx's reading, capitalism) has required abstractions in order to operate. "The state" is such an abstraction (Sayer 1987).

Thus I have written an ethnography of the abstraction "state" and the everyday practices and social relations of power that coincide with it in this particular historical conjuncture. In this sense, my analysis will not seem to differ too much from the historical materialism of Philip Abrams and Michael Taussig. As far as we decipher the history that coincides with the abstraction "state," we are on similar ground.

There is, however, a further issue involving the particular history under study here, and one unaddressed by historical materialism and post-structuralism. The abstraction that we have been endeavoring to deconstruct (the state) has shown to have a life of its own even beyond its public deciphering. The state dies and yet is resurrected. In contemporary Turkey, the notion of state is outliving the span predicted for it by historical materialists or post-structuralists. It survives the overcoming of false consciousness about the state as farce; it survives deconstruction. The notions of Turkey and the Turkish state still have force, still have effect on everyday practice, still work to operate social institutions, still commit violence despite the fact that they have been challenged in public life. Moreover, their potency exists despite the emergence of contradictions in a system that depended on their untouchable, sacred, and iconic status. Almost everyone, in different situational ways, as I have attempted to show, is conscious of the deceitful and violent social relations of power and interest that go into the manufacture of the notion of the Turkish state. Yet this notion has maintained potency beyond the dissolution of false consciousness and after deconstruction. People ridicule statesmen and women and they expose the social relations in which they are involved, but the idea of Turkey is stoutly defended. It is still the greatest taboo. As I hope to have shown through ethnographic examples, the signifier "Turkey" lives on, having recovered from several diagnoses and lethal diseases. Despite public consciousness about the entanglement of the abstraction in relations of social and self-interest, the abstraction, in itself, is able to pull people behind it. This is what Marx had not predicted for capitalism and what such historical materialists, as Abrams and Taussig, have not predicted for the state. This is what post-structuralists are unable to analyze. Unlike former historical formations, the state, like capitalism (up to this point), has shown itself capable of surviving crisis, conveniently refashioning itself where necessary. It is in this ability to have an afterlife where the actual danger of statism and nationalism is located.

How does the signifier endure? How does it survive when the social relations that are its constituent structure have toppled over themselves? Like the monster that Dr. Frankenstein created out of a corpse, immortal (at least so far), the state has shown itself to have many lives after death. The aura of "state" is more difficult to maintain today, after seventy years of a history of Turkey, when more people are conscious of the state's embeddedness in relations of interest and power and its role in a swamp of violence. But if the category "state" does not have false consciousness to depend on, what keeps it standing? A new manner of taking action upon the world is required to maintain the abstraction in its afterlife. Cynicism as a political culture provides the answer for the time being. Today in Turkey, as possibly in other states, people are conscious of the underside of "state," yet persist in carrying on with their everyday practices and in forging social relations as if this weren't there. It is on the historical site of what I have called the afterlife of the abstraction of "state" where my ethnography is located.

To amend the terms that historical materialists have used to study the state (Marx's "abstraction," Abrams's "mask," and Taussig's "fetish"), I will return to Lacan's concept of "fantasy" (as employed for the study of the political by Žižek). As I suggested in an earlier section, Lacan understands "fantasy" to be that psychoanalytic symptom that resists interpretation even after the patient has constructed his or her narrative about the past. Somehow, despite the labors of the psychoanalyst and the patient, the symptom persists. It does not disappear. Lacan explains this through the concept of *jouissance* or "surplus enjoyment" (Žižek 1995, 49–53).[31] The patient takes joy in his or her symptom and would have no personality, no consistency without it. She unconsciously fears that she might no longer exist. Hence, she persists in reproducing the symptom (as "fantasy") in order not to risk the unknown, even though she is well aware of having the symptom, having gone through psychoanalysis. Fantasy, this persistence of the symptomatic, is what Sloterdijk and Žižek have described as cynicism. "They know what they are doing, but they still do it." I will propose that public relations with the state, at least in contemporary Turkey, are at this "fantastical" stage, in the Lacanian sense. The state is no longer mask, fetish, image, or discourse as its former theorists have had it, but fantasy. It is what is surviving all efforts at consciousness and interpretation. If it hadn't this potential for phantasmatic recovery, the state would have disappeared long ago. It would not have survived the crashes and the crises. The state seems to be stronger than its theorists had imagined.

I have written an ethnography of an abstraction. Some anthropologists might object and be skeptical of the place of abstraction in everyday practice.[32] Yet I hope I have been able to illustrate the power of abstraction in the course of contemporary history. When I write of abstractions (such as "culture" and "the state"), I do not write of floating epiphenomena. As Richard Marsden has noted in citing Derek Sayer, "Categories are an integral part of social reality and, as such, as much in need of explanation as the social relations they express" (1992, 359).

To conclude this chapter in following and furthering Žižek's thought on the political, I will suggest that we employ "fantasy" (in Lacan's sense of it) as analytical framework because we still have to deal with the real effects of the abstraction or signifier "state." "The state" remains because it is a doer as much as it is a signifier. What we experience as our real world is a product of the structures and objects produced in the name of "Turkey" as signifier. Even when we know that the state as an abstraction does not exist, the objects and life processes that have been put into activity in the name of state continue to exist. Cynicism, as I mentioned before, is part and parcel of a practice of keeping the signifiers "Turkey" and "Turkish state" intact. And cynicism is located in acts of doing or of taking action upon the world. We are aware of our symptom of statism and yet we maintain it (what Lacan and Žižek call *jouissance*). Public *jouissance* is an activity of maintaining the state. We fantasize as we maintain our ordinary practice of everyday life, because knowing does not suffice. Many social theorists have approached the world in intellectualist terms, as if history is overthrown when we resolve things in our minds, when we lift false consciousness, when we deconstruct the discourses we are implicated in. But a materiality of statecraft and relations of power persist even when many of us have come intellectually to disentangle the political. The key to the endurance of the signifier state does not, then, lie in intellectual critique or deconstruction, but in its maintenance as object. We fix, rebuild, and maintain the state through our real everyday practices. It is because the state remains as an object and because we are still subjected to it that we resort to fantasy. Despite our consciousness about it as farce, the state as an object persists.

6

The Cult of Ataturk: The Apparition of a Secularist Leader in Uncanny Forms

> To expect help from the dead is a disgrace for a
> civilized society.
> —*Mustafa Kemal Ataturk, 1925*

> There are no rules by which intellectuals can
> know what to say or do; nor for the true secular
> intellectual are there any gods to be worshipped
> and looked to for unwavering guidance.
> —*Edward W. Said, 1993*

THIS CHAPTER explores the ethnographic and political context for the contemporary deployment of the image of a former head of state, or public reverence for Mustafa Kemal Ataturk, known as the founder of modern Turkey. In the mid-1990s and in the context of what was called the "politics of identity" among secularists and Islamists, the figure of Ataturk was widely used and massively reproduced by self-declared Ataturkists. The image of Ataturk that used to be an emblem of the sovereignty of the Turkish state, associated with institutions and rituals of state, took on a different dimension in the 1990s, with significant public participation in shows of veneration for the national father figure. At various sites of political conflict in public life, the image of Ataturk was employed in the making of posters, badges, protraits, photographs, busts, statues, and statuettes.[1] These items were extensively distributed and circulated in public and private secularist venues as well as at demonstrations. Following Michael Taussig's development of the idea of "state fetishism" (1992) to describe feelings of reverence for the state, I study the massive recourse to the image of Ataturk as Ataturk fetishism, or the cult of Ataturk.[2] This chapter explores the form and meaning of this aura around a dead secular head of state.

Anthropological work on what has alternatively been called "secular ritual," "civic religion," or "secular theodicy" has addressed the religiosity of state practices.[3] The object of literature on "secular ritual" was to employ the anthropological tools for the study of "ritual" in studies of modern secular politics. There are abundant studies of political ritual, in this framework, on Eastern Europe and many on Israel. No such ethnographic analysis is available for the phenomenon of Ataturkism in Turkey, one of the contexts for state-geared secularism in its most militarized form.

Mustafa Kemal Ataturk spent the latter part of his life secularizing and Westernizing state and society. In declaring a "Republic" (*Cumhuriyet*) in defiance of the dynastic rule of Ottoman heads of state, he organized a major transformation from a polity governed by Islamic law to one that strictly separated affairs of religion and state.[4] In the 1920s, under the governance of Ataturk and his associates, the seat of the caliph, last held by the fallen Ottoman sultan, was abolished. Attendance in Sufi orders and dervish lodges, wearing religious garb, and carrying religious titles was made punishable by state decree. Education was centralized and strictly secularized.

Studies of secularism and modernization in the Ottoman Empire and Turkey have generally employed a modernist historical trajectory, whereby the constructed distinction between religion and secularity, tradition and modernity has been naturalized (see Berkes 1964, Mardin 1962, Lewis 1969). Taking the mysticism / rationality opposition for granted, most scholarship on secularism in Turkey has reproduced the classical narrative of history utilized in modern social theory. The assumption is that Turkish national history developed, in the terms of "progress," on a linear path "from religion to science." Here, secularism is studied in the self-referential terms of secularism and is associated with other supposedly derivative terms such as "modernity," "rationality," and "democracy."

Scholars bent on critiquing modernization theory in the study of the Middle East by employing postmodern theory have at times ended up reproducing the very binarism—religion versus secularity, tradition versus modernity—which they had intended to deconstruct. Michel Foucault's narrative of history, a shift toward a rationalizing, ordering, and disciplining mode of power (1979), has influenced the work of some of the most important ethnographers of the region (see Rabinow 1989, Mitchell 1988, Messick 1993). In these studies, which take discursive rupture as their main historical referent, religion and secularity are implicitly interpreted as belonging to distinct and incommensurable, if consecutive, domains of culture and power.

The ethnographic material presented in this chapter leads us to situate secularism in a different trajectory. Within the context of Ataturk fetishism, such terms as "modernity," "rationality," "discipline," "order," or "bureaucracy" are inadequate for the purposes of ethnographic interpretation. In other words, the terms of secularism are not appropriate for the study of secularism. The material observed includes a peculiar phenomenon of invoking spirits in the name of secularism, employing numerology to validate it, seeing supernatural apparitions or images of Ataturk, and producing an aura around his image. "Belief," "magic," "mysticism": I suggest that these terms may be more appropriate for the study of contemporary secularist cultures in Turkey, especially those implicated in statism.

Much has been written on participation in Islamist or other religious movements. Less has been said, however, on public participation in secularist movements. To put it another way, the questions asked of communalism or "fundamentalism" have not been asked of secularism. The object of this chapter is to reverse the anthropological and sociological gaze so frequently directed at Islamists. In the mid-1990s, at the time of my field research, Islamists in Turkey complained of having been turned into objects for social scientific analysis. In shifting attention to their rivals, I studied that there was much misconception in analyses that isolated religion from the domain of secularity, or that approached Islamism as a history apart from Turkish secularism. Indeed, the ethnographic record calls for a deconstruction of the categories "secularity" and "religion," so pitted against one another in both public political discourses and social scientific analyses. This is precisely what this chapter endeavors to do.

Like a Cross That Stops the Devil . . .

A government formed under the consent of the army in 1997, the coalition between the right-wing ANAP and the social democratic DSP, began the process of abolishing the religious schools (*İmam-Hatip*) which were central to the production of Islamist activists and intellectuals. Compulsory elementary education was to be extended from five to eight years, and parents would be officially prevented from sending their children to the religious secondary schools. In reaction to this state-enforced decree, Islamists organized a major public demonstration in the capital city Ankara to argue for their democratic right to choose how to educate their children. As the demonstrators marched, voicing their anger over state-enforced secularism, a young woman who was standing on the side of the road, bewildered and taken aback, took out a framed portrait of Ataturk from her handbag and lifted it up against the Islamist demonstrators. She stood there for a little while, erect in posture with arm raised up high, holding the figure of Ataturk with his eyes directed at the marching Islamists. The young woman, Chantal Zakari, had raised the portrait of Ataturk as the expression of her protest of the Islamist movement and her commitment to the secularist and Westernist worldview of Ataturk. She had deployed the image of Ataturk, in that instance of built-up emotion and anxiety, to symbolize her identity, viewpoint, and feelings as if the portrait of the former head of state summed it all up. It was as if she were performing a formal religious rite or holding a cross to stop the devil.

On the following day, journalists of the mainstream secular press blew this event out of all proportion in praising the act of Chantal Zakari. Photos of the young woman in front of images of Ataturk were depicted on the front pages of every important and widely distributed newspaper.[5] Her story was narrated in the headlines of every mainstream TV channel. Chantal was turned into a public hero of Ataturkism. Columnists wrote in praise of her non-Muslim family from İzmir, saying that the greater enemies of the Turkish state were Islamists, and not Ataturkist non-Muslims like Chantal.[6] In reply, the Islamist press predominantly focused on the non-Muslimness of Chantal, mostly assuming that she was Jewish, and manufactured conspiracy theories charting connections between Ataturkism and non-Muslim minorities in Turkey.

This event, ardently discussed in public life, was only one expression among many in the political battle between secularism and Islamism that had developed in the 1980s and 1990s. Chantal had pulled a portrait of Ataturk from her handbag; others during this period developed a multiplicity of ways in which to commemorate Ataturk, reproducing his portrait as fetish in many forms and contexts.[7] Many of these Ataturkist manifestations took on magical, ritualesque, and mystical dimensions. The secularist founder of state was not remembered in a secular fashion.

"Visits to a Saint's Tomb"

A practice that had been institutionalized since 1953, visitations to Ataturk's mausoleum (Anıtkabir) in Ankara were reinvigorated in public life during the 1990s, with people organizing trips to the mausoleum in massive groups to voice complaints about the present state of affairs and to express loyalty to Ataturk. When Ataturk died in Istanbul on November 10, 1938, a huge state funeral had been organized, and large numbers of the public attended with expressions of grief and feelings of loss.[8] Those who have been socialized in the institutions of Turkey are familiar with pictures of a crying nation. In schools and public offices all over the country, formalized commemoration services have been practiced at 9:05 in the morning on every November 10 to remember the moment when Ataturk closed his eyes "to leave his nation behind."[9] The ritual of standing in a show of respect as the sirens sounded made November 10 into a symbol of the moment when Turks had been orphaned as a nation.

Anıtkabir, Ataturk's mausoleum, had been built over the course of fifteen years following his death. A massive neoclassical structure, somewhat resembling the Acropolis in Athens, it was erected on the topmost hill of Ankara. Visits to the mausoleum took on a ritualistic protocol; people would have to descend from their vehicles and walk toward the monument in silence and respect. Anıtkabir had been built in a site that was visible from all points in Ankara, a city founded by Ataturk to set Turkey's course in a direction that countered that of the former Ottoman palace in Istanbul.[10]

In the 1990s, when tension with Islamists was at its height, secularists from many walks of life began to organize group visits to Ataturk's place of rest. The commemoration of November 10th was significantly more popular among civil servants as well as laypeople in the mid-1990s than it had been in the 1980s. But even on other days of the year, less nationally symbolic occasions, people from different occupational sectors walked in groups to the mausoleum with written complaints in hand. If they had experienced injustice on the part of a state institution, for example, they wrote in the book of commemoration in Anıtkabir in symbolic complaint to the national father figure.[11] So went the visit of university professors, wearing scholarly cloaks, to Anıtkabir in 1994. When their rights were breached by the Institute of Higher Education (YÖK), professors wrote personal complaints in Ataturk's symbolic book and organized a public demonstration by walking together in a large group to the mausoleum.[12]

Such performances of loyalty to Ataturk were overinterpreted in public life. In the 1990s, Ataturk was turned into symbol of absolute justice by Ataturkists of different backgrounds, transcending the vagaries of particular governments. Those who employed the symbol of Ataturk as if it were a cure for their contemporary social and political ills conflated an overarching notion of "state" with his ghost. Ataturk was dead. But people visited his tomb in great numbers and wrote him personally addressed complaints, soliciting his help, as if he were still alive. Standing by his tomb, the imagination colored by mass-produced figures of Ataturk, visitors to the mausoleum personified their idea of state for themselves. In the act of paying a visit to Ataturk and speaking to him directly, they anthropomorphized the far-too-abstract notion of the state.[13]

Visits to Ataturk's mausoleum were ironically likened, by a parliamentarian of the Islamist Welfare Party in 1994, to saint's tomb visitations (türbe ziyaretleri).[14] Even though these practices were performed out of reverence for a secularist head of state by secular individuals, it would be wrong, I think, to construct a radical epistemological differentiation between the devotional Sufi practice of visiting a saint's tomb, on the one hand, and the act of visiting Ataturk's mausoleum, on the other hand. In a certain sense, it is difficult not to agree with the Islamist parliamentarian who used the image of a "saint's tomb" to characterize Anıtkabir. Journeys to Ataturk's mausoleum show a resemblance with the practice of visiting a sheyh's tomb as an expression of ongoing devotion and a desire for favors and support.[15]

Secularity and religion have been distinguished from one another too

categorically by social scientists working under the paradigm of modernization or rationalization. In contrast, a number of anthropologists have studied formalized and secular state ceremonies as forms of ritual comparable
to religious practice.[16] I build upon the work of such political anthropologists. However, I argue that the concept of secular ritual still operates from
within a discourse of secularism, validating secularism without politicizing
it or subjecting it to rigorous political critique. I propose, therefore, to
investigate the mystical propensity attributed to the "secular" image of Ataturk in terms other than those reified for "secularism." Far from being an
orderly state ritual, Ataturkism is expressed in the domains of excessive
emotion, waves of feeling for a central signifier of contemporary Turkish
identity, or reverence for a personified image of state. Secularism needs to
be studied within this culture of and for the state.

Mystical Apparitions

Yet further Ataturkist practices incited magic and mysticism. In different
parts of the country, people fashioned links of sorts between Ataturk and
supernatural forces. On October 30, 1994, the secularist *Hürriyet* newspaper reported that the silhouette of Ataturk's profile had appeared on a
mountain across the village of Gündeşli in Ardahan when a cloud cast
down its shadow (see figure 8). "Regularly, in the village of Gündeşli, the
profile of Ataturk appears on the mountain," according to the article in the
newspaper that was accompanied by a photograph of this apparition dated
June 1994. After the October 29th celebrations of Republic Day, *Hürriyet*
interpreted this event as proof for "the indivisible unity of our country."[17]
In the context of PKK bombings in İzmir earlier that month, this newspaper's editor was using the symbol of Ataturk to recall *Misak-ı Milli*, or
the 1920 declaration of Turkey's national borders and official construction
of Turkey as a country.[18] Moreover, Ardahan was a significant place for the
shadow of Ataturk to materialize. Nationalist poets always made reference
to Ardahan as the easternmost point of the country, stretching away from
Edirne in the west. Moreover, Ardahan is close to Kars, which is densely
populated by Kurds. Here, there was a recourse to mysticism in the effort
to legitimize and reinstate an Ataturkist nationalism. The secularist journalists of *Hürriyet*, as well as (reportedly) the villagers of Gündeşli, were
searching for mystical signs of a constructed transcendental truth of Turkey: the materialization and, therefore, affirmation of a central symbol of
identity. In this case, the apparition of Ataturk's profile as shadow on the
mountain was taken as supernatural proof of the unity of Turkey's borders
against claims made by Kurdish nationalists.[19] The imagining of mystical
clues about Ataturk arose out of a desire to render Turkey permanent on

Figure 8. Photo of Ataturk's profile, believed to have been reflected from a passing cloud in the village of Gündeşli (source: *Hürriyet* newspaper).

the landscape of this geography. Mysticism was deployed here to suggest the primordiality or naturalness of Turkey against arguments to the contrary.[20]

Calling Spirits

Another common magical link to Ataturk can be observed in the practice of calling upon spirits. Spirit calling is very popular, especially in urban places, and is undertaken by saying Kuranic prayers over a reversed Turkish coffee cup placed in the middle of a circle of Turkish-alphabet letters written in Latin script. Those who call upon spirits, sometimes with the help of a medium, recount the coded responses of the spirits through the movement of the coffee cup among the letters of the alphabet. It is interesting that, as common as it is to call upon spirits in urban Turkey, so is it not unusual to supplicate the spirit of Ataturk. And, invariably it is reported that Ataturk responds with only one sentence, spelling the letters of "Don't disturb me" (*Beni rahatsız etmeyin*) with the coffee cup. What is significant in these stories and practices is the widespread phenomenon of wanting spiritually to communicate with the ghost of Ataturk. It seems that those who partake in such spirit-calling sessions have been looking for mystical or supernatural clues for the existence of Turkey and the Turkish state. What is even more interesting to note is the unilaterally identical response of Ataturk. Most other spirits who are invited through such sessions communicate messages from the other world, including fatal information about the future of individuals in this one. Spirit callers narrate stories of dialogue with dead individuals in this way. But Ataturk always says "Don't disturb me." Unlike other spirits, Ataturk is untouchable, in the instance of these practices, even after his death. People attempt to forge spiritual connections with him without committing sacrilege or rendering him ordinary. A mystical contact of sorts is accomplished with Ataturk—an affirmation of his transcendental presence—and his "don't disturb me" serves in mystifying his image even further.

Numerology

In the context of cultural conflict between secularists and Islamists, as hyped up by the media and politicians in the mid-1990s, certain individuals attempted to forge a bridge of sorts between Ataturk and Islam. The number of people who turned to Islam in this period was so significant that certain Ataturkists found that they had to engage with (rather than reject) Islam if they wanted to relegimitize Ataturk's state and worldview. And they had to read Ataturkism into the original sources of Islam—the Kuran and the Prophet's sayings—as recognized by Islamists.

In October 1994, a few months after the Welfare Party assumed municipalities in Istanbul, Cenk Koray, a well-known journalist and public figure, published a book titled *Kuran, Islam, Ataturk, and the Miracle of 19*. The book was meant to present clues to Ataturk's positivist and scienticist worldview in the Kuran. In Cenk Koray's reading of verses of the Kuran, there were traces of scientific findings. He gave citations for inferences about the existence of oxygen in the air, the sphericity of the earth, the law of gravity, the chemical formation of petrol, the possibility of visiting the moon, and so forth. But most importantly, he drew attention to the "mathematical accuracy" of the Kuran through the "miracle of the number 19." By counting nineteen through the old numerical system (*cifr*) in the letters of the names of God and in verses of the Kuran, one could arrive at all the secrets of the Kuran. According to Koray, "The miracle of 19 will convince atheists as to the existence of God and will open the gates of faith." "It is not possible," he noted, "to find a human being who can devise such an extraordinary mathematical plan" (44). The account of nineteen, here, is taken as proof for God.

But Koray's real intentions lay elsewhere. To counter polarization between Ataturkism and Islam, he wanted to illustrate congruence. He wanted to recast a politics of culture in which belief in God had been posited as diametrically opposed to a commitment to Ataturk's principles.

What he called "the miracle of 19" was a guideline for his efforts to "prove" the supernatural (and particularly "Islamic") qualities of Ataturk. As it was in the life of the Prophet Muhammed, so was the number 19 prevalent in the life of Ataturk, in Koray's construction. Ataturk was born in the year 1881 and died in 1938, numbers exactly divisible by 19. His first military assignment was as "commander of the 19th army corps." The number of letters in his name, Mustafa Kemal Ataturk, amounted to 19. And Ataturk initiated the War of National Liberation on the memorable date of May 19, 1919. From all these calculations, Cenk Koray derived that "Ataturk was sent to Turkey by the orders of God in order to complete a particular mission" (45–6).[21] Between 1994 and 1997, Koray's book became a best-seller in Turkey. It was advertised in and promoted by mainstream secular newspapers.

Statues and Idols

Such interest in finding supernatural, mystical, or Islamic affirmation for the secularist and modernist worldview of Ataturk and for his successes in founding Turkey has to be placed in the context of a wider social phenomenon of organizing Ataturk events. Efforts to give magical or religious meaning to the Turkish state, to inscribe a lasting presence for "Ataturk's Turkey" in supernatural and natural space, arose in the middle of the 1990s out of anxiety over the possible disintegration of Turkey as a result of attacks from Kurdish and Islamist social movements. Accordingly, people joined forces to organize all sorts of Ataturk events. For example, in April 1994, Bedri Baykam, a well-known artist and Ataturkist activist, dedicated an exhibition to Republic Day and the memory of Ataturk. His paintings, against a backdrop of enlarged clippings from early republican newspapers, were meant to remind the public of the purpose of Ataturk's revolution, especially with regard to the building of Turkey out of a "War for National Liberation." The week of November 10, 1994 was officially organized as "Ataturk Week" (*Atatürk Haftası*) in memory of the death of the nation's founder. The most popular singers appeared in concert together to sing for Ataturk in an event sponsored by an Ataturkist civic organization, the Mustafa Kemal Foundation.[22] President Demirel ceremonially introduced Ataturk statues into four new schools in Ankara, including one in the neighborhood of Sincan, densely populated by Islamists. Ataturk statues were planted in the main school courtyards, with visitors to the state ceremonies carefully checked by security forces and watched by armed policemen from the roofs of nearby buildings. In his speeches on this occasion, President Demirel declared that "15 million young Turkish people are taking charge of Ataturk with love" and that "the statue of

Figure 9. Standard busts and statue of Ataturk, for sale to public and private offices and buildings.

Ataturk is a symbol of love."[23] The placing of Ataturk statues was the central defining activity of Ataturk Week events.

As institutionalized as these stately reaffirmations of the framework of Turkish statism were, activity around Ataturk's image was now more widespread among members of society. Demand for Ataturk busts, statues, portraits, posters, and badges grew in the mid-1990s, with people decorating their physical surroundings with images of Ataturk[24] (see figure 9). The image of Ataturk was mechanically reproduced in art studios and in civic gatherings of sorts. In reflecting on this frenzy over Ataturk, the Islamist *Yeni Şafak* newspaper likened the cult around Ataturk statues to "idolatry" (*putçuluk*) and *akit* declared that "statues do not fill hungry stomachs."[25]

Indeed, erecting Ataturk statues was an ordinary practice of statecraft in Turkey, undertaken by each new government to illustrate authority over different districts of the country and to reproduce an overpowering image of a unified Turkish statehood. More energy was channeled to such ceremonials than were geared to education and health. The head of Ataturk, whether in the form of bust, statue, portrait, or badge, was symbol of the existence and longevity of the Turkish state. And politicians at the time regularly made visits to different districts of the southeast, in which the Turkish army was at war with the PKK, to erect Ataturk statues.

The poignant place of Ataturk statues in the making of Turkish nationalism has been described by psychiatrist Vamık Volkan (1980, 151–154). Volkan describes the case of an eleven-year-old boy, Savaş, who, born to a nationalist poet in Cyprus during the ethnic conflict in 1963, was named for "War." His father had dedicated to him a book of poems interwoven with images of a weeping statue of Ataturk. In later years, Savaş would pass through a phase of excessive identification with the statue of Ataturk. Volkan, who analyzed him, writes that Savaş thought his skin, if scratched, would chip off like a statue's.

Though an extreme case, this story nicely illustrates the extent of symbolic weight attached to statues of Ataturk in the context of Turkish nationalism. Identification is not with a disembodied idea of an institution, but with the figure of a national hero rendered permanent, after death, by being carved in stone. Statues of Ataturk, though dead stone, have a life for those who revere them. With the aura that is ascribed to them in the political culture, they have the capacity to move people's innermost senses of personal identification. The state is personified and is therefore rendered closer to human experience. The statue of Ataturk, then, is paramount as a marker of Turkish statehood. Much more than a show of faith in secularism, fetishizing the statue is also an expression of loyalty to the project of the Turkish state.

Here, I have been illustrating the specific manner in which a particular group of people who conceive of themselves as a nation actually imagine their state. Rather than being imagined in the abstract terms suggested by Philip Abrams (1988), the Turkish state materializes in peoples' (semi-) consciousness in the figure of the person (man) of Ataturk, in the objectified form of statue, bust, portrait, or badge.

"Ataturk" has a central place in the imaginary lifeworld of those socialized in Turkish nationalist institutions. His life story is taught year-after-year with incessant repetition in schools. The birth, childhood, and growth of Ataturk into soldier and statesman is narrated very frequently in the political culture, whether it be in schools, on TV, or in newspapers, as metaphor for the birth of a state. Ataturk's life path, turned into mythology, is to be taken as representation of the Turkish state. "Running through the field and chasing crows with his sister, the little Mustafa in the vicinity of Salonica" is an image ingrained in the national imagining of everyone disciplined into subjecthood under the Turkish state. "The little Mustafa, called by his teacher to the front of the classroom and told, 'let your name be Kemal from now on, my child'" is another anecdote that rings in the ears of those socialized into Turkishness. He was called by his name, "Kemal," and the name has been blown up in proportion as though it had been given to the state. Oral recitation from memory of Ataturk's life story, performed throughout years of schooling, has created a common pool of national reference and identification points. The Turkish state is personified and imagined necessarily, now, through the symbolisms of Ataturk.

There is a widespread practice of resorting to sayings (*vecizeler*) of Ataturk for guidance, as if these were sayings (*hadis*) of the Prophet. There is an appropriate saying of Ataturk's for every context and situation. Politicians of various persuasions make regular references to Ataturk's recorded and canonized words. "*Ne Mutlu Türküm Diyene*," or "How Happy Is the One Who Declares Himself a Turk," is one of these. Public offices are decorated with framed quotations such as this one by Ataturk. Sayings are taught and memorized in schools. In the 1990s, Ataturk's sayings were repopularized. Ataturkists would sum up the lesson of their everyday conversations by asking, "What did Ataturk say?" before reciting his statements as though seeking validation in a book of religious commentary.

Heads of State

When contemporary "heads of state" are deemed incompetent or are criticized in public discourse, a reified "head of Ataturk" appears and reappears (sometimes mystically or religiously, as I have shown) on many sites in the arena of what has been called "society." Ataturkism, in the diversity of causes in which it is presently employed, is a serious and persistent sentiment and culture in contemporary Turkey. As the image of Ataturk is utilized in secularist struggles against Islamists, so is the figure of Ataturk used in struggles with corruption, in resistance against neoliberalism, in pan-Turkist reaffirmations of nationalism, as well as in union fights for workers' rights. The image of Ataturk lives on, materializing out of every corner, deployed for a whole diversity of contradictory causes and situations.

Conversely, in Islamist movements that define themselves against the secularism and Westernism of Ataturk, other heads of state are reanimated or brought into relevance. The figure of Fatih Sultan Mehmet, conqueror of Istanbul and Ottoman Sultan who set Turkish-Islam on a course of authority over Europe, has been especially popularized by members of the Islamist Welfare Party. In fact, the Welfare Party has been attempting to dispose of Ataturk as "figure of state" and replace it with the image of Fatih Sultan Mehmet. (Other, more politically conservative Islamists prefer the figure of Abdülhamid II of the late nineteenth and early twentieth centuries, known for his war with the modernist and constitutionalist Young Turks). In such movements to undermine the official image of "head of state" (Ataturk), a "head" of sorts is, no less, still apparent. If

Ataturk, as powerful symbol for a statist culture, is to be disposed of, his image and potency are replaced, by his adversaries, with that of another patriarchal figure of Turco-Islamic statecraft.

In its rise to popularity and quest for state power in the mid-1990s, the Welfare Party aimed at reforging public and state ceremonial.[26] Party leaders suggested new and alternative dates for national festivals. To shift attention away from the official etiquette of observing Republic Day or November 10th, for example, Welfarists emphasized the Muslim holidays of fast and sacrifice. Instead of erecting more Ataturk statues in their municipal zones, Welfarists invested in more mosques. There has been a widespread practice, among secularists, of naming institutions and places after Ataturk and after events or ideas associated with Ataturkism. The Yeşilköy airport in Istanbul has been renamed as "Ataturk airport" for example. Cultural centers, schools, and streets have been named after Ataturk or after the wars that he commanded or the ideals that he preached. To counter this practice of naming institution, object, and place after Ataturk, Welfarist mayors introduced state objects inflected with Ottoman-Islamic references. The void of Ataturkism had to be filled and a new "head" had to be reified. The Welfare Party capitalized on a constructed image of Fatih Sultan Mehmet.

May 29th had been annually celebrated as Conquest Day (*Fetih Günü*) in Istanbul, in remembrance of the day in 1453 when Istanbul had been captured from the Byzantines by the Ottomans under the command of Fatih Sultan Mehmet. Yet not much popular significance was attached to this date until it was appropriated by the Welfare Party. In 1994, a couple of months after Welfare took office in Istanbul, Conquest Day was organized as a major extravaganza. Welfarists wanted to mark new dates for public celebration and commemoration and they preferred what could be suggested ideologically from "conquest" to what was spoken in the name of "the republic." In the massively attended event filling up a whole soccer stadium in Istanbul, Welfarists declared that they had gathered in the memory of Fatih Sultan Mehmet to "conquer Turkey and the world."[27] Welfarists started the day by visiting the tomb of Fatih Sultan Mehmet, which stands in the courtyard of Fatih mosque, built according to the sultan's wishes, in Istanbul. The subsequent public ceremony began with a collective *namaz*, thus changing the course of official ceremonial, which was usually inaugurated with the singing of the national anthem. And after the speeches of Welfare's leaders, the conquest of Istanbul was brought to life on the stadium field by actors from the Welfare Party's youth foundation (MGV). A makeshift Byzantine city wall was attacked by men under the leadership of the character Fatih on horseback. And at the end of the play, "the keys of Istanbul" were symbolically handed to Erbakan, the leader of the Welfare Party. He was to succeed Fatih, in this production, as head of state. Istanbul was to be reinvented as the center of state, in opposition to republican Ankara and in line with the old Ottoman polity.

Welfarists posited themselves against the state, at least in the way they presented themselves in public discourse. And yet, they reinvented the state in new (or "old") form through their practices. Indeed, statism has shown itself to have a remarkable potential for self-preservation in Turkey at the level not only of state but also of society. The state endures at the level of signification and actuality as it is reemployed, reformulated, and adjusted after it has been deconstructed. More significantly, statism is reproduced on the ground level, as organizations, objects, institutions, political and economic processes, and lives centered on its methods live on. As the political economy that has been mobilized around the signifier "Turkish state" remains alive and functioning, in spite of its trips and turns, images of "heads of state" are sought time and again for what appear to be a variety of projects.

The state has particular significance in the ethnographic and historical context of Turkey, arguably more so than other contexts. More than any other symbol of identity, the state (*devlet*) has been central to the constitution of Turkish identity. The practice of statecraft was primarily reserved for the Muslim subjects (whether born as such or converted) of the Ottoman empire, with some exceptions. This has been the case in the Turkish republic, as well. For many centuries, Turkishness was associated with the practice of statecraft by those subjects of the empire who were marginalized from it. Turkish identity under nationalism was not, unlike other nationalisms, imagined in the absence of state, but in the enduring presence of stately practices. Up to this day, Turkish national identity is developed in school history books through accounts of a so-called lineage of Turkish states from the Göktürks and Huns in medieval Central Asia to Ataturk's Republic of Turkey. Any study of secularism and Islamism in Turkey, then, would be significantly misplaced without an ethnographic depiction of the specific culture of statism here. I define statism as something beyond nationalism, as an identification not only or even necessarily with a nation, but with a reified and exalted state.

Secularist Excesses

The study of nationalism as a mode of discipline (Mitchell 1988) fails to explain the excess of emotion through which nationalism is felt and expressed, the search for mystical reassurance, the hallucination of supernatural presence, the cult of Ataturk. Even at times when modern techniques of ordering power are not successfully implemented or fully internalized, or when the organizing operations of nationalism are resisted

(Fahmy 1997), there is still what could be called an effect of nationalism that survives. Slavoj Žižek has coined the concept of "fantasy" for the psychoanalytic symptom that persists in spite of analysis. I locate "excess" in this domain of "fantasy," after construction and deconstruction. Perhaps, then, the site for the study of nationalism ought to be sought not in the rubric of modernity (institutions, bureaucracy, order), but of excess.[28] Nationalism (including its secularist versions) also, and significantly, operates through the medium of excess (Aretxaga 2000).

In "The Work of Art in the Age of Mechanical Reproduction," Walter Benjamin (1990) had written about "the contemporary decay of the aura." He had related this to "the increasing significance of the masses in contemporary life" (325). Benjamin was optimistic about contemporary times, surprisingly so, given the historical circumstances in which he was caught. He believed that photographs that grew out of the technique of mechanical reproduction destroyed the "aura" that characterized traditional works of art. Because it could be reproduced without detracting from its value, the photograph bespoke of a more egalitarian society. Indeed, Benjamin imagined the photograph to hold an antifascist potential.

More than sixty years later, at a time when many new forms of mechanical reproduction are widely available, it is not possible to make the same observation as did Benjamin about images. In the age of consumable goods, the figure of Ataturk, widely reproduced, invokes what could still be called an "aura." And in the personified figure of Ataturk it is the Turkish state, Turkey, that is being reified. There is symbolic excess around the Turkish state, expressed in intense and vast proportions in public life. How appropriate is it, then, to study and interpret the culture of secularism outside the terms of statism?

In Turkey, the army is the most persistent secularist institution, much more so than political parties or governments, which strategically shuffle their relations with religious constituencies. This army, which uses the terms of "secularism," "democracy," "modernity," "rationality," "stability," and "order" under the rubric of "Ataturk" to counter the Islamist movement, is the same army that employs violence in its war against Kurds in southeastern Turkey and against Cypriots in Cyprus. Thus the discourse of secularism is coeval with violence. Secularism in Turkey is the discourse of state power employed by the army. It would be a mistake to evaluate secularism, then, without studying its politics as practiced in the context of a statist culture of violence.

The aura around Ataturk is enforced through specific state practices. In 1951, the Turkish National Parliament passed a law on "Crimes Against Ataturk." Law number 7872, still on the books in the 1990s, punishes all those who "insult the memory of Ataturk" through words or actions to three years in prison. Those who damage busts or statues of Ataturk are similarly punished with confinement. Through the years, antisecularist sentiment in Turkey has revolved around the figure of Ataturk, whereby Islamist groups have often expressed their dissent by disfiguring Ataturk statues. It is in response to such actions that the law on "Crimes Against Ataturk" was originally developed and why it was still in place during the 1990s. Islamists who target the image of Ataturk in their critiques of secularism nurture the cult around his figure by default. But the aura around Ataturk is not just produced spontaneously by the public. The fetishism of Ataturk is also fed by legal prohibition.[29]

Secularism has often been represented through the imagery of sobriety in distinction from religious fundamentalism or communalism, especially in scholarship on India.[30] It has explicitly been differentiated from such concepts as statism, nationalism, or fascism. However, at least in the historical context of Turkey, secularism has been manifest not only in the rational and ordered terms of an analytically reified modernity, but also in the medium of excessive expression, mystical, ritualesque, and religious.

Notes

Introduction
Semiconscious States

1. The most important reference on "the public sphere" is, of course, the work of Habermas (1989). For the term "public culture," see Appadurai (1988). For recent anthropological work on "civil society," see Hann and Dunn (1996).

2. Jacqueline Rose, merging psychoanalytic theory with a study of the state, has developed the notion of "states of fantasy," identifying statehood as "the symptom of the modern world" (1996, 12).

3. Careful readers will notice my reference to Europeanist critics like Sloterdijk and Žižek in situating and studying the political in Turkey. Indeed, there are parallels, and one would be grossly misconceived in attempting a cultural relativist distinction between the political in Turkey and in Europe.

4. Hall et al. define moral panic as follows: "When the official reaction to a person, group of persons or series of events is out of all proportion to the actual threat offered, when 'experts,' in the form of police chiefs, the judiciary, politicians and editors perceive the threat in all but identical terms, and appear to talk 'with one voice' of rates, diagnoses, prognoses and solutions, when the media representations universally stress 'sudden and dramatic' increases . . . and 'novelty,' above and beyond that which a sober realistic appraisal could sustain, then we believe it is appropriate to speak of the beginnings of a moral panic" (1978, 16).

5. The project at hand is distinct and different from Kemalism or Ataturkism, represented by some of the characters who are studied in this ethnography. It is important to note that at the present time, now that the EU has granted candidacy to Turkey, those who are defensive and skeptical about joining the EU are the Westernist and secularist Kemalists (in high-ranking positions in the state and the army) who would like to maintain their power in a Turkish status quo. Curiously, Islamists are generally in favor, presently, of Turkey's still possible membership in the EU.

6. Kelly (1991) makes a similar point on the postmodernist reification of the notion modernity.

7. For this, see Anderson (1991). Malkki (1994) has studied nationalism as an inter-national (between nations) discourse.

8. Berkes (1964) notes that Turkish nationalists acquired their information about their supposed racial, cultural, and linguistic links with the peoples of Central Asia through the publications of West European Orientalists. Here too, then, we can interpret that "national culture" was formulated in the context of power-laden relations with Europe.

9. Dirks (1990) has argued that this, in fact, was not even a paradox, for the projects of nationalism and modernity were integral.

10. This is according to Lewis (1969, 8).

11. Distinction between the Turkish and Greek nation-states, for example, was primarily defined around religion. In the exchange of populations that took place in 1922 between Greece and Turkey after the war, the criterion was religion. Indeed, in this event, Greek-speaking Muslim inhabitants of Crete were forced to move to Western Anatolia, while Turkish-speaking Orthodox inhabitants of Anatolia, such as certain gypsy groups, were forced to migrate to Western Thrace and Macedonia. Turkey was left, as a result of historical agency and not as a matter of fact, as predominantly Muslim. But the Muslim members of this newly defined "mother-land" were of mixed background, many having Albanian, Slavic, Greek, Arab, Circassian, Tatar, Armenian, Kurdish, Jewish, and other ancestries. It is only by force of historical agency that all these people who lived in or came to inhabit the new Turkey were defined as "Turkish" or as "Turks" (*Türk*).

12. The "Community Houses" (*Halk Evleri*) were founded under the early republic to educate Turkey's citizens in the values of the new nation.

13. In his book, Stirling describes his effort to select a relatively typical Turkish village for study, one distant from the influence of the urban metropolises and representative of what he defined as "the Sunni Muslim traditional majority." For a critique of holistic approaches to culture and society, see Gupta and Ferguson (1992).

14. For examples of such ethnography, see Hann (1990, 1993) and Shankland (1993). Some of Sirman's earlier work (1990) also reflects aspects of this British tradition. Beller-Hann and Hann's most recent work (2000) is still surprisingly conventional in this sense.

15. Delaney (1991) distinguishes herself to a certain extent from Clifford Geertz. Yet her project is very much placed and informed by the interpretivist search for "the native's point of view."

16. For a critique of nativism in anthropology, see Kuper (1994).

17. For an excellent analysis of positivism in interpretive anthropology, see Adams (1997).

18. Hall (1993, 392) studies "identity as a 'production'."

19. Lederman (1989), for example, draws attention to internal contestation among the Mendis, taking issue with ethnographies which produce holistic cultural accounts.

20. These othering discourses are situated, of course. The encounters that Istanbul Greeks, Armenians, or Kurds have had with the principle of "nativity" is different and definitely more drastic.

Chapter One
Prophecies of Culture

1. There had been some public controversy over Ayasofya at the time. The imposing structure of building, dome, and minarets had originally been built as a Byzantine church, transformed into a mosque upon the Ottomans' conquest of Istanbul, and finally converted into a museum in Turkey's early republican period. Islamists have been demanding ever since that Ayasofya be turned back into a mosque. Ayasofya is at the top of the must-see list in tourists' itinerary of Istanbul. While for most secularist Turkish visitors, it represents a museum of "a time past,"

an Islamist visiting Ayasofya would most likely be lamenting its former state as a mosque.

2. Contrary to the implication of Pierre Bourdieu's notion (1991) of "habitus," people in Turkey at this juncture were not just habitually living out their everyday practices with lack of consciousness, but were thinking abstractly about their culture and producing public commentary about tradition. And it was not only intellectuals who were involved in this sort of expressive disagreement over the disciplines of "proper" Turkish culture.

3. Upon learning my Jewish name on a first meeting, many informants' almost instinctive response, whether they were of Islamist or secularist affiliation, would be, "*Ha yabancı!*" (Oh foreigner!) showing surprise at my native use of the Turkish language.

4. The Turkish-Islamic synthesis is a version of Turkish nationalism that developed in Turkey during the twentieth century. Advocated by certain Islamists as well as by certain activists of pan-Turkism, it maps out a Turkish and Muslim heritage for Turkey, externalizing Europe as well as all elements deemed "non-Turkish" or "non-Muslim" within Turkey.

5. In a similar manner, Foucault (1980) identifies and studies what he calls a "modern" time of heightened interest in discoursing on sexuality.

6. Many scholars have studied and theorized the centrality of gender to the constitution of nationalisms. We build upon the works of Kandiyoti (1993), Göle (1991), Chatterjee (1993), Jayawardena (1988), Mohanty, Russo, and Torres (1991), Alexander and Mohanty (1997), Yuval-Davis and Anthias (1989), and Sangari and Vaid (1989). Aided by these texts, we are now able to study the implication of gendered relations in the making of nationalisms and colonialisms. In this chapter, I study the implication of a gendered historical contingency in competing versions of nationalist discourse.

7. Since then, there has been change in discourses on Turkey's culture and my account suggests possible ways to analyze these changes, but does not endeavor to study them.

8. Welfarists were much more accurate, it turned out, in their poll research. In fact, they pretty much knew ahead of time that they would win. Until the very day of the elections, on the other hand, the secular mainstream press was announcing the candidates of the Social Democratic Peoples' Party (SHP) and The Motherland Party (ANAP) to be the favorites.

9. Islamists were aware of this mode of discoursing about them. They in turn joked about what they called secularists' exaggerated "nightmares." For example, the monthly magazine *Bülten* (1994) published by members of an educational foundation for young Islamist intellectuals (Bilim ve Sanat Vakfı) entitled its post-elections issue "The Nightmare: The 27th of March, the most Exciting Adventure after Friday the 13th."

10. Careful distinction has to be made between Islam(s) and Islamism(s). Readers will notice that in this chapter I often use the terms "Islam," "Islamism," "Islamic culture," and "Islamic order and administration" as if they were interchangeable. I do so only because in the popular secularist discourse that I am untangling, the distinction between these terms is blurred. This study is not about what Islam or Islamism essentially are, but about what they were made to be in Istanbul's public life in the 1990s.

11. There was, simultaneously, *serious* discussion of the premises and misdeeds of secularism and Islamism. In fact, at the time of Welfare's takeover, private and public TV channels were organizing one forum after another for intellectual representatives from the secularist and Islamist communities to discuss their differences with one another. TV has been a central institution of public life in Turkey. It is one of the only media of entertainment for poor people (most families try to get a TV as soon as they can assemble some money), and in many homes as well as in public places it is common to keep the TV on at all times. The broadcasted forums on secularist-Islamist politics of identity were watched by a great number of people, who sat after-hours listening to the grim and monotonous speeches of intellectual talking heads. One particular discussion forum, the "Political Arena" (*Siyaset Meydanı*), was very popular. It was watched very widely in Turkey and my informants made regular references to its arguments. Mainstream newspapers also reserved much space in their layouts for the humorless discussion of the possibilities for Istanbul under an Islamist administration.

12. This main question of my ethnography here is the counter-face of Bora's (1995) question about the perception of an Islamic administration on the part of Islamists themselves.

13. For a detailed historical ethnography of the Girls' Institutes and the institution of home economics classes in early republican Turkey, see Navaro-Yashin (2000).

14. For this interpretation of Ataturk's reforms regarding women, see Tekeli (1982). For a study of these reforms as symbolic, see Kandiyoti (1987).

15. Indeed, since then, the Welfare Party did win the national elections of December 1995, too, and led a coalition government until the summer of 1997.

16. "Kuran" is the Turkish spelling of the Koran.

17. Frankenberg (1993) has done a similar ethnographic exercise in studying the racialized identity of white American women. Race had mostly been studied as an issue that concerned African-Americans. Frankenberg drew attention to the implication of white women's lives in racialized identity, writing about "the social construction of whiteness." Like the Turkish-secularists whom I study who did not perceive their lifestyles to be cultural but normal or neutral, white American women thought that race was not their issue but that of black women. Like Frankenberg, who reverses the object of analysis in studying race and racism, in this book I study Turkey's secularist community (along with the Islamist) as culturalized.

However, I do not fully endorse Göle (1991), who likens Islamists to "Turkey's blacks" and draws analogies between Turkish secularists' approach to Islamists and whites' racism against blacks in the United States and Europe. Although the analogy is rhetorically useful and has an important political point, I would not endorse it ethnographically or historically, for racism against blacks in the United States and Britain is different from secularist Turks' attitudes against Islamists. Islamists have more power than African-Americans currently do in claiming the nationalism of their country to themselves. There are stakes over versions of nationalism, and Islamists work for a more Islamic-centered definition (i.e., the Turkish-Islamic synthesis). Islamists are able to assume presence and power within organs of the state, unlike most African-Americans.

18. The Turkish language has two forms of past tense. One, expressed with the suffix "-di," is used in speaking of past events that were either experienced firsthand by the narrator or that are known to have certainly taken place. The other, expressed

with the suffix "-miş," is used in the narration of stories, fairytales, and past events overheard only secondhand. History is always written with the suffix "-di," rumor is exchanged with the suffix "-miş." The specific gossip that I cite here reached my ears in the "-miş" form and was inscribed in my notes in the form of "-di." In other words, I am saying that these rumors certainly did circulate, saying that such and such an incident was apparently experienced by such and such person.

19. "Yobazlar İstanbul'da otobüs kaçırdı," *Cumhuriyet*, April 1, 1995, p. 1.

20. When I use the term "mainstream secular" for media, I refer to the newspapers *Sabah, Milliyet, Hürriyet*, and *Yeni Yüzyıl*, and the TV stations aTV, SHOW TV, Interstar TV, Channel 6, and Channel D as well as the state's TRT. These television channels have the highest rating and they are distinct from the Islamist channels Channel 7, Samanyolu, and TGRT. The mainstream secular press represented in the newspapers cited above is once again distinct in political discourse from Islamist newspapers such as *Milli Gazete, Türkiye, Yeni Şafak, Vakit* (later *akit*), and *Selam*. For a study of the construction of knowledge about Islam in commercial television in Turkey, see Öncü (1994).

21. In this sense, the contingency studied here is distinct from that in Adams's (1996) ethnography on the relation between Sherpas and Westerners. In the historical context that Adams studies, Western discourse on "authentic Sherpas" produces the Sherpas that are desired by Western tourism, spiritualism, and consumerism. In the case of the relation between Turkish secularists and Islamists that I address, secularists have had ways of effecting and influencing what they fear.

22. Lockman (1996) approaches history relationally, whereby he studies Arab and Jewish workers in Palestine not in isolation from each other, but in relation to and cognizance of each other.

23. "'RP'ye Oy Vermedik," *Milliyet*, April 1, 1994, p. 3.

24. Interviews with Nusret Bayraktar, April 2, 1994, the Beyoğlu municipality building.

25. "Kozakçıoğlu: 'Keyfi İşlem Durdurulur'," *Milliyet*, April 1, 1994, p. 9.

26. "Dualı-Kurbanlı Devir," *Cumhuriyet*, April 1, 1994, p. 7.

27. "Belediye'de Olay," *Milliyet*, April 16, 1994, p. 9.

28. These two scholar / journalists are very well known as "experts on Islamism" in France. Their work has been translated into English as well as Turkish.

29. I am not suggesting that this was a conspiracy on the part of the two French journalists who first used the term "fatwa." The two scholars probably thought that they were being accurate in their characterization of Khomeini's statement. They probably half-consciously wanted to think that Khomeini had declared a fatwa, being themselves part of the French public.

30. For an excellent study of the event of the "burning of the book" in Britain in 1989 during the Rushdie affair, as placed in the context of postcolonial British discourse on immigrant Muslims, see Rajasingham (1993).

Chapter Two
The Place of Turkey

1. A history of the word "region" in its Turkish context, as inspired by Raymond Williams's historiography of concepts, would be of utmost interest. However, I do

not endeavor this in what follows. This section on the history of "region" is my summary of the early republican construction of "regionalism." A historical study on regionalism in the Ottoman Empire based on primary sources would be invaluable. For insights into this from the particular perspective of the Balkans, see Todorova (1997).

2. For a history of population exchanges across the Aegean, see Ladas (1932). For ethnography on the impact of this exchange on the Greeks of Asia Minor, see Hirschon (1989) and Voutira (1997). I do not use the terms "mixed" and "hybrid" here assuming that there is a pristine state of ethnic or religious purity. I use it only to emphasize the complex backgrounds of those who were singularly defined as "Muslim" or "Christian" in that modern period of cultural classification. For a critique of the theoretical notion of hybridity, see Spivak (1996, 169).

3. For a history of population transfers between cosmopolitan groups of Christians and Muslims in the eastern Black Sea zone, see Ascherson's (1996) history and travel book, especially chapter 7. For a study of the Pontic Greek diaspora in the Soviet Union, see the work of Eftihia Voutira (1997). Pontic Greeks had a state of their own in the eastern Black Sea region of what is now Turkey for a duration of over 3,000 years until they were forced to immigrate toward Caucasia or, in 1922, to what became modern Greece. Their history of diaspora from Trebizond did not end there: under Stalin, they were sent in massive groups from Georgia to Siberia. More recently, Pontic Greeks have been moving to modern Greece, as if that were the place where they belonged.

4. The Turkish state and, by and large, Turkish public opinion still refuses to acknowledge the atrocities committed against the Armenians as a genocide. In turn, for Armenians, the genocide has become a central historical marker of national memory and identity. The Hemşins, Armenian-speaking Muslims of the eastern Black Sea region of Turkey, were able to escape persecution because of their religion.

5. One of the best accounts of the place of school books in the construction of official history is the work of Ersanlı-Behar (1992).

6. For a critique of the narrative of decline in Ottoman historiography, see Kafadar (1995).

7. A history of early republican Turkish anthropology waits to be written. For an example of anthropological work from the period of national formation, see İnan (1939). Most anthropologists working for the newly established Turkish state were physical anthropologists interested in the skull and skeleton measurements of villagers of Anatolia. İnan, a foster daughter of Ataturk, for example, was sent specially to Switzerland to study physical anthropology, and her monograph includes this sort of racialized data. Later, the discipline of archaeology took more central stage in Turkish nationalists' attempts to construct a Turkish heritage in Anatolia. Some nationalist archaeologists went so far as to argue that the ancient civilization of the Hittites was Turkish.

8. For a study of the centrality of folklore studies in the construction of national cultures, see Herzfeld (1982).

9. It is the early republican nationalists' commitment to cultural Westernization that differentiates their project from nationalisms elsewhere. In postcolonial India, as studied by Partha Chatterjee (1993), there was more splitting, an adoption of

Western technology with an attempt to maintain Indian culture through the domestication of women.

10. This trend has been undergoing radical change (since summer 1997), with the military-backed reenforcement of strict secularism in the educational system as a backlash against the popular Welfare (later Virtue) Party.

11. At certain points in the history of republican Turkey, Jews have attempted to identify themselves as Turks. At present, certain Jews do identify themselves as Turkish (*Türk*), claiming the category of Turkishness as a secular category of citizenship. But most Muslim-born Turks do not really accept Jews as such. For a history of the Turkification of Jews in Turkey, see Bali (1999).

12. For a study of the mapping of modernity onto the nation-state in another context, see Dirks (1990).

13. This is according to the news piece published in the secular / libertarian *Yeni Yüzyıl* on August 16, 1995, p. 8.

14. This is not the first time that the image of Saudi Arabia has been used as a means of crafting a regional and cultural distinction for Turkey. See, for example, an article that preceded the event of August 1995 by one year. The article was authored by secularist lawyer Arif Çavdar and is entitled "The Saudi Arabianization of Turks" (*Cumhuriyet*, September 20, 1994, p. 2).

15. See *Hürriyet*, August 17, 1995, p. 1.

16. It is interesting to note that this comparison, as such, was made by radical Islamist writer Emine Şenlikoğlu, who is reported to have said that "the cutting of heads with a sword is scary. When one thinks about it, the Americans' electric chair is more civilized (*çağdaş*)." Note that the term *çağdaş*, which Şenlikoğlu uses in this interview is one commonly used by secularists with the intention of judging Islamism. The word *çağdaş*, like "modern," is a moral judgment in Turkey, and Şenlikoğlu, who wears a black veil, has been attacked several times for not being *çağdaş*.

17. Such critical counter-discursive pieces on the part of secular mainstream journalists were rare. Almost no journalist or intellectual compared the Saudi legal system with the Turkish. Almost none asked the question of whether the modern forms of punishment in Turkey, routine torture in prisons, for example, were more just. But see for example, the article by Can Dündar in *Yeni Yüzyıl* (August 20, 1995, p. 2), in which the writer asks citizens of Turkey to turn and consider how just the Turkish legal system is and leave aside the ridicule of the Saudi system. In making reference to the movie *Midnight Express*, Dündar notes that Turkey's human rights record is one of the worst in the world. Dündar is implying that Turkey has not matched Western standards of justice well enough to be able to critique Saudi Arabia.

18. See secular mass media from those particular dates, eg. *Hürriyet, Sabah, Yeni Yüzyıl, Milliyet*, and *Cumhuriyet*.

19. See for example Yalçın Doğan's article, "İşte şeriat budur!" *Milliyet*, August 17, 1995, p. 15. Also see headlines in *Hürriyet* on August 17, 1995, p.1, speaking of "*çağdışı kafa kesme*" (uncivilized beheading).

20. This is what certain Islamists have been proposing under the rubric of a "multilegal system" for Turkey, whereby everyone would be judged by the law that she or he chooses. This contemporary construction of "plural legalities" is a presen-

tist Islamist reading and rendering of "the *millet* system" in the Ottoman Empire, where each was judged under the law of his religion. Those categorized as *dhimmi* under the Ottoman state, a legal term that designated non-Muslim subjects, had the right, in certain matters, to employ their proper communal law, in return for paying a higher tax than Muslims to the Ottoman authorities (Rodrigue 1997, 46).

21. Gülay Göktürk, "Bedevi Kimliği," *Yeni Yüzyıl*, August 20, 1995, p. 3.

22. This rather resembles the categorization of immigrant communities and minorities as "ethnic" in North America and Western Europe.

23. Here Hasan Pulur is referring to Islamists in general and Welfarists in particular.

24. See *Milliyet*, August 17, 1995, p. 15. Abdurrahman Dilipak edits a radical Islamist daily newspaper, *akit* (formerly *Vakit*). This newspaper specifically positions itself in critique of the Saudi regime, differentiating dictatorship from Islam. See, for example, a news piece that appeared in *akit* on January 9, 1996, p. 6.

25. Ibid.

26. Ibid.

27. *Zaman*, December 14, 1995, p. 15.

28. *Cumhuriyet*, December 13, 1995, p. 3.

29. *akit*, December 14, 1995, p. 8.

30. *Milli Gazete*, December 14, 1995, p. 1, 8.

31. *Yeni Şafak*, December 14, 1995, p. 5.

32. *Milli Gazete*, December 14, 1995, p. 1.

33. *Zaman*, December 14, 1995, p. 5.

34. *Yeni Şafak*, December 13, 1995, p. 1.

35. *akit*, December 14, 1995, p. 1.

36. The Patriarchate of the Greek Orthodox church is placed in the Fener neighborhood of Istanbul. Islamists have been making a big issue out of this, writing scenarios of conspiracy involving the Patriarchate. When the Patriarchate applied for a new building, not being able to fit in its current premises, numerous Islamist publications wrote of Greek Orthodoxy's plot to invade Turkey from within. Dilipak is speaking from that perspective.

37. For the best account on Sabbetai Zevi, his movement, and the history of *dönme*s in Thessaloniki, İzmir, and Istanbul, see the work of Gershom Scholem (1995). In Turkey, Ilgaz Zorlu (1995), identifying himself as *dönme*, is one person who began, in the 1990s, to publish sensationalist pieces on the history of *dönme*s. Otherwise, most of the literature on *dönme*s published in Turkish is antisemitic conspiracy theory, forging links between Jews, converts, the Freemasons, and secularist Turkish politics.

38. The *namaz*, main form of prayer in Islam, is performed five times a day.

39. The *hazırol* position is taken when listening to and singing the national anthem. It consists of standing up straight with arms stretched formally down. It is normally done in public.

40. Here this nephew is revealing a common fear among such secularist families about the Islamicization of a family member, cases when sons or daughters of secularist families had joined Sufi orders (*tarikat*s) and taken up religious practice.

41. Fatma was showing her concern about the prospects for Turkey's joining in the European Union.

42. For an excellent ethnography of *arabesk* music and musicians in Turkey, see Stokes (1992); also Özbek (1994). Many secularist upper-middle-class families like Fatma's have a denigrating attitude to *arabesk*, looking down upon it as low culture or as the culture of immigrants from Anatolia into the cities.

43. Later on, more of the public in Turkey would learn about the Aczmendi Sufi order to which these particular men belonged. As Aczmendis got involved in demonstrations in protest of a ballet performance in the archaeological museum near the Topkapı Palace and as they increasingly appeared wearing turbans and robes on the streets, many of them were caught by police and convicted in courts for breaching the Hat Law of 1925, which was still in place, the law instituted by Ataturk forbidding the wearing of head gear other than the bowler hat. In the fall of 1996, journalists of the mainstream press barged into the house of an Aczmendi sheyh, found him naked with a young woman, and printed his photograph. The sheyh had temporarily married the young woman through a religious wedding (*muta evliliği*). It is legally forbidden in Turkey to get married through noncivil ceremonies. The sheyh and the young woman were taken to court. But at the time of the incident on the streets of Fatih, the public had not yet come to know about the Aczmendis in this sensationalized journalistic way.

44. While the İmam Hatip schools are attached to the state, Kuranic schools are generally funded by religious foundations or personalities. Many Kuranic schools are "unofficial." In the summer of 1997, the government that overtook power (under military directions) from the coalition between the Welfare and True Path parties, started a major attack on the İmam Hatip and Kuranic schools, in suggesting to transform compulsory elementary education from five to eight years. This way the secularist new ministers wanted to ensure that children underwent 8 years of secularist education in Ministry of Education schools: an attempt on the part of statesmen and the military to curb the strength of religious education in general and the Islamist movement in particular. My walk through Fatih with Fatma took place two years before these new arrangements, but Fatma would, then, make associations between these schools and the Islamist movement.

45. Spencer (1997) has made a similar point about "landscape," arguing that "landscapes are results of human action, and not of nature."

46. Greeks refer to the same war as "the Great Catastrophe." The war in western Anatolia was won by the Turkish army and west Anatolian Greeks were forced to migrate out of their homeland to Greece. What for Turks is "liberation," is therefore "catastrophe" for Greeks in the respective nationalist discourses of the two nation-states.

47. For a critical history of the condition of non-Muslims in Turkey, see Yelda (1996).

48. On September 6–7, 1955, xenophobic riots took place especially against the Greeks of Istanbul, but also against Jews and Armenians, after an unidentified sabotage attempt on Ataturk's house of birth in Thessaloniki, Greece. Many of Istanbul's Greeks, whose past in the city preceded the Ottoman conquest of Istanbul all the way back to the Byzantine era, were forced, out of fear, to leave Turkey permanently for Greece. In 1974, after Greek-Cypriots' attacks against Turkish-Cypriots, many Turkish nationalists turned their gaze against Istanbul's Greeks once again, in retaliation. Until 1971, the Greek government discouraged Istanbul Greeks from moving to Greece. But, almost all the rest of Istanbul's Greeks left

Turkey in the latter half of the 1970s, leaving a very small population of about 3,000 behind.

49. The minority status was granted to Jews, Greeks, and Armenians in Turkey according to the Lausanne Agreement of 1923. This particular conceptualization of minority was an extension of the Ottoman *dhimmi* law, which recognized these separate communities as cultural entities of their own (*millets*). Yet, unlike Ottoman law, after the Lausanne agreement, minorities were not granted the right to practice their own legal systems and had to be judged under what became a unified and secular Turkish law of the state.

50. What was conceptualized in Turkish occidentalism as "Europe" in early republican years—with special reference to France, Italy, Germany, and England—would later be transformed into a notion of "the West" with the United States as a central reference, after Turkey joined NATO following the Second World War.

51. For the concept of "situated knowledge," see Haraway (1990).

52. The work of Jenny B. White (1994) could be considered an exception. Her book concerns itself with working-class women in urban Turkey. There has been developing interest in the study of Alevi women as well, work that could be evaluated as an exception to the proposition I have put forward. However, as much as studies of Alevis have the power to counteract scholarly discourse on Muslim women, they do not say much about Sunni Turkish women who do not practice Islam, ending up (by default) marginalizing the lifestyles of Alevis as "the culture of a minority." Anthropological work on Turkish women has been focused mostly on villages and has not addressed, from this locus, the issues of identity politics as they are played out between secularist and Islamist women in urban Turkey. See for example, Delaney (1991), Sirman (1990), Yalçın-Heckman (1990), Onaran İncirlioğlu (1993), and Hann (1993). A more historically attuned study of contemporary villages would have to deal with the ramifications of nation-wide political conflicts on the periphery, and account for the diminishing distinction between rural and urban life, due especially to the presence of TV and other social institutions.

53. For studies of Turkish-Islamist women, see Göle (1991), İlyasoğlu (1994), Aktaş (1992). Only the last reference here is a study by an Islamist woman of Islamist women in Turkey. The other references are to works and research conducted by secular women scholars.

54. Frankenberg (1993) makes a similar point about the lack of study of the intrinsically racialized aspect of white American women's lives.

55. See, for example, the work of Durakbaşa (1987). The Turkish Economic and Social History Foundation started an oral history project a few years ago. Elite Kemalist women were prime on the list for interviews by scholars of oral history affiliated with the foundation.

56. The word *konuştuk* is used by rural migrants to the city to indicate flirtation before marriage. The word *çıktık* is modern urban slang. Zeynep alternated in using the two idiomatic verbs.

57. Eyüp contains the grave of Eyüp Sultan, one of Prophet Muhammad's closest allies in war and one of only a handful of descendants in the Prophet's line to be buried within the borders of today's Turkey.

58. There is a highly competitive track system in Turkish education. At the end of elementary school, in grade five, those children who are to be sent to good

schools are trained to take a centralized exam prepared by the Ministry of Education. Those who score highly may enroll either in private foreign schools such as Robert College, St. Michel, or the German Lycée or in the state-funded Anatolian lycées. The private foreign schools are attended mostly by elites who can afford to take private lessons to prepare for the exam and to pay the tuition for seven or more years. The Anatolian lycées are good schools, but hard to enter. Most high school graduates in Turkey go to what I called the normal lycées, of the sort Zeynep had attended. These schools are sometimes called "the Turkish lycées" (*Türk liseleri*) and they are state schools.

59. I study the market for veils in chapter 3.

60. "Selling snails in a Muslim neighborhood" is my literal translation of a Turkish saying, "*Müslüman mahallesinde salyangoz satmak*." This refers to attempts at introducing something foreign to a Muslim place. Zeynep's boss interprets this particular form of veiling as a pretense of Islam. She is angered with this woman for wanting to preach Islam to Muslims.

61. I study the public celebration of Republic Day 1994 in chapter 4.

62. *Lahmacun* is a layer of pastry sprinkled with spiced meat in the style of southeastern Turkey's food.

63. Spencer (1990) theorizes a similar convergence between anthropology and Sri Lankan national debates.

64. In another article (1991), Abu-Lughod favors the analytical category "discourse" to that of "culture."

65. I argue this in spite of Abu-Lughod's theoretically attuned statements about representation (1990, 85).

66. Shohat (1988) has written about the reluctant migration of Middle Eastern Jews, who left their countries of origin for Israel, with the encouragement and manipulation of Zionists of European origin, in the first decade of the Israeli nation-state.

67. In Abu-Lughod' review (1990), there are only two references to a non-Arab subject of study within the region that she reifies: one is to the work of Deniz Kandiyoti on Turkish women, and the other is to that of Michael Meeker on Black Sea Turks. On this particular subject, see especially Herzfeld (1987). Hirschon (1989) reveals the ambiguities of identity among Greek immigrants from western Anatolia to the Greek nation-state. Faubion's work (1993) could be read as an ethnography of an urban space and its place in the history and politics of region.

68. On this particular subject, see especially Herzfeld (1987). Hirschon (1989)

69. Excellent literary critiques of nationalism and regionalism are also emerging on Greece and the Balkans. See, respectively, Gourgouris (1996) and Todorova (1997).

Chapter Three
The Market for Identities

1. Kopytoff (1986, 73) distinguishes culture from commodification.

2. I use the term "Muslim," here, to refer to Islamist and / or religious individuals. This is in keeping with the ways of the religious, identifying themselves as

"Muslims" in Turkey, so as to distinguish themselves from secularists or others who do not practice Islam. "Muslim" (*Müslüman*) is also the colloquial Turkish reference for "a religious person."

3. *Zekât*, as it is spelled and pronounced in Turkish, is one of the five precepts for being a Muslim. It refers to giving alms to the poor.

4. Another central commodity of the market for "Islamic identity" that was fashioned by Islamist-owned businesses was books.

5. I use the term "covered" (in quotation marks) as the literal translation of the colloquial Turkish term (*kapanmak, kapalı*) for veiling.

6. For an ethnography of Turkish women's headscarves and xenophobia in Germany, see Mandel (1989).

7. The intention, here, is to anthropologize the everyday practices of Turkish secularists as I do those of Islamists. As I note here, there was a tendency among secularists to view their lives as supra- or extra-cultural. Secularists thought that they had transcended "culture" to meet a "global" (European) norm. In writing about the production of secularism here, I culturalize or put into context the life practices of secularists. The approach can be compared to that of Ruth Frankenberg (1993), who studied "racialized identity" not among black, but among white American women. Also see Rajasingham's study (1993) of white British women's ways of othering.

8. The term *çağdaş* in secularist-Turkish usage literally means "contemporary" or "modern," signifying a state of being up with the times or of keeping in step with progress. In daily usage, however, in the 1990s, *çağdaş* was used to mean "civilized" in the Eurocentric sense of the term. A particular section of society, those who associated themselves with Ataturk's vision, use the term "*çağdaş*" to refer to themselves and their aspirations in contradistinction to Islamists. Note that one of the biggest Ataturkist civic organizations is called "Çağdaş Yaşamı Destekleme Derneği," or "The Society to Promote Civilized Life."

9. In early republican years the *tayyör* was adopted by young nationalist women as the proper modern dress for the nation's new Turkish woman. For more on this, see Durakbaşa (1987).

10. George Yudice (1995) makes a similar observation, drawing attention to the parallels between politics of culture, race, and identity on the one hand and consumerism on the other.

11. *Hürriyet*, October 18, 1994, p. 7. The Turkish original for my translation of the last sentence is striking: *İnsanlar burada çağdaşlığı yaşıyor*.

12. *Milli Gazete 2*, November 7, 1994, p. 1. The article was making a reference to Turgut Özal's phrase "*çağ atlamak*," used in his promise to make Turkey "jump a century ahead."

13. Ibid. Note that the writer of this article is attempting to appropriate the terms of "being civilized" to the ways of ordinary believers. He does not use the word *çağdaş* to signify "civilized." Instead, he uses the older, Ottoman-Turkish word *medeni* to describe the lifestyle of those who frequent the Topkapı market. In this usage, a more modest life in an Islamic sense of the term is what being "civilized" is about.

14. *Aksiyon*, December 10–16, 1994, p. 34; see also pp. 32–5. I would here like to draw attention to the similarity between this nostalgic discourse of an Islamist

intellectual with versions of anthropological critiques of modernity. Kandiyoti (1996, 16–17) cautions us against this sort of coincidence. Likewise, Hammoudi (1993, viii) draws attention to the coincidence between colonial and postcolonial discourses on what is authentic to a Muslim society. My intention in this chapter is to illustrate the emdeddedness of Islamists in the everyday practices of the "modernity" (here understood as market-oriented capitalism, materialism, and consumerism) that they critique.

15. Beside the Eyüp mosque, there is a line of eight or nine shops, most of which sell religious commodities. Previously, these particular shops were owned by toymakers, according to the old residents of Eyüp, who recount the history of small trade in this district. These craftsmen used to be known with their special wooden toys for children. It is commonplace in Istanbul for circumcized boys to be brought to Eyüp mosque for a visit of blessing. It is hence that toy shops had flourished in this particular place, to provide gifts for the little boys. In 1960, one of the toymakers turned his shop into a religious bookshop. This shopowner had gone on the haj and upon his return could no longer trade in toys, according to his account. He found it morally ill-fitting to sell toys beside such a holy site as Eyüp. He also noted that the market for religious goods was much more profitable for him. By the 1980s and 1990s, all but two of the shops by the mosque were transformed into shops for religious goods. Some of the owners were still the same, those who had put toymaking aside, seeing that the market for religious objects was more prolific and profitable. Not all of them practiced Islam piously. "With the spread of religiosity in the last ten or fifteen years," one of the shop owners said, "the demand for religious goods grew." The fathers and grandfathers of most of the young shopkeepers there used to be artisans of toys, but the sons now said that they would not be able to survive any longer if they were to trade only in handmade toys. Mass production had taken over the toy industry in Istanbul, and there was no longer any demand for the wooden trinkets.

The shops were owned by small traders and not by big production companies. In the new shops selling religious goods, Muslims could meet almost all of their religious needs. There were prayer mats imported from Saudi Arabia, prayer muslins for women brought from India, China, and Thailand, prayer caps for men, non-alcoholic perfumes, special toothbrushes made from root (*misvak*) for believers who wished to imitate the manner in which the Prophet Muhammad brushed his teeth, light soleless boots (*mest*) to be worn after ablutions (*abdest*) in the tradition of certain Sufi orders, automatic clocks that indicate the times of prayer (*namaz saatleri*) and the rhythm for the repetition of God's name in Sufi ritual (*zikir saatleri*).

Believers bought miniscule books of prayer to carry under their shirt for spiritual protection when in travel (*cevşen-ül kebir*), as well as prayer mats (*seccade*) that exposed the picture of the house of God in Mecca (Kâbe). Most of the customers of the Eyüp shops were women who came to visit the many nearby saints' tombs to make wishes or to pray. Yet, in the 1990s, especially after the Friday noontime prayer when Eyüp mosque became well attended, religious men also frequented the shops in large numbers. Shopkeepers said that in the last ten years many young people, especially students who had turned to religion, were customers of these shops.

"Previously," one of the shopowners said, "there didn't use to be such shops that met all the particular needs of the Muslim. The one who went on the haj brought all that he needed back with him. In those times, it was possible to travel to Mecca by car and the haj-goers could pile up their trunks with religious goods. Now it is only possible to go by plane and you are allowed to carry only 30 kilograms with you. So we now provide all these things that are necessary for the haj right here in Turkey in these specialized shops."

The Eyüp shops exposed their goods on wooden stalls that extended onto the sidewalk. The shops had windows, but these were not where things were to be displayed. Some items were hung up from the rooftops of the shops as well. Spatially and physically the shops were different from the windowshops in the shopping centers in other parts of town.

16. Aksoy and Robins (1994, 71) use the phrase "dual city, *alaturka.*" The following quote may give a sense of these critics' narrative: "In their differences, in the contrast between the villa new towns and the *gecekondus* [shanties], we can see the growing polarisation that is making a dual city" (ibid.).

17. Here Mustafa Karaduman is referring to the veil (*çarşaf*) in distinction from the headscarves and overcoats (*türban* and *pardösü*) more commonly worn by Islamist women in Turkey today. The black veil, which is made of one piece of cloth from head to toe, is worn by religious women who would like to refrain from ornament in their covered clothing.

18. "Aygaz" is a standard brand for gas in Turkey, pretty much a monopoly. Karaduman's example can be compared to the common use of the word "xerox" in the United States for photocopying.

19. "Sana" is a standard brand of butter in Turkey, used very widely.

20. "Open" ("*açık*") is my literal translation for the colloquial Turkish adjective for women who do not cover.

21. The reason for the enthusiastic applause for the model who wore the black veil in particular can be interpreted in the following way: The fashion show organized by Islamists was taking place in the midst of othering secularist discourse about the "backwardness" of the Islamist headscarf. Secularists frequently used the black veil (*kara çarşaf*) as a symbol to critique "the position of women under Islam." So when the model in Tekbir's fashion show appeared so beautiful in the black silken veil, Islamists in the audience rose up in enthusiasm. The appearance of the model wearing such a style represented a reversal of secularist discourse for those Islamists who were clapping. The people in the audience, along with the managers of Tekbir, were rewriting the meaning of the signifier "black veil" as it circulated in Turkey's political culture.

22. The *saz* is a Turkish musical instrument used in Turkish folk and classical music.

23. The haj is the pilgrimage to the holy sites in Mecca and is one of the five prescriptions of Islam, required for the Muslim who can afford it.

24. The newspapers *Milli Gazete* and *Yeni Şafak* have wider circulations compared to *Vakit* and the weekly *Selam*. *Milli Gazete* is read by supporters of the Welfare Party, those who influenced the wins of the party in municipal and national elections. *Yeni Şafak* is the newspaper of Islamist intellectuals who are in dialogue with leftist and secularist intellectuals. Generally, *Yeni Şafak* has been supportive of the Welfare Party. *Vakit* and *Selam* are radical Islamist newspapers, both of which

are quite critical of Welfare for being too pragmatic and modernist and for compromising on the requirements of Islam. One of *Vakit*'s main editors, the popular Islamist intellectual Abdurrahman Dilipak, had written a column in critique of the wedding of Necmettin Erbakan's daughter. The wedding had been held in the Istanbul Sheraton and the bride's dress was covered, but highly extravagant.

25. Indeed, such shows were not organized only by Tekbir, Inc. The Welfare Party had also taken up such organization of veiling fashion shows all over Turkey.

26. The Turkish words that Özdür used in this section to describe Islamic principles were *tevazu*, *züht*, and *takva*.

27. The original Turkish of the last of Özdür's statements on "selling Islam" is *birbirimize İslam satacağız*.

28. A reprint of this article appeared in *Selam*, November 28–December 4, 1994.

29. For an account of this exhibition, see the newspiece in the secular mainstream newspaper *Sabah*, November 11, 1994, p. 33.

30. For a historical ethnography on the Girls' Institutes and their students, see Navaro-Yashin 2000.

31. For the concept of social life in reference to commodities, see Appadurai (1986).

32. Alfred Gell (1986) has observed that "consumption involves the incorporation of the consumed item into the personal and social identity of the consumer." He thinks of "consumption as the appropriation of objects as part of one's personalia" (112).

33. It would be interesting to compare contemporary Islamists' discourse on secularist traders with early republican Kemalists' discourse on non-Muslim traders in Turkey. Indeed, Islamists have been accusing secularists for being compradors. In nationalisms in the Middle East, cultural difference has too easily been mapped onto difference in access to financial resources. In early republican Turkey, the wealth tax (*varlık vergisi*) was forced onto non-Muslims to create a Turkish capitalist class. Non-Muslims severely suffered from the measures instituted by the wealth tax. We need more complex, ethnographically based assessments that do not reproduce nationalist discourses. Kandiyoti (1998) suggests fresh and new directions for conceptualizing the relation between wealth and cultural difference in the Middle East.

Chapter Four
Rituals for the State

1. For the best study of pan-Turkists, see Bora and Can (1994).

2. Important theorists of "civil society" in Turkey are Göle (1994), Heper (1994), Robins (1996), and Öncü (1994).

3. In 1999, the MHP won one of the highest percentages of votes in its history and is presently sharing government with two other parties. The events recounted in this chapter refer to the period before the MHP won governmental parliament seats.

4. The MHP has received many of its votes from really marginalized segments

of society, including inhabitants of shantytowns in the big cities and dwellers of smaller Anatolian towns.

5. For a good study of the different meanings ascribed to the Turkish flag in contemporary Turkey, see Seufert (1997).

6. See Abrams (1988) for the notion of "the state as an idea."

7. The notion of "state fetishism" is Michael Taussig's (1992).

8. The state owns five TV channels and a number of radio channels all under the initials TRT, which stand for "Turkish Radio and Television." The state had a monopoly over TV until the liberalization of the mid-1980s, when private channels were legalized. Since then, many private channels have been founded, most of which are much more popular than the state-run TRT. The TRT tries to function as "the voice of the state," even at times of highest confusion as to the content and meaning of the state (e.g., during coalition debates and corruption scandals).

9. The Turkish national anthem, "The March of Liberation" (*İstiklal Marşı*), is an adaptation from a poem that was written in the early part of the last century by poet Mehmet Akif Ersoy. It was selected in the foundational years of the republic as national anthem from among a number of other possibilities. For all those socialized in Turkey, especially those who have been subject to the discipline of state institutions—through schools, the army, work in public offices, watching TV—the sound of the national anthem is second nature. School children are taught the tune early on and have to sing it on Monday mornings when beginning the school week and on Friday afternoons when ending it. The anthem is central to army discipline as well. In Turkey, it still stands as one of the most salient symbols of the existence of state.

10. For a historical account on the invention of Turkish national holidays in early republican years (1923–40), including the story of the Youth and Sports Day, see Öztürkmen (1996a, 1996b).

11. For cultural studies of sports in Turkey of the 1980s, especially the promotion of sports by the state in this period, see Kozanoğlu (1990) and Bora, Horak, and Reiter (1993).

12. With its history of regular interventions (conducted in 1960, 1971, and 1980, to date), the Turkish army has presented itself (or has constructed an image of itself) as "the only pillar of secularism and democracy in Turkey." Generals have performed military coups arguing that, as it stood in the hands of civil politicians, "Turkish democracy was in danger" and that only the secular-minded generals could save it from damage. Certain social scientists have been reproducing this military ideology in their works (see, for example, Heper 1994). I use the term "secular democracy" only rhetorically in this passage, to indicate a discourse or an ideology and not a social fact.

13. *Zaman*, August 4, 1996, p. 1.

14. The 1980s and 1990s, as a period of economic liberalization prompted by the opening of Turkey's borders to free trade, also proved to be the boom time for Turkey's advertising industry. The term "image" (in Turkish, *imaj*, as in the French pronounciation) entered public discourse with the influence of the culture of commercials. There was a proper image for everything: for the businesswoman, the politician, the academic, the lover-to-be. So could there be a better image for the state. For the first time in the 1980s, politicians began to professionalize themselves

in terms of world standards of politics by taking advice from advertisers during election campaigns as well as during their political terms. If there was a better image to be had for competing individuals in the world of free trade, so there was one for the state. The advertising industry in Turkey succeeded, in the 1980s, in transforming the notion of the image of Turkey (in relation to the West, of course) into a popular concern. Hence the reference to "the image of Turkey" in the domain of sports. For an interesting study on the uptake of a culture of representation in Turkey during the 1980s, see Gürbilek (1992) and Kozanoğlu (1992). So much emphasis has been discursively loaded onto the notion of Turkey's image vis-à-vis the West, that it has turned out to be the matter at stake in every public and publicized issue in Turkey.

15. Renata Salecl (1994) has similarly analyzed the shift of opinion among Serbian mothers of soldiers who, when they protested about conscription initially, were convinced afterwards that it was necessary for the national good (p. 14). I find Salecl's study highly important in the ways it illustrates the participation of women in nationalism.

16. The DEP was, in turn, the continuation of a former Kurdish Party, the Peoples' Labor Party (HEP), which had been banned. Founding extensions of banned parties, organizations, and publications under new names and symbols is a common practice among the socialist and Kurdish movements in contemporary Turkey.

17. Because membership in parliament officially requires at least 10 percent of countrywide votes, HADEP was not granted any seats in the currently running parliament.

18. Much resistance literature in anthropology has been written following the work of Scott (1985).

19. I would argue similarly with regard to the secular mainstream of privately owned newspapers such as *Sabah*, *Milliyet*, *Hürriyet*, and *Cumhuriyet*, also represented, in scholarly studies of civil society and by self-proclaimed journalistic personifications of it, as illustrations of the realm of a free circulation of ideas in Turkey during the 1980s and 1990s. In that they published information unavailable in the state's organs of culture, these privately run newspapers have also developed a certain sort of support for an established idea of the Turkish state, one that does not contradict the army's ideals for it. These mainstream newspapers have heralded Ataturkist secularism and Westernism; they have also left official political lines unchallenged. Even though there isn't direct censorship on the press, as there used to be in the period of martial law between 1980 and 1983, there is effective self-censorship in contemporary mass media.

20. Among these scholars, see especially the works of Metin Heper (1994), Şerif Mardin (1993), and Nilüfer Göle (1994).

21. The term "the return of the repressed" has been used by Robins (1996) to describe the rise of the Islamist movement in Turkey.

22. This analysis can be read as a critique of Foucault's periodizing dissociation of "productive" from "repressive power" in *History of Sexuality: Volume One* (1980). I use the concept of "statesmen" not in reference to specific government or political party officials. The reference is more theoretical; it refers to individuals who are implicated in a particular mode of state practice, or habitus of statecraft (see Bourdieu [1972] 1991).

23. I am skeptical of "democracy" and, following Foucault, study it as a technique of power. The critique of democracy as mode of power also benefits from Gramsci (1989), as well as from Frankfurt School critics of modern models of power (Adorno and Horkheimer 1994).

24. In critiquing Habermas, as I do here, I do not intend to lump secularism and Islamism together, nor to overlook the differences between these varied ideologies. I mean only to challenge exclusivist Eurocentric searches for the space of communication and democracy in the realms of secularism. For the likes of Habermas, secularism would categorically be superior to Islamism in proximity to interactive communication. The specific historical situation in contemporary Turkey has shown that Islamists may at times be more communicative in the public sphere, in Habermas's sense, than secularists. Kemalist secularism has been deployed at times by the army to produce extremely antidemocratic results. What I am arguing is that neither Islamism nor secularism are categorically democratic or antidemocratic. Different historical contingencies have produced different historical results.

25. I do not refer to anthropological literature on resistance in this book, but my critique of literature on civil society rising out of Turkish academia and of scholarship on the Middle East produced in the West should be taken as a critique of resistance literature, as well. As theorists of civil society have reified the notion of society in distinction from the state, so have ethnographers of resistance been mostly digging for sites that escape the access of power. I am as skeptical and critical of the state / society distinction as I am of the power / resistance one. Scott (1985) has been pivotal in the development of studies of resistance, pulling many anthropologists (and political scientists) behind it.

26. This article by Mitchell is an excellent critique of James Scott's *Weapons of the Weak* and of resistance literature.

27. My use of the term "Welfarist" is an English translation of the colloquialism *Refahlı*.

28. For a study of Islamists' uses of Western social theory, see Navaro 1993.

29. My use of the term "Ataturkist" in this article is a translation of the colloqualism used by secularist activists in the self-designation *Atatürkçü*.

30. There are a number of Ataturkist women's manifestos on "the original Turkish woman" or "the Anatolian woman," some written in early republican years and recently reprinted and others published recently for the first time. See, for example, Taşkıran (1976) and Arat (1980). Introduced as scholarly or academic works by Ataturkist women professors, writers, and researchers, most of these works draw a nonreligious (almost non-Islamic) picture of women in Anatolia. The elite women writers argue that Anatolian women do not and historically did not let themselves be oppressed, secluded, or mistreated by men, that they did not veil, that they invariably worked outside the home, and that they were independent-minded and strong. Certain of these Ataturkist narratives are more pan-Turkist than others in arguing the historical freedoms of Turkish women in Central Asia, typically described to have rode on horses along with their men before the advent of Islam in Turkish culture. In writing such narratives about Turkic, Turkish, or Anatolian women, Ataturkist elites wrote a specific history for the Turkish nation, claiming one sort of primordial culture over another. In this version of the story of Turkish culture, Islam is alien, nonindigenous, and foreign.

31. This is not the first time in history that an Ataturkist agenda is presented in specialized curricula for women. An important institution in early republican years were the Girls' Institutes, where girls and young women had been taught all sorts of "female" skills, sewing, cooking, embroidery, and childcare, along with the principles of Kemalism. See Navaro-Yashin (2000). Certain of the elderly activists in The Society to Support Civilized Life were themselves trained in Girls' Institutes of the early republican period.

32. I must note the specifically urban context of this relation between Ataturkist elites and Alevi activists. Shankland (1993) notes the different relations that rural Alevis forge with the state in juxtaposition with urbanized Alevis. In this account, Alevi villagers find it difficult to accommodate to the everyday life of statecraft due to their loyalty to their own alternative personas of authority (the *dedes*, or elderly men who have traditionally been solicited for all sorts of advice and to lead ritual ceremonies). Urbanized Alevis, on the other hand, have found a way to reconcile themselves with the state by embracing secularism and Kemalism against the threat of Sunni Islamism. It is hence that the old urban Kemalist elites think they have found their "society" in Alevi shantytowns in the city.

33. "Cumhuriyet Şenliği," *Sabah*, October 28, 1994, p. 1.

34. Secular mainstream TV channels were blowing Republic Day attendance out of proportion partly as a counterpoint to the Taksim meeting organized by Prime Minister Tansu Çiller on February 28, 1994, months before October 29, when an event meant to belittle the Welfare Party and the ousted Kurdish political party DEP turned out disastrously, as it was attended only by schoolchildren in uniforms who were brought by their teachers. On October 29, the media wanted to portray a better image for Republic Day vis-à-vis Welfarists and Kurdists.

35. The more recent attempts to incorporate "organizations of civil society" in the celebration of the seventy-fifth year of the Turkish Republic were an extension of this first attempt for a "people's holiday" in October 1994 and could also be analyzed along the critical theoretical framework I have employed in this chapter.

Chapter Five
Fantasies for the State

1. Michael Taussig's work on fetishism (1992, 1997) is inspired by Walter Benjamin's reading of Marx's work on commodity fetishism. Taussig also builds on anthropological work on the fetish.

2. I do not wish to conflate, here, the post-structuralisms of Foucault and Derrida. Indeed, in an important chapter, "Cogito and the History of Madness," Derrida (1978) had critiqued Foucault for reproducing (by default) a metaphysics of presence (Derrida's term for humanist politics of truth) in his work. In this passage, I mention the two theorists together duly to differentiate their projects from those of the Marxist. I do think Anderson and Taussig's projects (perhaps unwillingly now) are more akin to the politics of Marxism than that of poststructuralism.

3. A number of symbolic anthropologists have written ethnographies of the ritualistic aspect of statecraft, comparing practices of the state to those of religions. See

for example the works of Moore and Myerhoff (1977), Handelman (1990), Aronoff (1977), Geertz (1980), and Herzfeld (1992).

4. On this point he differs from Georges Bataille whom he follows. Bataille does believe in the sacred.

5. To be more precise, Žižek would like to shift the theoretical debate from a Habermas-Foucault to an Althusser-Lacan axis (1995, 1–4).

6. One could compare this analytical insight about contemporary history with Mikhail Bakhtin's (1984) faith in laughter and irony (as in the carnivalesque) as forces that contradict orthodoxies of power. Žižek, in contrast to Bakhtin, is arguing that laughter and irony (in the contemporary contingency that he studies) enhance, rather than challenge, ideologies of power. Unlike Žižek but like Bakhtin, Michael Taussig (1987) has drawn attention to the liberating aspects of irony and laughter. In the carnivalesque healing practices of shamans in yagé nights in South America, in the jokes, reversals of discourse, and the joy, Taussig finds the kernel for reenchantment amid colonialist discourse. Of course, the location and history of Bakhtin and Taussig's studies are different from mine in contemporary Turkey or, for that matter, from the context of Žižek's work, emerging out of postsocialist Eastern Europe. Differing approaches to irony and laughter must have to do with different contexts of history, ethnography, and their particularities. Important studies of the carnival, laughter, and irony have shown that these domains, rather than being expressions of cynicism, may be, in certain historical contexts, grounds for political contest. See especially Hammoudi (1993).

7. This Enlightenment framework in traditional psychoanalysis can be well compared with narratives of emancipation in Marxisms of the same period.

8. Žižek analyzes this state through an example. In Syberberg's film version of Wagner's opera *Parsifal*, the main character Amfortas cries, "Here I am—here is the open wound!" Žižek advises that this line should be understood literally: "All his being is in his wound; if we annihilate it, he himself will lose his positive ontological consistency and cease to exist" (1995, 77–8).

9. Unlike clinical uses of Lacanian theory, Žižek's and other Slovenian critics' use of Lacan is distinguishably philosophical and political. (See Ernesto Laclau's preface to Žižek 1995, ix–x).

10. Indeed, in much of Taussig's work, there is a constructed dualism between power, on the one hand, and resistance, on the other—colonialism versus healing. Taussig (1987) finds the emancipatory energy he looks for in the healing practices of shamans in Colombia. Some have criticized him for reading Benjaminian montage into his description of yagé nights or for finding his ideal of a Western critical discourse among the people whom he studies (Hevia 1992, 119). I do not argue here, as I suggested in a preceding footnote, with the historicity of Taussig's ethnography or with the power of healing. I am only more skeptical in my ethnographic, historical, and existential case about identifying such a site for enlightenment and liberation. So, in this case, instead of positing the state against civil society, or power against resistance, I study the complex *in between* in which public life in Turkey seems to be located. It is in the muddled middle ground that I have observed cynicism of the sort studied by Žižek and Sloterdijk.

11. One could use this insight in dialogue with Pierre Bourdieu's notion of "habitus" (1991). One could demonstrate that in the present historical contingency or

contemporary experiences of the political, we know that we are caught in "habiti," yet we persist in practicing them. Bourdieu does not allow the subject much capacity for consciousness. Instead, I argue, following Žižek, that much more consciousness is available to social individuals than is usually allowed by social analysts. And yet, and this is the twist, what could be called the psychic manifestation of the political, in following Žižek, contradicts and overcomes this available realm of critical consciousness.

A similar argument could be made with regard to our cynical contemporary relation to the habiti of statecraft, as in the act of voting. We are aware that the activity of voting will not amount to very much, and yet we persist in practicing it. Even though Bourdieu's work has been taken as a stepping stone for a theory of practice and agency, in fact, as far as he interprets us to be ever subconsciously immersed in habitus, Bourdieu does not really grant that much agency to the subject. In contrast, with Žižek's work on psychoanalysis and politics, it is possible to study the more complex relation between political consciousness and the unconscious.

12. In a more recent study, Žižek (2001) has radically critiqued the notion of "totalitarianism."

13. I suggest the term "totalitarian democracy" as a category for the study of the contemporary Turkish political order, which subverts the totalitarianism / democracy dichotomy. I mean to imply, with this concept, that even though the Turkish republic runs through a procedural democracy of sorts, a totalitarian (military and militarized) system still defines what this "democracy" is going to look like. This system, especially after the military coup of 1980, works effectively in an ambiguous zone between totalitarianism and democracy. Because one cannot know to which side power is more tilted at any one time, one has to self-regulate one's ideas and actions.

14. Here I am drawing attention to the difficulty of finding historical illustrations for Weber's ideal types of power in the context of contemporary Turkey. Weber (1949), of course, had meant for his "ideal types" only to be used as categories of measurement that were to be discarded as soon as they proved to be useless or misconceived. He did not mean for his ideal types to be taken as discriminating descriptions of three possible states of legitimation in the world. In following his caution for the use of these types, I maintain that one cannot characterize the present political situation in Turkey in privileging one of Weber's "authoritarian," "charismatic," or "legal-rational" types over another.

I will suggest even further, however, that it is hard, in a description and analysis of the contemporary Turkish state system, to pick between Foucault's (1979, 1980) "repressive" and "productive" hypotheses about power, as well. Important ethnographers of the Middle East have juxtaposed temporally variant modes of power in borrowing from Foucault (e.g., Mitchell 1988, Messick 1993). In studying Turkish modes of politics in the 1990s, I am unable to select between the violent versus the manipulative or the enforcing versus the rationalizing. It appears in this historical context that both these modes of power are simultaneously relevant.

15. I do not agree with Sloterdijk about the irreversibility of consciousness-raising. At least in Turkey, in certain particular cases, former leftist radicals of the student movement of the 1960s and 1970s turned out to be supporters of neo-liberalism. Sloterdijk's comments would have to be particularized to speak about a

group of former leftists who took up jobs in business and yet who maintained their critical approach to society. In Turkey, such a social group has been at the center of the culture industry in the 1980s and 1990s.

16. Sloterdijk borrows his image of "kynicism" (versus "cynicism") from the Greek kynic Diogenes, who subverted the state through a satiric relation to life. Sloterdijk's faith in irony, satire, and laughter can be compared with Bakthin's depiction of the carnivalesque. In both these histories, there is a dualism of power versus resistance, a construction that I would argue, in following Timothy Mitchell (1990), is power-laden in itself or is an effect of a specific mode of power.

17. In 1983, more than 90 percent of the population in Turkey voted in favor of the military coup in a referendum.

18. The Turkish words for these expressions of experience under alarm are *galeyan, hengâme, sansasyon, panik*.

19. See, for example, *Cumhuriyet*, November 15, 1996 as well as other newspapers from the aftermath of the Susurluk accident of November 3.

20. Uğur Mumcu, one of Turkey's most important political researchers and journalists who was a columnist for the secular-leftist newspaper *Cumhuriyet*, was assassinated in early 1993 when a bomb exploded in his car, in front of his home in Ankara. He was known for his exposés of the state's undercover dealings. In January of 1997, four years after he was murdered and a few months after the Susurluk accident, his wife and brother, who had all along been saying that the murder had been committed under the orders and / or knowledge of certain representatives of the state or the army, noted that Mumcu had written specifically about Abdullah Çatlı's mafia relations with politicians. Kutlu Adalı, an important Turkish-Cypriot journalist known for his critique of the Turkish army's presence in northern Cyprus and the soldiers' looting of Greek-owned property, was assassinated in the summer of 1996 in Nicosia. Both these political assassinations, like all others of this sort in Turkey, were not explained. The perpetrators of the murders have still not been found or revealed. Such incidents are commonly referred to as "murders where the agent is unknown" (*faili meçhul cinayet*). It has been commonplace in Turkey for political murders to remain unsolved, in spite of pressure applied by organized political resistance.

21. *Milliyet*, January 22, 1997, pp. 1, 10. After this incident, Abdullah Öcalan, leader of the PKK, was captured by Turkish Secret Service in an international operation.

22. Slavoj Žižek interprets the reception of the sinking of the *Titanic* with similar insights. He writes, "The sinking of the *Titanic* had a traumatic effect, it was a shock, 'the impossible happened,' the unsinkable ship had sunk; but the point is that precisely as a shock, this sinking arrived at its proper time—'the time was waiting for it': even before it actually happened, there was already a place opened, reserved for it in fantasy-space. It had such a terrific impact on 'social imaginary' by virtue of the fact that it was expected" (1995, 69). Michel Foucault uses a comparable concept in his analysis of history. He writes about "conditions of possibility" or about an epistemological context that makes certain forms of knowledge more possible than others (1973, 346, 364). Here, I argue that the "fantasy-space" in Žižek's terms or "the conditions of possibility" in Foucault's, were ripe in November of 1996 for the uproarious reception of the Susurluk accident in Turkey. As Euro-

peans found a symbol in the *Titanic* to represent their fears of a fin de siècle, were people in Turkey over interpreting "Susurluk" because they were already worried of a cataclysm of the Turkish state? Is there a kernel of the "symptomatic" (or, more properly, the "fantastic") in the Lacanian sense in such excessive worries about the end of state? Is this perhaps a form of cynicism?

23. The Turkish originals of the nouns I cite here respectively are: *bataklık, çürümüşlük, kirlenme, kokuşmuşluk, pespayelik, yamukluk, hastalık,* and *yozlaşma.* See articles from the press published in that period, as well as recordings of TV programs. *"Burası bir bok çukuru"* and *"Bu üzerine kusulacak bir devlet"* are the Turkish originals for the popularly made statements.

24. *Cumhuriyet,* November 15, 1996, p. 19.

25. The army played a major role, in this stage, in enforcing a shift in media coverage and the public agenda and changing the terms of the debate.

26. ÖDP is a political party of socialist groups, intellectuals, and feminist and gay groups who have recently gathered under an umbrella organization after years of amoebic factionalism in the 1980s' aftermath of the military coup, when leftist groups had been eradicated and undermined.

27. See *Milliyet,* November 6, 1996, pp. 1, 10.

28. My reference to "people with power" in this section in this particular way might reflect upon some of my readers as an argument that resembles conspiracy theory. Unlike Foucault, I study discourse as it takes shape in the agency and practices of actual people. In this particular aspect, my approach to "discourse" resonates more with that of Edward Said (1985 and 1978).

29. Derrida (1978, 31–63) criticizes Foucault for maintaining a margin of "truth" in his labors to transcend it. According to Derrida, Foucault is still a metaphysicist of presence, where Derrida would like to illustrate the eternal deferrence of meaning (as in his deliberately misspelled *"différance"*) in an endless string of signifiers. Derrida would like to warn against finding truth under any signifier. Everything we think we know is already entextualized, according to Derrida, that is, it is already a secondary, tertiary, or further order of knowledge and there never was a primary form of knowing or truth. So would he critique Marx for finding the mode of production under all signs and Foucault for reading the history of discipline into his theory of discourse.

30. Sayer (1987) describes Foucault as a follower of Marx. He notes, "Other sociologists have picked up on this complementarity of individualization and state formation, and the connection of both with capitalism, and in some cases elucidated its phenomenology more thoroughly than does Marx. I think of Foucault and Elias, as well as Weber and Durkheim" (138).

31. Žižek (1995) insightfully outlines the difference between Marx and Lacan in the following passage: "Herein lies the difference with Marxism: in the predominant Marxist perspective the ideological gaze is a partial gaze overlooking the totality of social relations, whereas in the Lacanian perspective ideology rather designates a totality set on effacing the traces of its own impossibility" (49).

32. I would argue that the notions of everyday life or everyday practices, so popular among anthropologists, are abstractions too. One could deconstruct these abstractions and show their implications in modern relations of power as well. Anthropologists who insist on everyday practice in arguing against studies of discourse

are themselves implicated in a modern discourse that works by dividing concepts into binary oppositions, as if everyday practice could be independent of discourse and vice versa. The anthropological notion of practice, like civil society, is an abstraction of power.

Chapter Six
The Cult of Ataturk

1. For this, see also chapter 3.

2. Other anthropologists have studied cults around living or dead political leaders. See Wedeen (1999) and Verdery (1999).

3. See Moore and Myerhoff (1977), Aronoff (1977), Herzfeld (1992), Handelman (1990).

4. For an anthropological study of legal transformations in the Ottoman Empire / Turkey, see Starr (1992). Secularizing reforms, in the "Westernizing" sense, had precedent in the Ottoman Empire. Yet these were intensified and systematically and ideologically promoted as the national ideal only in the formative years of Turkey as a nation-state.

5. See for example headlines of *Hürriyet*, August 2, 1997, p. 1.

6. See, for example, Ekşi (1997).

7. For the concept of state fetishism, see Taussig (1992).

8. For a study of the public funeral organized for Ataturk, see Seufert and Weyland (1994).

9. Only in the late 1980s had a government, that of Turgut Özal, lifted the obligation to practice November 10 as a date of commemoration. But in the 1990s, civic organizations were observing the ritual once again.

10. For an ethnography of Anıtkabir as architectural and symbolic site, see Meeker (1997).

11. Delaney (1995) has written about the gendered dimension of statism in Turkey with reference to patriarchal attachments to Ataturk. Although I find her work far too essentialist in its theory of culture and gender, the article is interesting in its focus on gendered ascriptions to land and state.

12. *Sabah*, November 8, 1994, pp. 33, 40.

13. For a study of the state as an abstract idea, see Abrams (1988).

14. The parliamentarian, Hasan Mezarcı, was involved in many heated affairs between secularists and Islamists.

15. Abdellah Hammoudi (1997) has studied the more direct links between Moroccan Sufism and monarchism. I do not claim such direct links between Turkish traditions of Sufism, on the one hand, and Ataturkism, on the other hand, in this ethnography simply because I am not sure that such cultural continuity could be cited in the Ottoman-Turkish case in terms of a culture of statism. This question would require separate ethnographic research, as exhibited in the work of Hammoudi. My claim in the above paragraph is more modest. I mean only to juxtapose saint's tomb visitations with visitations to Anıtkabir so as to reshuffle the boundaries between what we, still in contemporary politics of culture, assume to be the separate spheres of secularity and religion.

Despite a state decree that abolished saints' tombs and dervish lodges (in the 1920s), saint's tomb visitation has been a popular and common practice all over Turkey. This practice is periodically reprimanded both by the secularist state's Ministry of Religious Affairs and by Islamist movements in search of religious puritanism. Though it is not possible to draw direct links between popular religion and popular visitation of Ataturk's mausoleum, a metaphorical comparison is, I think, very appropriate.

16. See Moore and Myerhoff (1977), Aronoff (1977), Handelman (1990, 1992).

17. *Hürriyet*, October 30, 1994, p. 5.

18. The borders and territories indicated in *Misak-ı Milli* were decided by members of the Erzurum and Sıvas Congresses who were leading the War for Turkey's liberation from occupying Allied forces. In 1920, after its foundation, the Turkish parliament (TBMM) vowed to defend the principles of *Misak-ı Milli*. Since then, the declaration has been officially defined as a founding construction of Turkey as a country. Ataturk had defined *Misak-ı Milli* as an agreement that guaranteed the wholesomeness and independence of the country, lifting all obstacles to its achievement.

19. In contrast to public consciousness in Greece vis-à-vis Turkey, in Turkey "threats to the country's unity," as they are called, are generally perceived to be internal, rather than external. Significantly, there does not exist, in public consciousness in Turkey, a general fear of possible attack by Greece.

20. Such apparitions of Ataturk have been reported by residents of other locations in Turkey, as well. Kozanoğlu (1997) gives several other examples of this phenomenon of searching for Ataturk mystically. For example, he notes that on a hill close to Sivrihisar, bushes grow in a manner that resembles the profile of Ataturk, and they remain that way no matter how one tries to cut them. And in İzmir, residents have reported that a UFO appeared on the spot from which Ataturk had historically seen İzmir for the first time at 6:20 in the morning (51).

21. Koray's efforts to inscribe Ataturkism in Islam and therefore to legitimize and naturalize it in the eyes of believers is not an original phenomenon. Koray's work is heir to a tradition of "scholarship" in this line, dating back to the years 1950. Nationalist Turkish writers had attempted to read Ataturkism into verses of the Kuran before. See for example Saygın (1952) and Çerman (1958). In the 1950s, Osman Nuri Çerman led a movement of reform to reinterpret the Kuran in the light of Ataturkism, an effort that is to be observed in the state-geared Ministry of Religious Affairs' textbooks on Islam for schoolchildren of the early republican period. This movement was called "reform in religion" (*dinde reform*) and it has been countered by contemporary Islamists such as Abdurrahman Dilipak in his book *This Is Not My Religion* (*Bu Din Benim Dinim Değil*). For our present purposes, it is interesting that Koray is reviving the tradition of "reform in religion" in the year 1994, amid intensified strife between secularists and Islamists. By 1997, the "reform in Islam" ("*İslamda reform*") movement was fully revived, with Turkish secularists upholding an Ataturkist, as opposed to an Islamist Islam, model for a "modern Muslim identity," inspired by the charisma of Yaşar Nuri Öztürk. With the phenomenon of "reform in Islam," a religious ground was constructed for the work of Ataturk in an effort to counter an Islamist monopoly over Islamic symbols and identity.

22. See *Hürriyet, Istanbul Eki*, November 15, 1994, p. 1.

23. *Cumhuriyet*, November 14, 1994, p. 15.

24. For a comparable study of objects of nationalism with emphasis on uses of the Turkish flag, see Seufert (1997).

25. *Yeni Şafak*, November 11, 1996 and *akit*, November 11, 1996. Islamist intellectual Abdurrahman Dilipak (1988) had compiled a reference book of primary sources on what he called the "deification of Ataturk" (see especially 375–408). Journalists of *Yeni Şafak* and *akit* (where Dilipak is editor-in-chief) would have been aware of this book.

26. Connerton (1996) has found "commemorative ceremonies and bodily practices" to be central to the making of history.

27. *Cumhuriyet*, May 31, 1994, p. 1, 7, *Zaman*, May 30, 1994, p. 14. For a study of the Welfare Party's celebration of Conquest Day, see Bora (1995).

28. By making this point, I depart from the terminology of Peter van der Veer (1994). I think that the concept of "religious nationalism," which van der Veer has coined, is misleading in that it assumes separate spheres of religion and secularity and fails to study what could be called the religion-like operations of secularism.

29. See the article "Ataturk Law" in Cem Encyclopedia (1986).

30. For an account of secularism in India, see Khilnani (1997).

Bibliography

Abrams, Philip. 1988. "Notes on the Difficulty of Studying the State (1977)." *Journal of Historical Sociology* 1 (1): 58–89.

Abu-Lughod, Lila. 1988. In *Arab Women in the Field: Studying Your Own Society*, ed. Soraya Altorki and Camillia Fawzi El-Solh, Syracuse, N.Y.: Syracuse University Press.

———. 1990. "Anthropology's Orient: The Boundaries of Theory on the Arab World." In *Theory, Politics, and the Arab World*, ed. Hisham Sharabi. New York: Routledge.

———. 1991. "Writing Against Culture." In *Recapturing Anthropology: Working in the Present*, ed. Richard G. Fox. Santa Fe, N.M.: School of American Research Press.

———. 1998. *Remaking Women: Feminism and Modernity in the Middle East.* Princeton: Princeton University Press.

Adams, Vincanne. 1996. *Tigers of the Snow and Other Virtual Sherpas: An Ethnography of Himalayan Encounters.* Princeton: Princeton University Press.

———. 1997. "Dreams of a Final Sherpa." *American Anthropologist* 99 (1): 85–98.

Adorno, Theodor, and Max Horkheimer. 1994. *Dialectic of Enlightenment.* New York: Continuum.

Ahmad, Aijaz. 1994. *In Theory: Classes, Nations, Literatures.* London and New York: Verso.

akit. 1995. December 14, pp. 1, 8.

———. 1996. January 9, p. 6.

———. 1996. November 11.

Aksiyon, 1994. December 10–16, pp. 32–35.

Aksoy, Asu, and Kevin Robins. 1994. "Istanbul Between Civilization and Discontent." *New Perspectives on Turkey* 10: 57–74.

Aktaş, Cihan. 1992. *Tesettür ve Toplum: Başörtülü Öğrencilerin Toplumsal Kökeni.* Istanbul: Nehir.

Alexander, Jacqui M., and Chandra Talpade Mohanty, eds. 1997. *Feminist Genealogies, Colonial Legacies, Democratic Futures.* New York and London: Routledge.

Anderson, Benedict. 1991. *Imagined Communities: Reflections on the Origin and Spread of Nationalism.* London and New York: Verso.

Appadurai, Arjun. 1986. "Is Homo Hierarchicus?" *American Ethnologist* 13 (4): 745–61.

———. 1988. "Why Public Culture?" *Public Culture* 1 (1): 5–9.

Arat, Necla. 1980. *Kadın Sorunu.* Istanbul: Edebiyat Fakültesi Matbaası.

Aretxaga, Begona. 1997. *Shattering Silence: Women, Nationalism, and Political Subjectivity in Northern Ireland.* Princeton: Princeton University Press.

———. 2000. "A Fictional Reality: Paramilitary Death Squads and the Construction of State Terror in Spain." In *Death Squad: The Anthropology of State Terror*, ed. Jeffrey A. Sluka. Philadelphia: University of Pennsylvania Press.

Argyrou, Vassos. 1997. "'Keep Cyprus Clean': Littering, Pollution, and Otherness." *Cultural Anthropology* 12 (2): 159–78.

Aronoff, Myron J. 1977. *Power and Ritual in the Israel Labor Party: A Study in Political Anthropology*. Assen: Van Gorcum.

Ascherson, Neil. 1996. *Black Sea: The Birthplace of Civilisation and Barbarism*. London: Vintage.

Bakhtin, Mikhail. 1984. *Rabelais and His World*. Bloomington: Indiana University Press.

Bakiler, Yavuz Bülent. 1996. *Türkiye*. November 16, p. 10.

Bali, Rıfat N. 1999. *Bir Türkleştirme Serüveni: Cumhuriyet Yıllarında Türkiye Yahudileri (1923–1945)*. Istanbul: İletişim.

Baudrillard, Jean. 1996. "The System of Objects." In *Selected Writings*, ed. Mark Poster. Cambridge: Polity Press.

Beller-Hann, Ildiko, and Chris Hann. 2000. *Turkish Region*. Oxford: James Currey.

Benjamin, Walter. 1990. "The Work of Art in the Age of Mechanical Reproduction." In *Photography in Print*, ed. Vicki Goldberg. Albuquerque: University of New Mexico Press.

———. 1968. "Theses on the Philosophy of History." In *Illuminations*. New York: Harcourt, Brace, and World.

Berkes, Niyazi. 1964. *Development of Secularism in Turkey*. Montreal: McGill University Press.

Blok, Anton. 1987. *The Mafia of a Sicilian Village, 1860–1960: A Study of Violent Peasant Entrepreneurs*. Cambridge: Cambridge University Press.

Bora, Tanıl. 1995. "'Fatih'in İstanbul'u': 'İslam Şehri' ile 'Dünya Şehri' arasında İslamcıların İstanbul Rüyası." *Birikim* 76: 44–53.

Bora, Tanıl, and Kemal Can. 1994. *Devlet Ocak Dergâh: 12 Eylül'den 1990'lara Ülkücü Hareket*. Istanbul: İletişim Yayınları.

Bora, Tanıl, R. Horak, and W. Reiter, eds. 1993. *Futbol ve Kültürü*. Istanbul: İletişim Yayınları.

Bourdieu, Pierre. 1991. *Outline of a Theory of Practice*. Cambridge: Cambridge University Press.

———. 1984. *Distinction: A Social Critique of the Judgment of Taste*. Cambridge: Harvard University Press.

Brown, Wendy. 1995. *States of Injury: Power and Freedom in Late Modernity*. Princeton: Princeton University Press.

Bulaç, Ali. 1990. *Din ve Modernizm*. Istanbul: Endülüs Yayınları.

Bülten. 1994. 5, no. 34.

Çakır, Ruşen. 1994. *Ne Şeriat Ne Demokrasi: Refah Partisini Anlamak*. Istanbul: Metis Yayınları.

Can, Kemal. 1997. "'Yeşil Sermaye' Laik Sisteme Ne Yaptı?" *Birikim* 99: 59–65.

Çandar, Cengiz. 1996. *Sabah*. November 17, p. 9.

Çavdar, Arif. 1994. "Türklerin Suudi Arabistanlaşması." *Cumhuriyet*. September 20, p. 2.

Cem Büyük Ansiklopedi. 1986. "Atatürk." Istanbul: Cem Ansiklopedik Yayınlar.

Çerman, Osman Nuri. 1958. *Dinde Reform ve Kemalizm Işığı Altında Dinimiz'in Esasları*. Istanbul: Tan Matbaası.

Chatterjee, Partha. 1993. *The Nation and Its Fragments: Colonial and Postcolonial Histories*. Princeton: Princeton University Press.

Clifford, James, and George E. Marcus. 1986. *Writing Culture: The Poetics and*

Politics of Ethnography. Berkeley, Los Angeles, and London: The University of California Press.

Connerton, Paul. 1996. *How Societies Remember*. Cambridge: Cambridge University Press.

Cumhuriyet. 1994. April 1, p. 7.

———. 1994. May 31, pp. 1, 7.

———. 1994. November 14, p. 15.

———. 1995. April 1, p. 1.

———. 1995. December 13, p. 3.

———. 1995. December 14, p. 10.

———. 1996. November 15.

Delaney, Carol. 1991. *The Seed and the Soil: Gender and Cosmology in Turkish Village Society*. Berkeley: University of California Press.

———. 1995. "Father State, Motherland, and the Birth of Modern Turkey." In *Naturalizing Power: Essays in Feminist Cultural Analysis*, ed. Sylvia Yanagisako and Carol Delaney. New York and London: Routledge.

Derrida, Jacques. 1978. *Writing and Difference*. Chicago: The University of Chicago Press.

Devji, Faisal Fatehali. 1992. "Hindu / Muslim / Indian." *Public Culture* 5 (1): 1–18.

Dilipak, Abdurrahman. 1988. *Bir Başka Açıdan Kemalizm*. Istanbul: Beyan Yayınları.

———. 1995. "Artık Avrupalı Olduk!" *akit*. December 14, pp. 1, 9.

Dirks, Nicholas. 1990. "History as a Sign of the Modern." *Public Culture* 2 (2): 25–32.

Doğan, Yalçın. 1995. "İşte şeriat budur!" *Milliyet*. August 17, p. 15.

Dündar, Can. 1995. *Yeni Yüzyıl*. August 20, p. 2.

Durakbaşa, Ayşe. 1987. "The Formation of 'Kemalist Female Identity': A Historical-Cultural Perspective." Master's thesis, Boğaziçi University.

Ekşi, Oktay. 1997. "İki Genç İnsan." *Hürriyet*, August 2, pp. 1, 7.

Ersanlı-Behar, Büşra. 1992. *İktidar ve Tarih*. Istanbul: Afa Yayınları.

Fahmy, Khaled. 1997. *All the Pasha's Men: Mehmed Ali, His Army and the Making of Modern Egypt*. Cambridge: Cambridge University Press.

Fardon, Richard, ed. 1990. *Localizing Strategies: Regional Traditions in Ethnographic Writing*. Edinburgh: Scottish Academic Press.

Faubion, James D. 1993. *Modern Greek Lessons: A Primer in Historical Constructivism*. Princeton: Princeton University Press.

Foucault, Michel. 1973. *The Order of Things: An Archaeology of the Human Sciences*. New York: Vintage.

———. 1979. *Discipline and Punish: The Birth of the Prison*. New York: Vintage.

———. 1980. *The History of Sexuality: Volume One*. New York: Vintage.

Frankenberg, Ruth. 1993. *White Women, Race Matters: The Social Construction of Whiteness*. Minneapolis: University of Minnesota Press.

Geertz, Clifford. 1980. *Negara: The Theater State in Nineteenth-Century Bali*. Princeton: Princeton University Press.

———. 1983. "From the Native's Point of View: On the Nature of Anthropological Understanding." In *Local Knowledge: Further Essays in Interpretive Anthropology*. New York: Basic.

Gell, Alfred. 1986. "Newcomers to the World of Goods: Consumption Among Muria Gonds." In *The Social Life of Things: Commodities in Cultural Perspective*, ed. Arjun Appadurai. Cambridge: Cambridge University Press.

Gilroy, Paul. 2000. *Between Camps: Nations, Cultures and the Allure of Race*. Allen Lane: Penguin.

Göktürk, Gülay. 1995. "Bedevi Kimliği." *Yeni Yüzyıl*. August 20, p. 3.

Göle, Nilüfer. 1991. *Modern Mahrem: Medeniyet ve Örtünme*. Istanbul: Metis Yayınları.

————. 1994. "Towards an Autonomization of Politics and Civil Society in Turkey." In *Politics in the Third Turkish Republic*, ed. Metin Heper. Boulder: Westview Press.

Gourgouris, Stathis. 1996. *Dream Nation: Enlightenment, Colonization, and the Institution of Modern Greece*. Stanford: Stanford University Press.

Gramsci, Antonio. 1989. *Selections from the Prison Notebooks*. ed. and trans. Quintin Hoare and Geoffrey Nowell Smith. New York: International Publishers.

The Guardian. 1997. March 7.

Gupta, Akhil. 1995. "Blurred Boundaries: The Discourse of Corruption, the Culture of Politics, and the Imagined State." *American Ethnologist* 22 (2): 375–402.

Gupta, Akhil, and James Ferguson. 1992. "Beyond 'Culture': Space, Identity, and the Politics of Difference." *Cultural Anthropology* 7 (1): 6–23.

Gupta, Akhil, and James Ferguson, eds. 1997. *Anthropological Locations: Boundaries and Grounds of a Field Science*. Berkeley: University of California Press.

Gürbilek, Nurdan. 1992. *Vitrinde Yaşamak: 1980'lerin Kültürel İklimi*. Istanbul: Metis Yayınları.

Habermas, Jürgen. 1989. *The Structural Transformation of the Public Sphere: An Inquiry into a Category of Bourgeois Society*. Cambridge: Polity Press.

Hall, Stuart. 1993. "Cultural Identity and Diaspora." In *Colonial Discourse and Post-Colonial Theory: A Reader*, ed. Patrick Williams and Laura Chrisman. New York and London: Harvester Wheatsheaf.

Hall, Stuart, C. Critcher, and T. Jefferson. 1978. *Policing the Crisis: Mugging, the State, and Law and Order*. London: Macmillan.

Hammoudi, Abdellah. 1993. *The Victim and Its Masks: An Essay on Sacrifice and Masquerade in the Maghreb*. Trans. Paula Wissing. London and Chicago: University of Chicago Press.

————. 1997. *Master and Disciple: The Cultural Foundations of Moroccan Authoritarianism*. Chicago and London: University of Chicago Press.

Hançerlioğlu, Orhan. 1984. *İslam İnançları Sözlüğü*. Istanbul: Remzi Kitabevi.

Handelman, Don. 1990. *Models and Mirrors: Towards an Anthropology of Public Events*. Cambridge: Cambridge University Press.

Hann, Chris. 1990. *Tea and the Domestication of the Turkish State*. Huntingdon, UK: Eothen Press.

————. 1993. "The Sexual Division of Labor in Lazistan." In *Culture and Economy: Changes in Turkish Villages*, ed. Paul Stirling. Hemingford, UK: Eothen Press.

Hann, Chris, and Elizabeth Dunn, eds. 1996. *Civil Society: Challenging Western Models*. London and New York: Routledge.

Haraway, Donna J. 1990. *Simians, Cyborgs, and Women: The Reinvention of Nature*. London: Free Association.

Hell, Julia. 1997. *Post-Fascist Fantasies: Psychoanalysis, History, and the Literature of East Germany*. Durham and London: Duke University Press.

Heper, Metin. 1994. *Politics in the Third Turkish Republic*. Boulder: Westview Press.

Herzfeld, Michael. 1982. *Ours Once More: Folklore, Ideology and the Making of Modern Greece*. Austin: University of Texas Press.

————. 1984. "The Horns of the Mediterraneanist Dilemma." *American Ethnologist* 11 (3): 439–54.

————. 1987. *Anthropology Through the Looking Glass: Critical Ethnography in the Margins of Europe*. Cambridge: Cambridge University Press.

————. 1992. *The Social Production of Indifference: Exploring the Roots of Western Bureaucracy*. Chicago and London: University of Chicago Press.

————. 1995. "Hellenism and Occidentalism: The Permutations of Performance in Greek Bourgeois Identity." In *Occidentalism: Images of the West*, ed. James G. Carrier. Oxford: Clarendon Press.

Hevia, James L. 1992. "History, Theory, and Colonial Power: The Critical Method of Michael Taussig in Shamanism, Colonialism, and the Wild Man." *Journal of Historical Sociology* 5 (1): 104–25.

Hirschon, Renée. 1989. *Heirs of the Greek Catastrophe: The Social Life of Asia Minor Refugees in Piraeus*. Oxford: Clarendon Press.

Hürriyet. 1994. October 18, p. 7.

————. 1997. August 2, p. 1.

————. 1994. October 30, p. 5.

Hürriyet: İstanbul Eki. 1994. November 15, p. 1.

İlyasoğlu, Aynur. 1994. *Örtülü Kimlik*. Istanbul: Metis Yayınları.

İnan, Afet. 1939. *L'Anatolie, le Pays de la 'Race' Turque: Recherches sur les Caractères Anthropologiques des populations de la Turquie (Enquête sur 64,000 Individus)*. Genève: Georg.

Jayawardena, Kumari. 1988. *Feminism and Nationalism in the Third World*. London: Zed.

Kafadar, Cemal. 1995. *Between Two Worlds: The Construction of the Ottoman State*. Berkeley: University of California Press.

Kandiyoti, Deniz. 1987. "Emancipated but Unliberated? Reflections on the Turkish Case." *Feminist Studies* 13 (2): 317–37.

————. 1993. "Identity and its Discontents: Women and the Nation." In *Colonial Discourse and Post-Colonial Theory: A Reader*, ed. Patrick Williams and Laura Chrisman. New York and London: Harvester Wheatsheaf.

————. 1996. "Contemporary Feminist Scholarship and Middle East Studies." In *Gendering the Middle East: Emerging Perspectives*. London and New York: I. B. Tauris.

————. 1997. "Gendering the Modern: On Missing Dimensions in the Study of Turkish Modernity." In *Rethinking Modernity and National Identity in Turkey*, ed. Reşat Kasaba and Sibel Bozdoğan. Seattle and London: University of Washington Press.

———. 1998. "Afterword: Some Awkward Questions on Women and Modernity in Turkey." In *Remaking Women: Feminism and Modernity in the Middle East*, ed. Lila Abu-Lughod. Princeton: Princeton University Press.

Kasaba, Reşat, and Sibel Bozdoğan, eds., *Rethinking Modernity and National Identity in Turkey*. Seattle and London: University of Washington Press.

Kelly, John D. 1991. *A Politics of Virtue: Hinduism, Sexuality, and Countercolonial Discourse in Fiji*. Chicago and London: University of Chicago Press.

Khilnani, Sunil. 1997. *The Idea of India*. London: Hamish Hamilton.

Kopytoff, Igor. 1986. "The Cultural Biography of Things: Commoditization as Process." In *The Social Life of Things: Commodities in Cultural Perspective*, ed. Arjun Appadurai. Cambridge: Cambridge University Press.

Koray, Cenk. 1996. *Kur'an-İslamiyet, Atatürk ve 19 Mucizesi*. Istanbul: Altın Kitaplar Yayınevi.

Kozanoğlu, Can. 1990. *Bu Maçı Alıcaz!* Istanbul: İletişim Yayınları.

———. 1992. *Cilalı İmaj Devri*. Istanbul: İletişim Yayınları.

———. 1997. *İnternet Dolunay Cemaati*. Istanbul: İletişim Yayınları

Kuper, Adam. 1994. "Culture, Identity and the Project of Cosmopolitan Anthropology." *Man: The Journal of the Royal Anthropological Institute* 29 (3): 537–54.

Kuran-ı Kerim ve Türkçe Anlamı (Meal). 1973. Ankara: Diyanet İşleri Başkanlığı.

Ladas, S. P. 1932. *The Exchange of Minorities: Bulgaria, Greece and Turkey*. New York: Macmillan.

Lederman, Rena. 1989. "Contested Order: Gender and Society in the Southern New Guinea Highlands." *American Ethnologist* 16 (2): 230–47.

Lewis, Bernard. 1969. *The Emergence of Modern Turkey*. London, Oxford, and New York: Oxford University Press.

Lockman, Zachary. 1996. *Comrades and Enemies: Arab and Jewish Workers in Palestine, 1906–1948*. Berkeley: University of California Press.

Malkki, Lisa. "Citizens of Humanity: Internationalism and the Imagined Community of Nations." *Diaspora* 3 (1): 41–68.

Mandel, Ruth. 1989. "Turkish Headscarves and the Foreigner Problem." *New German Critique* 46: 27–46.

Marcus, George. 1995. "Ethnography in / of the World System: The Emergence of Multi-Sited Ethnography." *Annual Review of Anthropology* 24: 95–117.

Mardin, Şerif. 1962. *The Genesis of Young Ottoman Thought: A Study in the Modernization of Turkish Political Ideas*. Princeton: Princeton University Press.

———. 1993. "Europe in Turkey." In *Where Does Europe End?* ed. Taciser Belge. Istanbul: Helsinki Citizens' Assembly.

Marsden, Richard. 1992. "'The State': A Comment on Abrams, Denis and Sayer." *Journal of Historical Sociology* 5 (3).

Meeker, Michael E. 1997. "Once There Was, Once There Wasn't: National Monuments and Interpersonal Exchange." In *Rethinking Modernity and National Identity in Turkey*, ed. Reşat Kasaba and Sibel Bozdoğan. Seattle and London: University of Washington Press.

Messick, Brinkley. 1993. *The Calligraphic State: Textual Domination in a Muslim Society*. Berkeley: University of California Press.

Milli Gazete. 1995. December 14, pp. 1, 8.

Milli Gazete 2. 1994. November 7, p. 1.

Milliyet. 1994. April 1, p. 3.
——. 1994. April 1, p. 9.
——. 1994. April 16, p. 9.
——. 1995. August 17, p. 15.
——. 1996. November 6, p. 1 and 10.
——. 1997. January 22, p. 1 and 10.
——. 1997. March 6, p. 12.
Mitchell, Timothy. 1988. *Colonising Egypt*. Cambridge: Cambridge University Press.
——. 1990. "Everyday Metaphors of Power." *Theory and Society* 19 (5): 545–77.
——. 1991. "The Limits of the State: Beyond Statist Approaches and Their Critics." *American Political Science Review* 85 (1): 77–96.
——, ed. 2000. *Questions of Modernity*. Minneapolis and London: University of Minnesota Press.
Mohanty, Chandra Talpade, Ann Russo, and Lourdes Torres, eds. 1991. *Third World Women and the Politics of Feminism*. Bloomington: Indiana University Press.
Moore, Sally Falk, and Barbara G. Myerhoff, eds. 1977. *Secular Ritual*. Assen, The Netherlands: Van Gorcum.
Mozaffari, Mehdi. 1996. "The Fatwa that Wasn't." *The Guardian*. November 13, p. 16.
Narayan, Kirin. 1993. "How Native is a 'Native' Anthropologist?" *American Anthropologist* 95 (3): 671–86.
Navaro, Yael. 1993. "Islam and Deconstruction? Turkish-Islamist Readings and Uses of Western Social Theory." Paper presented at the annual meeting of the American Anthropological Association, Washington, D.C.
Navaro-Yashin, Yael. 2000. "'Evde Taylorizm:' Cumhuriyet'in ilk Yıllarında Evişinin Rasyonelleşmesi." *Toplum ve Bilim* 84: 51–74.
Norton, Augustus Richard, ed. 1995. *Civil Society in the Middle East: Volume One*. Leiden, New York, and Koln: E. J. Brill.
Onaran İncirlioğlu, Emine. 1993. "Marriage, Gender Relations and Rural Transformation in Central Anatolia." In *Culture and Economy: Changes in Turkish Villages*, ed. Paul Stirling. Hemingford, UK: Eothen Press.
Öncü, Ayşe. 1994. "Packaging Islam: Cultural Politics on the Landscape of Turkish Commercial Television." *New Perspectives on Turkey* 10: 13–36.
Öz, Yılmaz. 1982. *Quotations from Mustafa Kemal Atatürk*. Ankara: Ministry of Foreign Affairs.
Özbek, Meral. 1994. *Popüler Kültür ve Orhan Gencebay Arabeski*. Istanbul: İletişim Yayınları.
Özdür, Atilla. 1994. "Bu son yazıdır." *Vakit*. November 11, p. 4.
Öztürkmen, Arzu. 1996a. " Milli Bayramlar: Şekli ve Hatırası - I." *Toplumsal Tarih*, April.
——. 1996b. "Milli Bayramlar: Şekli ve Hatırası - II." *Toplumsal Tarih,* May.
Pandolfo, Stefania. 1997. *Impasse of the Angels: Scenes from a Moroccan Space of Memory*. Chicago and London: University of Chicago Press.
Pulur, Hasan. 1995. "Şeriat ve Din Kardeşlerimiz." *Milliyet*. August 20, p. 3.
Rabinow, Paul. 1989. *French Modern: Norms and Forms of the Social Environment*. Cambridge: MIT Press, 1989.

Rajasingham, Darini. 1993. "The After Life of Empire: Immigration and Imagination in Post-Colonial Britain." Ph.D. diss., Princeton University.

Robins, Kevin. 1996. "Interrupting Identities: Turkey / Europe." In *Questions of Cultural Identity*, ed. Stuart Hall and Paul du Gay. London: Sage.

Rodrigue, Aaron. 1997. *Türkiye Yahudilerinin Batılılaşması*. Ankara: Ayraç Yayınları.

Rosaldo, Renato. 1989. *Culture and Truth: The Remaking of Social Analysis*. Boston: Beacon.

Roscoe, Paul B. 1995. "The Perils of 'Positivism' in Cultural Anthropology." *American Anthropologist* 97 (3): 492–504.

Rose, Jacqueline. 1996. *States of Fantasy*. Oxford: Clarendon.

Sabah. 1994. October 28, p. 1.

———. 1994. November 8, pp. 33, 40.

———. 1994. November 11, p. 33.

———. 1996. November 16.

Sadowski, Yahya. 1993. "The New Orientalism and the Democracy Debate." *Middle East Report* 183: 14–21, 40.

Said, Edward. 1985. *Beginnings: Intention and Method*. New York: Columbia University Press.

———. 1978. *Orientalism*. New York: Pantheon.

———. 1978. "The Problem of Textuality: Two Exemplary Positions." *Critical Inquiry* 4: 673–714.

———. 1981. *Covering Islam: How the Media and the Experts Determine How We See the Rest of the World*. New York: Pantheon.

———. 1994. *Representations of the Intellectual: The 1993 Reich Lectures*. London: Vintage.

Saint-Exupéry, Antoine de. 1971. *The Little Prince*. San Diego, New York, and London: Harcourt Brace.

Salecl, Renata. 1994. *The Spoils of Freedom: Psychoanalysis and Feminism After the Fall of Socialism*. London: Routledge.

Sangari, KumKum, and Sudesh Vaid, eds. 1989. *Recasting Women: Essays in Colonial History*. New Delhi: Kali Press.

Sayer, Derek. 1987. *The Violence of Abstraction: The Analytical Foundations of Historical Materialism*. Oxford: Basil Blackwell.

Saygın, Celal. 1952. *Dini Bahislerden: Diyanet Cephesinden Atatürk İnkılapları*. Ankara: Türk Tarih Kurumu.

Scholem, Gershom. 1995. "The Crypto-Jewish Sect of the Dönmeh (Sabbatians) in Turkey." In *The Messianic Idea in Judaism and Other Essays in Jewish Spirituality*. New York: Schocken.

Scott, James. 1985. *Weapons of the Weak: Everyday Forms of Peasant Resistance*. New Haven and London: Yale University Press.

Seufert, Günter. 1997. "The Sacred Aura of the Turkish Flag." *New Perspectives on Turkey* 16: 53–61.

Seufert, Günter, and Petra Weyland. 1994. "National Events and the Struggle for the Fixing of Meaning : A Comparison of the Symbolic Dimensions of the Funeral Services for Atatürk and Özal." *New Perspectives on Turkey* 11: 71–98.

Shankland, David. 1993. "Alevi and Sunni in Rural Anatolia: Diverse Paths of

Change." In *Culture and Economy: Changes in Turkish Villages*, ed. Paul Stirling. Hemingford, UK: Eothen Press.

Shohat, Ella. 1988. "Sephardim in Israel: Zionism from the Standpoint of Its Jewish Victims." *Social Text* 19–20: 1–35.

Sirman, Nükhet. 1990. "State, Village and Gender in Western Turkey." In *Turkish State, Turkish Society*, ed. Nükhet Sirman and Andrew Finkel. London: Routledge.

Sloterdijk, Peter. 1988. *Critique of Cynical Reason*. London and New York: Verso.

Spencer, Jonathan. 1990. "Writing Within: Anthropology, Nationalism, and Culture in Sri Lanka." *Current Anthropology* 31 (3): 283–300.

———. 1997. "People in a Landscape: Writing Anti-Essentialist Histories of Sri Lanka." Paper presented in the Department of Anthropology, University College London, February 5.

Spivak, Gayatri Chakravorty. 1996. "Interview." In *A Critical Sense: Interviews with Intellectuals*, ed. Peter Osborne. London and New York: Routledge.

Starr, June. 1992. *Law as Metaphor: From Islamic Courts to the Palace of Justice*. New York: State University of New York Press.

Stewart, Kathleen, and Susan Harding. 1999. "Bad Endings: American Apocalypsis." *Annual Review of Anthropology* 28: 285–310.

Stirling, Paul. 1965. *Turkish Village*. London: Weidenfeld and Nicolson.

———, ed. 1993. *Culture and Economy: Changes in Turkish Villages*. Hemingford, UK: Eothen Press.

Stokes, Martin. 1992. *The Arabesk Debate: Music and Musicians in Modern Turkey*. Oxford: Oxford University Press.

Strathern, Marilyn. 1990. "Negative Strategies in Melanesia." In *Localizing Strategies: Regional Traditions in Ethnographic Writing*, ed. Richard Fardon. Edinburgh: Scottish Academic Press.

Taşkıran, Tezer. 1976. *Women in Turkey*. Istanbul: Red House Press.

Taussig, Michael. 1987. *Shamanism, Colonialism, and the Wild Man: A Study in Terror and Healing*. Chicago: University of Chicago Press.

———. 1992. "Maleficium: State Fetishism." In *The Nervous System*. New York and London: Routledge.

———. 1997. *The Magic of the State*. New York and London: Routledge.

Tekeli, Şirin. 1982. *Kadınlar ve Siyasal Toplumsal Hayat*. Istanbul: Birikim Yayınları.

Todorova, Maria. 1997. *Imagining the Balkans*. Oxford: Oxford University Press.

Toptaş, Hasan Ali. 1999. *Bin Hüzünlü Haz*. Istanbul: Adam Yayınları.

Turner, Bryan S. 1984. "Orientalism and the Problem of Civil Society in Islam." In *Orientalism, Islam, and Islamists*, ed. Asaf Hussain, Robert Olson, and Jamil Qureishi. Brattleboro, Vt.: Amana Books.

Uzun, İsmail. 1994. "Tekbir Giyim'in Dikkatine." *Vakit*. November 16, p. 13.

van der Veer, Peter. 1994. *Religious Nationalism: Hindus and Muslims in India*. Berkeley, Los Angeles, and London: University of California Press.

Verdery, Katherine. 1999. *The Political Lives of Dead Bodies: Reburial and Postsocialist Change*. New York: Columbia University Press.

Volkan, Vamık D. 1980. *Cyprus—War and Adaptation: A Psychoanalytic History of Two Ethnic Groups in Conflict*. Charlottesville: University Press of Virginia.

Voutira, Eftihia. 1997. "Population Transfers and Resettlement Policies in Inter-war Europe: The Case of Asia Minor Refugees in Macedonia from an International and National Prespective." In *Ourselves and Others: The Development of a Greek Macedonian Cultural Identity Since 1912*, ed. Peter Mackridge and Eleni Yannakakis. Oxford and New York: Berg.

Warren, Kay B. 1998. *Indigenous Movements and Their Critics: Pan-Maya Activism in Guatemala*. Princeton: Princeton University Press.

Weber, Max. 1949. *The Methodology of the Social Sciences*. Ed. Edward A. Shils and Henry A. Finch. New York: Free Press.

Wedeen, Lisa. 1999. *Ambiguities of Domination: Politics, Rhetoric, and Symbols in Contemporary Syria*. Chicago: University of Chicago Press.

White, Jenny B. 1994. *Money Makes Us Relatives: Women's Labor in Urban Turkey*. Austin: University of Texas Press.

Williams, Raymond. 1958. *Culture and Society, 1780–1950*. New York: Columbia University Press.

———. 1985. "Culture." In *Marxism and Literature*. Oxford and New York: Oxford University Press.

Wittfogel, Karl. 1978. *Oriental Despotism: A Comparative Study of Total Power*. New Haven and London: Yale University Press.

Yalçın-Heckman, Lale. 1990. "Kurdish Tribal Organization and Local Political Processes." In *Turkish State, Turkish Society*, ed. Nükhet Sirman and Andrew Finkel. London: Routledge.

Yelda. 1996. *Istanbul'da, Diyarbakır'da Azalırken*. Istanbul: Belge Yayınları.

Yeni Şafak. 1994. November 12, p. 16.

———. 1995. December 13, p. 1.

———. 1995. December 14, p. 5.

———. 1996. November 11.

Yeni Yüzyıl. 1995. August 16, p. 8.

Yıldız, Lütfi. 1997. *Bizim Çatlı*. Kayseri: Karaca Yayın Dağıtım.

Yudice, George. 1995. "Civil Society, Consumption, and Governmentality in an Age of Global Restructuring: An Introduction." *Social Text* 14 (4): 1–25.

Yuval-Davis, Nancy, and Floya Anthias, eds. 1989. *Woman-Nation-State*. London: Macmillan.

Zaman. 1994. May 30, p. 14.

———. 1995. December 14, pp. 5, 15.

———. 1996. August 4, p. 1.

Žižek, Slavoj. 1995. *The Sublime Object of Ideology*. London and New York: Verso.

———. 1997. *The Plague of Fantasies*. London and New York: Verso.

———. 2001. *Did Somebody Say Totalitarianism? Five Interventions in the Mis(use) of a Notion*. London and New York: Verso.

Zorlu, Ilgaz. 1995. "Gizli Bir Etnik Cemaat: Türkiye Sabetaycıları." *Birikim* 71–72: 168–72.

Index

Abdülhamid II: as contemporary political symbol, 199

Abrams, Philip, 5, 155–57, 185–86, 198, 228n.13

Abu-Lughod, Lila, 8, 14, 73–77, 215 nn. 64, 65, and 67

Afghanistan: in Turkish public discourses, 63–64

Alevis, 68, 214n.52, 223n.32; in secularist discourses, 145–46

Anatolia: in public discourses, 46–48, 50, 61

Anderson, Benedict, 49, 65, 126, 156–57, 161, 182, 205n.7, 223n.2

Anıtkabir. *See* Ataturk, mausoleum for

anthropology at home. *See* native anthropology

Arab World: as anthropological category, 73–77, 215n.67; in Islamist discourses, 50; in Turkish public discourses, 49–50. *See also* Arabs

Arabs: as analytical category, 74, 76; in Europe, 9–10; in Islamist discourses, 54–55, 141; Turkification of, 49, 206n.11; in Turkish public discourses, 44–45, 48–55, 58–59, 61, 66, 71, 146

area studies, 73–77. *See also* region; regionalism

Aretxaga, Begona, 4, 15, 175, 182, 202

Armenians, 47, 49, 65, 75, 206 nn. 11 and 20, 210n.4, 213–14n.48, 214n.49; in Islamist discourse, 57

army. *See* military; militarism

Asia: as social construct, 46. *See also* Europe; Middle East; region; regionalism

Ataturk, Mustafa Kemal: ceremonial for, 37–38, 60, 86, 228 nn. 8 and 9, 106–7, 146–52, 154, 190, 196–97; commodification of symbol of, 79–80, 85–90, 93, 149, 202; cultural reforms of, 19–21, 25–26, 48, 98, 106–7, 208n.14; as emblem of Turkish statehood, 22, 71, 72, 152, 175, 188, 192–95, 197–202; as founder of state, 11, 47–48, 188; identification with, 190, 192, 198; in Islamist discourses, 58; law on crimes against, 202–3; marches

for, 72; mausoleum for, 37, 191–93, 228n.10, 228–29n.15; memorials for, 38; monuments for, 1, 147, 151; as political symbol, 188–92, 199, 202–3; portraits of, 37–39, 70, 86, 93, 149, 188, 190, 197; in public discourses, 27, 60, 71, 152, 167, 169, 171, 175; reverence for, 188–92, 199, 202–3; sayings of, 151, 188, 199; statues of, 2, 89–90, 188, 196–98, 200, 202–3

Ataturkism. *See* Ataturk; secularism; secularist(s); statism

authenticity. *See* culture: in public discourses; nativeness; politics of culture

authoritarianism, 6, 126, 138, 140

Bakhtin, Mikhail, 224n.6, 226n.16

Baudrillard, Jean, 110–11

Benjamin, Walter, 4, 15, 23, 202, 223n.1, 224n.10

Berkes, Niyazi, 10, 189, 205n.8

Bourdieu, Pierre, 207n.2, 224–25n.11

Byzantines, 9, 10

Central Asia: in Turkey's public discourses, 11–12, 47, 50, 57, 63, 68, 118, 205n.8, 222n.30

city. *See* municipalities; urban space

civil society: as analytical category, 1, 2, 5, 119, 122, 126, 129, 130–37, 143, 152–54, 159, 205n.1, 221n.19, 222n.25, 224n.10, 227–28n.32; in Islamist public discourses, 133, 136–44; in public discourses, 128, 132, 136, 143, 152–54, 223n.35; in secularist public discourses, 136–37, 144–52. *See also* resistance: as analytical category; public sphere: as analytical category; state: as analytical category

Clifford, James, 13

clothing reforms. *See* Hat Law

commodification, 78–82, 90, 110–13, 219n.32; Islamists and, 79, 81–85, 93–113, 216–17n.14, 217–18n.15; in Islamist public discourses, 79, 81–85, 91–92, 95–97, 103–6, 111–12; and politics of culture, 79, 80, 93, 110–13; secularists and,